D1253414

FROM GAUTIER TO ELIOT

ENGLISH LITERATURE

Editor
PROFESSOR BASIL WILLEY
M.A., F.B.A., HON.LITT.D.
*King Edward VII Professor of English Literature
in the University of Cambridge*

By the same author

VERHAEREN
(Paris de Boccard)
Couronné par l'Académie Française; Prix Narcisse Michaut

BAUDELAIRE
(Gollancz)

RIMBAUD IN ABYSSINIA
(Oxford, The Clarendon Press)

ARTHUR RIMBAUD
(Faber & Faber)

RIMBAUD EN ABYSSINIE
(Paris, Payot)

A LADY'S CHILD
(Faber & Faber)
Autobiography

BAUDELAIRE: LES FLEURS DU MAL
(Oxford, Basil Blackwell)
A Critical Edition with Introduction and Notes

ARTHUR RIMBAUD
(Hamish Hamilton)
Entirely revised

THE GOD THAT FAILED
(Hamish Hamilton)
The part concerned with André Gide

PETRUS BOREL EN ALGÉRIE
(Oxford, Basil Blackwell)

ANDRÉ GIDE
(Cambridge, Bowes & Bowes)

RIMBAUD 1854–1954
(Oxford, The Clarendon Press)

PETRUS BOREL
(Faber & Faber)

BAUDELAIRE
(Faber & Faber)

ARTHUR RIMBAUD
(Faber & Faber)

PR
129
.F8
S8

FROM GAUTIER TO ELIOT

THE INFLUENCE OF FRANCE ON ENGLISH LITERATURE
1851–1939

ENID STARKIE
M.A., D.Litt., F.R.S.L.

Reader in French Literature in the University of Oxford

HUTCHINSON UNIVERSITY LIBRARY

LONDON

WITHDRAWN

146510

HUTCHINSON & CO. (*Publishers*) LTD
178–202 Great Portland Street, London, W.1

London Melbourne Sydney
Auckland Bombay Toronto
Johannesburg New York

First published 1960
Second impression 1960
This edition 1962

© Enid Starkie 1960

*This book has been set in Times New Roman type
face. It has been printed in Great Britain by The
Anchor Press, Ltd., in Tiptree, Essex, on Antique
Wove paper and bound by Taylor Garnett Evans
& Co., Ltd., in Watford, Herts*

To

MARCELLE FOURNIER

devoted daughter of France
and staunch friend of Britain
this book is dedicated
with love and admiration

CONTENTS

CONTENTS

ACKNOWLEDGEMENTS

The author is grateful to the following for their permission to use copyright material:

Mr. Richard Aldington and George Allen & Unwin Ltd for an extract from 'Evening' in *Des Imagistes, an Anthology*; the Owner of the Copyright and Cassell & Co. Ltd for an extract from *Journals* by Arnold Bennett; The Bodley Head Ltd for extracts from 'To the Reader' in *English Poems* by Richard Le Gallienne and from articles in *The Yellow Book* by Max Beerbohm; Chatto & Windus Ltd for an extract from 'Dulce et Decorum' in *Poems* by Wilfred Owen; Mr. T. S. Eliot and Faber & Faber Ltd for extracts from *After Strange Gods*, 'The Hollow Men' and 'Prufrock and Other Observations' in *Collected Poems*, *Essays Ancient and Modern*, *The Sacred Wood* and *Selected Essays*; John Farquharson Ltd on behalf of the Estate of the late Henry James for extracts from *The Art of the Novel* and *Partial Portraits*; Librairie Gallimard (all rights reserved) for extracts from *Alcools* and *Calligrammes* by Guillaume Apollinaire, *Traité du Narcisse* by André Gide, *À La Recherche du Temps Perdu* and *Le Flacon* by Marcel Proust and *Mémoires d'un Poème* by Paul Valéry; Mr. David Gascoyne and Faber & Faber Ltd for an extract from the English translation of *Manifeste du Surréalisme* by André Breton; the Executors of the James Joyce Estate and Jonathan Cape Ltd for an extract from 'The Dead' in *Dubliners*; Mr. Louis MacNeice and the Oxford University Press for an extract from the Introduction to *Modern Poetry*; Contesse Renée Maeterlinck for extracts from *Chansons*, *Serres Chaudes* and *Le Tragique Quotidien* by Maurice Maeterlinck; Mr. W. Somerset Maugham and William Heinemann Ltd for an extract from *Altogether*; Mr. C. D. Medley and William Heinemann Ltd for extracts from *Confession of a Young Man*, *A Drama in Muslin* and *A Mummer's Wife* by George Moore; Mercure de France for an extract from *Les Ailes Rouges de la Guerre* by Émile Verhaeren; Mrs. Morgan and Macmillan & Co. Ltd for an extract from *Ode to France* by Charles Morgan; Mr. Ezra Pound and Faber & Faber Ltd for an extract from *Mauberly I*; The Richards Press Ltd for *The Man with a Hammer* by Anna Wickham; Routledge and Kegan Paul Ltd

for 'Above the Docks' and an extract from 'Autumn' in *Poems* and an
extract from *Speculations* by T. E. Hulme; Dame Edith Sitwell and
Macmillan & Co. Ltd for extracts from 'Aubade', 'Fantasia for a
Mouth-Organ', 'Popular Song', 'Romance' and 'Sleeping Beauty' in
Collected Poems; Mr. Stephen Spender and Hamish Hamilton Ltd
for an extract from *The Creative Element*; Mr. Arthur Symons and
William Heinemann Ltd for extracts from 'Days and Nights', 'London
Nights' and 'Silhouettes' in *The Poems of Arthur Symons, Volume I*
and from *The Symbolist Movement in Literature*; Mr. Leonard Woolf
for extracts from *The Common Reader*, *The Waves* and *A Writer's
Diary* by Virginia Woolf; and Mrs. Yeats and Macmillan & Co. Ltd
for extracts from *The Autumn of the Body*, 'He hears the Cry of the
Sedge', 'The Municipal Gallery Revisited', 'O Do Not Love Too Long',
'The Poet pleads with the Elemental Powers', 'The Shadowy Waters',
'Vacillations' and 'When You are Old and Grey' in *Collected Poems*,
Essays, *Magic*, *Symbolism in Poetry* and from the Introduction to the
English translation of *Axël* by Villiers de l'Isle Adam, all by W. B.
Yeats.

PREFACE

It is difficult to do justice to the subject of this monograph within such restricted limits. It is not possible to deal with the whole of French and English literature during the period, and so only those writers are studied who indubitably gained something from their connection and sympathy with France, and her literature, only those who definitely experienced her seminal influence; and they are dealt with solely from the point of view of the impact which France made upon them.

It is not a book intended for specialists. Each section, each subdivision, could be the subject of a whole book, and occupy a lifetime of research. It can serve only as a signpost for those who are not well informed, to point the way and indicate the direction which literature has taken. Those who are interested can continue along the same road, lingering at will at the various stages, to get to know the territory better, and finally make a longer stay when they reach their destination.

I have tried to chart the large currents, to indicate the trend of influences, and have avoided long lists of names which would mean little to those who have not read their works. My endeavour has been to generalize, to indicate movements and to suggest atmosphere. I do not intend to estimate relative merit—or indeed worth at all—I am only investigating the prevalence and extent of the influence of France on English literature, between the Second Empire and the Second World War.

The book is primarily addressed to readers of English literature rather than to those who specialize in French. It is more important to realize whence the literature of a country comes, than where it is going.

I have adopted a different plan for each of the two parts of the book. At first the influence of France drifted over to England in a haphazard manner, the seeds carried on the air without conscious sense of direction. At that moment movements are more important than the various forms of literature. Moreover, at the end of the nineteenth century, all the arts and forms of literature tended to merge into one another, aspiring to the ideal of unity between all the arts. That is the first part, which ends with the advent of the First World War. The influence of France was firmly established in England when war broke out, and it was then evident what immense strides had been made, since the beginning of the nineteenth century, in understanding and sympathy with France.

There arose, between the two wars, a period of extreme nationalism amongst the different arts—as amongst the various countries—when each wanted to assert its independence and its rights, its 'autarky'. That was the time when pure music, pure painting, and pure poetry were the fashion. Then the seeds, which had floated over the Channel from France, took root in the various forms of literature—poetry, fiction, and drama. The merging of the atmosphere from France with that of England took place in the different literary *genres*. At this point it seemed more fruitful to treat these separately, rather than the currents.

The theory of influences must not, however, be exaggerated. The establishment of influences is one of the more pernicious aspects of modern academic research, for, with a little ingenuity, an influence can always be proved where there may have been no more than an affinity. It should be remembered that no influence can take place unless the soil is prepared for the seed, unless there is affinity. Pascal, in his *Pensées*, makes God say to man: 'Thou wouldst not be seeking me, if thou hadst not already found me!' While Gide declared: 'Influences do not create anything; they merely awaken what is already there!' And Baudelaire, writing to Manet, who had been accused of imitating Goya, whose work he had not even seen, said: 'Are you sceptical about the possibility of such mathematical parallelism in nature? Well! don't they accuse me of imitating Poe? And do you know why, with such infinite patience, I translated Poe? It was because he was like me! The first time I ever opened a book by him I discovered, not only subjects which I'd dreamt, but whole phrases which I'd conceived, written by him twenty years before!' One must, therefore, not make too much of such resemblances. There are, in any and every age, currents of ideas, seeds of new conceptions, which float about in the air, in the different parts of the world, carried on any breeze, like feathery dandelion seeds, and they strike root in any suitable soil on which they may alight. If they did not find this suitable soil, they would fall to the ground and die sterile— many do in fact perish in this manner.

Nevertheless, English literature did obtain from France, in the period under review, more than from any other country. I shall hope to demonstrate that, in the second half of the nineteenth century, the influence of France gradually ousted that of Germany, and that French influence and prestige stood supreme during the twenty years which separate the two world wars. It is also hoped that my final chapter will suggest that our two countries have much yet to give each other, and even that the future of European culture depends on this understanding and interdependence.

I have quoted more freely from unfamiliar authors and texts than from those that are well known and of easy access, trusting that my readers will refer to these of their own accord.

I would like to tender my grateful thanks to all those associated with the Taylor Library at Oxford—to its librarian, Donald Sutherland, in particular—for the help they have so tirelessly afforded me, without which it would have been impossible for me to complete the book in the time at my disposal.

ENID STARKIE

PART I

THE SEED

From the Second Empire to the First World War

1

INTRODUCTION

IN THE early years of the nineteenth century interest in French literature amongst the English was almost non-existent. During the seventeenth and eighteenth centuries they had admired the culture of France but, later, considered that it had been desecrated by the outrages of the revolution, the tyranny of the upstart Napoleon, and finally by her defeat and humiliation in 1815, with the restoration of the effete Bourbon dynasty through foreign arms.

During the Restoration in France, as happened so often in that country in the course of her history, the young and progressive writers were inspired by the wish to know something of the literature of the nations by which they had been defeated—the literature of Germany and of England. Thus it came about that Anglomania sprang up in France, with adulation of such writers as Shakespeare, Scott, and Byron, as well as Wordsworth and the Lake poets. The travellers from England to France, however, did not reciprocate this admiration—they even despised it. France was generally held in universal contempt by the English—except as a playground for frivolous pleasure. The Rev. F. Eustace, writing in 1814, in his *Letter from Paris*, declared that it was cheaper to enjoy oneself in Paris than to be bored in England. This state of affairs continued all through the Restoration, right into the July Monarchy, and little was known in England of the new Romantic Movement in France until the late eighteen-thirties—and very little even then.

It is true that certain of Chateaubriand's works had been translated into English by 1820—*Atala*, *Le Génie du Christianisme*, *Voyage en Orient*, and *Essai sur les Révolutions*—and that an article reviewing his writings had appeared in the *Edinburgh Review* in November 1820, which, however, was far from favourable. Thomas Moore, the writer of this article, claimed that, although the state of France might be favourable for commerce, it was, with certain exceptions, lamentable in the realm of literature.

17

Most English writers agreed with Moore's contempt for French literature, and Southey declared that poetry was as impossible in the French language as in the Chinese.

There were nevertheless some exceptions. *The New Monthly Magazine* and *The London Magazine* commissioned Stendhal to contribute to their columns. He was a fervent admirer of the English and he did something to arouse in them an interest in the literature of France—especially in such prose artists as Mérimée who, in the midst of the exaggerations of Romanticism, kept some traces of the dignity of sober classicism.

After this, other magazines followed suit. Articles on French literature began to appear in *The Foreign Quarterly Review*, *The Foreign Review*, *The Westminster Review*, *The Athenaeum*, and *The Literary Gazette*.

The verdict of most English critics, at this time, was that the Romantic Movement in France had come too late. There were reasons to explain why it had not developed there as early as in England or in Germany. Romanticism had sprung up in the eighteenth century all over Europe—in France as well as elsewhere, in the works of Rousseau, Bernardin de Saint Pierre, and others of the same persuasion—but its natural development had been retarded, first by the revolution and then by the dictatorial government of Napoleon, who had regulated literature as everything else. He considered—rightly—that French classicism, in the age of Louis XIV, had been one of the great glories of France, and he wished to give her back the same prestige which she had enjoyed at that time. However, the day for that form of literature was past, and all he did was to shore up, for a time, the crumbling edifice of classicism, and hide its decay beneath stucco ornamentation. He supported waning classicism, the pseudo-classicism of the late eighteenth century, and this retarded the full flowering of Romanticism for nearly a generation, until his final defeat in 1815.

But it was only after the revolution of 1830 that English interest in France and her culture began to revive. The English approved of this revolution which seemed to them a step forward towards democracy and liberty, for they considered that it had been merciful, and had shown none of the excesses of its predecessor in 1789.

The revolution stimulated an interest in the new writers in France who had been implicated in it, for 1830 marked not only the final defeat of the Ancien Régime politically, but also the defeat of classicism at the Battle of Hernani, and the victory of the new literature. This was recognized also abroad, and Victor Hugo's play was translated into English by James Kennedy and acted with great success in London in

April 1831. Later, in the same year, there was a further translation, by Lord Francis Leveson Gower—in verse this time—which was performed before the royal family. He also translated Dumas' *Henri III et Sa Cour*. At the same time Hugo's novel, *Notre-Dame de Paris*, was reviewed in *The Foreign Quarterly* and rated higher than any novel by Walter Scott.

However, the most highly esteemed novelists at that time in France —George Sand and Balzac—were only to be known in England in the later eighteen-forties when Elizabeth Barrett, writing to Browning on 27 April 1846, declared that, since she had read the works of Balzac, she had said farewell to the English novel.

Now, in the eighteen-thirties, many periodicals were founded in England which studied French literature and interpreted it to English readers. There were: *The Critic*, *The Foreign Monthly Review*, *The British and Foreign Review*, *The Dublin Review*, *The Dublin University Review*. There were, as well, joint Anglo-French productions—*The Paris Literary Gazette*, founded in 1835, *Le Panorama de Londres* of 1836, *Le Paris-Londres*, *ou Keepsake Français* of 1837, and *Paris and Continental Spectator* of 1844.

Nevertheless, there were still many readers in England who would not tolerate what they called the immorality and cynicism of George Sand and the coarseness of Balzac. This nullified, for them, the good impression created by the revolution of 1830. Some tried to be broadminded—as did Bulwer Lytton, as befitted an aristocrat—but only succeeded in being condescending. Mrs. Trollope frankly indulged her prejudices in her disapproval of *Les Jeunes-France*, in 1835, and declared that Victor Hugo was the 'champion of vice, shame, and degradation' who transgressed the bounds of decency. *The Quarterly Review*, through the pen of a critic called Croker, violently attacked the immorality of France in a series of articles between 1834 and 1836. G. W. Reynolds, writing in 1839, in the Preface to his *Modern Literature of France*, calls them 'the most desperate attack ever made upon a foreign nation by the pen' and said that 'this assault was disgraceful in the extreme'. Croker declared that the revolution of 1830 was to be attributed to the depraved taste of the nation with regard to literature, for French drama was lamentable, the novel even worse, and he gave examples of the state of depravity reached by Dumas, Hugo, Balzac, and George Sand. He claimed that the revolution had effected a sudden change in the morality of the French by emancipating women from all etiquette and reserve; that is to say, from all modesty.

Reynolds deplored this ignorance on the part of his fellow-countrymen and said that the books written on France in England 'originated

in the most deplorable ignorance, the worst feeling of spite and malig-
nity, or an extraordinary facility of misapprehension and mistake'.

He was, however, an exception, and Thackeray, in his *Paris
Sketches*, published the same year as Reynolds' book, treated French
literature with ironical contempt. He declared that there were only
three kinds of drama in France. The old classical drama, 'well-nigh
dead, and full time too!' That is to say the old tragedies, in which 'half-
a-dozen characters appear and spout sonorous Alexandrines for half-
a-dozen hours'. Rachel, according to him, had been trying to revive this
genre and 'untomb' Racine, but it was comforting to reflect, he thought,
that he could never come to life again, and that she was only able to
galvanize the corpse, but not to revivify it. Then, Thackeray explained,
there was contemporary comedy of which Scribe was the main exponent. 'Playwrights,' he added, 'have handled it for about two thousand
years, and the public, like a great baby, must have the tale repeated to it
over and over again.' Finally there was the *drame* said to be fathered
by Shakespeare, which had sprung to life of late years, and Thackeray
said that 'after having seen most of the grand dramas which have been
produced in Paris for the last half-dozen years, the fictitious murders,
rapes, adulteries, and other crimes, a man may take leave to be heartily
ashamed of the manner in which he has spent his time; and of the
hideous kind of mental intoxication in which he has permitted himself
to indulge'.

On the whole, the best-informed interest of English readers in
French literature, between 1830 and 1850, lay in the realm of philo-
sophical thought, in works such as those by Cousin, Michelet, and
Comte. Carlyle, in his *French Revolution*, expressed appreciation of
Cousin's writings, but this may have been because his form of idealism
was almost Germanic, and thus more likely to appeal to the English.
John Stuart Mill read Guizot, Michelet, and Comte; he was particularly interested in the latter, with whom he corresponded between 1841
and 1846, and about whom he wrote his *Auguste Comte and Positivism*.

The first major English writer of the period to show any appreciation
of France and her literature was Matthew Arnold. Being half Celtic he
had perhaps more affinity and sympathy with a Mediterranean race
than his Anglo-Saxon fellow-countrymen. His father was one of the rare
Englishmen, at that time, to rate the civilization of France higher than
that of Germany, and he had a warmer sympathy for it. The English, at
this time, on the whole, considered the French a frivolous people, and
thought that Germany was the fount of all wisdom. Dr. Arnold, on the
contrary, believed that the anti-French policy of Palmerston in 1840
was unwise as well as wrong, and he uttered a warning against it, con-

stantly defending the desirability of friendly relations between England and France. He introduced the teaching of modern languages into Rugby, and put the study of French on equal footing with that of the classics. He enjoyed foreign travel and crossed the Channel twelve times between 1815 and his death in 1842.

Matthew Arnold, as a boy, was taken by his father, with two of his brothers, on a holiday to France in 1837, when they visited Chartres, Versailles, and Paris; and again in 1841, when they saw Angoulême, Bordeaux, Bourges, and revisited Paris.

Arnold went up to Balliol in 1841, graduating in 1844, and was awarded a Fellowship at Oriel College in 1845. That year he saw the French actress Rachel in the part of Hermione, in Racine's *Andromaque*, when she visited Britain, and was transported with enthusiasm for her acting, which appealed more to him than the actual play, for he was never to become an admirer of French classical drama. In 1846 he went to France for the express purpose of seeing her again, and he was there from December 1846 until February 1847, living a gay and frivolous life, and spending sixty-five pounds in less than three months, which was a very large sum for a young man in those days.

Whilst he was in France he came across the novels of George Sand, which moved him greatly, and he was never to lose his admiration for her writings. He visited her at Nohant, and that was his only meeting with her—he tells us this in the article he wrote, after her death in 1876, republished in *Mixed Essays* in 1880—but he preserved, for thirty years, the impression he had formed of her as a young man. He recalls that she had given him tea, that 'boisson fade et mélancolique', as Balzac called it, and that she was not wearing men's apparel, as she was always reputed to do, but a country dress such as any woman might have worn.

What attracted Arnold to Sand was her warm idealism and her concern for the betterment of others. He was, in his youth, a Romantic—though his education had been more classical than hers. He was later to describe this period of his life, nostalgically and a little ironically, as his 'Lélia days'—after the title of her most famous novel. George Sand also kept a vivid memory of the young poet's only visit to her and, many years later, she spoke of him as a young and wandering Milton. Senancour had died the year that she met Arnold, and she introduced his most famous work *Obermann* to the young Englishman, which was to exercise a permanent effect on him. It is probable that he read it in the edition prefaced by her, published in 1840, for it was always from that one that he quoted.

Obermann had appeared nearly half a century earlier, in 1804. It had passed almost unnoticed, for it had arrived too soon; but, at the height of Romanticism, between 1830 and 1850, it came into its own, and seemed to reflect to perfection the romantic and subjective mood of the age. George Sand also introduced Arnold to the writings of Sainte-Beuve, who was to have an influence on him later when he became a critic. Sainte-Beuve also had brought out an edition of *Obermann*, which was published in 1833, the same year as his own novel *Volupté*, which owes much to it. In that subjective age, readers made a habit of searching through literary works—particularly poetry and fiction—on the look-out for personal confessions of their authors, and *Obermann* was generally accepted as an autobiographical record—though Senancour himself always protested against such an interpretation.

Arnold's first published work, a collection of poems entitled *The Strayed Reveller*, appeared in 1849, and it contains many reminiscences and reflections of Senancour. A second collection, *Empedocles on Etna*, appeared in 1852. This borrowed its title from Sainte-Beuve's article on Senancour—written in 1832 and published in the first volume of his *Portraits Contemporains*—and many of its poems are inspired by *Obermann*. Further collections of poems appeared in 1853, 1854, 1857, and the final one in 1867. They are all reprints of the earlier collections, with the addition of new poems. The most significant and persistent influence in all these collections is that of Senancour, which the poet himself admits, addressing him as 'thou master of my wandering youth!' It is found in such poems as *Resignation*, in *A Summer's Night*, in *Moonlight*, in *To a Gypsy Child*, and especially in his most beautiful and perfect poem, *Dover Beach*. In the final poem of the last collection, written in 1867, and entitled *Obermann Once More*, he gives his final tribute to Senancour, composed many years after he had first encountered his work.

Arnold found in Senancour, at a vital stage in his own intellectual and artistic development, a fruitful influence, a kindred spirit, who was at the centre of his experience of France, at the heart of it, so that all other connecting influences radiated out from him and were—as Sainte-Beuve might have said—of the same spiritual family. Arnold was attracted, for instance, to the moralist Joubert, of whom Sainte-Beuve had written, and to the Swiss writer Amiel, also a moralist, and the author of an intimate journal—he studied them in his *Essays in Criticism*.

Through Senancour Arnold came into contact with Eugène Burnouf, who was the most important source of orientalism and exoticism in French literature at the middle of the century. He possessed a copy of his *Introduction à l'Histoire du Bouddhisme Indien*, published in 1844, and this provided him with many of his favourite themes of resignation and impassibility. It is however from Sainte-Beuve that he obtained the material for his long oriental poem *Sohrab and Rustum*, published in 1853. In a note to its re-publication he declared that it owed its birth to a passage in Sainte-Beuve's review of Jules Mohl's translation of *Le Livre des Rois* by the Persian poet Firdousi, which had been the subject of his *Lundi* for 11 February 1850.

Up to 1857, when he was elected Professor of Poetry at Oxford, Arnold had been primarily a poet, but he now became a critic—a similar literary evolution to that of his master Sainte-Beuve—and it is probably as a critic that he is most significant; it is also there that the influence of France is most evident. From a study of the French critics, he introduced into England a similar system based on intellectual and aesthetic laws. His lectures as Professor of Poetry mark an important step in the development of an English school of criticism, and led, later, to his *Essays in Criticism*, probably his chief claim to a permanent niche in the temple of fame. Saintsbury, in his tortuous and circumlocutory style, calls it 'the first full and varied, and perhaps always the best, expression and illustration of the author's critical attitude, the detailed manifesto and exemplar of the new critical method, and so one of the epoch-making books of the later nineteenth century in English'. What Saintsbury intends to convey is that Arnold had envisaged criticism as a deliberate and formal art—as it was in France—with laws and methods of its own, and with standards of taste by which other works of literature could be judged.

Arnold directed the literature of England towards France. Quiller-Couch declared that it had been the misfortune of the Victorian period, before the advent of Arnold, that its men of genius wrote with their eyes fixed upon German literature which, for all its qualities, 'must ever be dangerous to Englishmen, because it flatters and encourages their special faults'.

Arnold, as the first writer in England, in the nineteenth century, to be profoundly affected by France, was accused by his fellow-countrymen of being too French in his outlook. He was the self-appointed apostle of French culture, and he said, when lecturing in New York in 1883, that he had always felt very much attracted towards France, and was thus condemned, in certain quarters, for having too great a liking for France and things French. Sainte-Beuve realized that he had taken on some of the colouring of France and, in his *Lettres à mon Exilée*, he wrote in 1860: 'I know Arnold! He used to be very fond of us when he was young. He was truly a Frenchman, a Romantic, somewhat lost over there!'

Arnold, however, had his limitations as a critic. In taste he was not very adventurous and he tended to remain within the same narrow circle of writers, amongst those who resembled him in mind and personality. He had more liking for French prose than for French verse, and he was incapable of appreciating the real quality of French poetry—the only poet in France whom he seems to have enjoyed was Béranger. He did not care for Hugo or Racine, and was completely deaf to the melody of the French Alexandrine, which he considered inadequate as a poetic metre. He found pleasure in the writings of Maurice and Eugénie de Guérin, after George Sand and Sainte-Beuve had brought *Le Centaure* —a prose poem by Maurice—to his notice, and he devoted articles to the brother and sister in his *Essays in Criticism*, but these deal with their personal rather than with their artistic qualities, with morals rather than with aesthetics, and he admits that he is more drawn to their prose than to their verse.

The ten years during which Arnold held the Chair of Poetry at Oxford were vital years in French poetry—they marked the maturity of Baudelaire and the beginnings of Mallarmé and Verlaine—and, in 1857, the year of his election as Professor, there occurred Baudelaire's trial for obscenity with the consequent banning of a number of his poems; yet Arnold never mentions him and, when he lectured on the modern element in poetry, he gave no hint that he realized what Baudelaire had achieved in this field, nor the interest of his aesthetic doctrine.

In the first series of his *Essays in Criticism* Arnold had urged on his barbarian fellow-countrymen emulation of the French state of mind. Later his enthusiasm somewhat waned, and, when France was defeated by Germany in 1870, he saw this disaster as the result of her moral decay. At the end of his life he ranked Germany higher, and, in this, eventually came into line with typical English feelings. In the third series of the *Essays in Criticism* he wrote: 'A nation's intellectual place depends upon its having reached the very highest rank in the very highest lines of spiritual endeavour; this is what, in the end, makes its ideal; this is what fixes its scale of intellectual judgment, and what it counts by in the world!' France did not, for him, fulfil these requirements, and he quoted a line from one of his own poems: 'France, famed in all arts, in none supreme'.

Towards the end of his life Arnold no longer found favour with the new lovers of France who had previously admired him. Swinburne, on arriving at Oxford, had been prepared to follow his example because, as a boy, he had liked some of his poetry, but, after meeting him, and hearing him lecture, he turned against him and denied him competence to discuss French poetry, since he was deaf to it. He added ironically that Arnold 'had a good faith in the French Academy, and in the *Revue des Deux Mondes*, which is nothing short of pathetic; he seems actually to take them at their own valuation'.

Nevertheless, in spite of his ultimate recantation, Arnold had done his work well, in certain directions, in being the interpreter of France to English readers at a moment when interest in her literature was at a very low ebb, and he marks an important stage in the development of French literary influence in England. Lionel Trilling believes that, by bringing French influence into English letters, Arnold had broken down the provincialism of English criticism. And Eliot, as late as 1920, said in *The Sacred Wood* that 'Arnold is still a bridge across the Channel'.

2

ART FOR ART'S SAKE

THE Romantic Movement in France was virtually over by the middle of the eighteen-forties. Indeed the failure of Hugo's play, *Les Burgraves*, in 1843, from which so much had been hoped, is generally accepted as the official date of the demise of the movement. There were, however, even before that, signs that its supremacy was being questioned, and it could be claimed that the Battle of Hernani, which established its victory —after which the movement became middle-aged and set in its ways, traditional and sure of itself—marked the beginning of its decline. 1830 was the highest peak of the Romantic Movement and, although some, if not most, of its greatest works were produced between 1830 and 1840, the movement had become static.

At the time of the Romantic battle in 1830 the political field was equally disturbed, and politics and literature were closely interwoven. The political revolution of 1830 was linked with the literary revolution, and most of the men of letters of the time were implicated in it, in opposition to the Bourbon government.

There were, however, two revolutionary parties—those who wanted a republic, and those who would have been satisfied with the removal of Charles X, and his replacement by Louis-Philippe, the liberal Duke of Orleans.

It was the Republicans who fought in the streets and at the barricades, but it was the Orleanists who gained the prize of victory, for they had weight and wealth on their side—the big bankers and the business men—and the prestige of the veteran General Lafayette.

The older writers, those in their thirties at the time of the revolution, accepted the Orleanist régime with seeming willingness, and decided to work with it. It is noticeable that, during the July Monarchy, the best-known writers, such as Lamartine, Hugo, and Vigny, took an active part in politics.

There were, however, others, amongst those in their twenties, who refused to accept the Orleanist dynasty, and who lived, during the first

years of the reign of Louis-Philippe, in a state of violent revolt. In literature they stood outside the regular stream of Romanticism, and, in
poetry, were nearer to the dissident Romantic, Sainte-Beuve, than to
the leaders, Lamartine, Hugo, and Vigny.

A characteristic amongst the elder Romantics, which became very
marked after 1830, was their moral attitude to literature, and their
desire to teach an edifying lesson. Hugo, in the Preface to his play
Lucrèce Borgia performed in 1833, wrote: 'Il y a beaucoup de questions
morales dans les questions littéraires. Le théâtre est une tribune, le
théâtre est une chaire. Le drame, sans sortir des limites impartiales de
l'art, a une mission nationale, une mission sociale, une mission
humaine.'

Those who refused to accept this prosaic ideal formed a group of
their own, on the fringe of society. They despised material prosperity
and the necessity of flattering the general public in order to obtain it—
Hugo was frequently accused of doing precisely that. They held a well-
ordered life in contempt, also the conventional morality of the bourgeois régime. They preferred to live for Art alone—Art with a very large
'A'.

In the early years of the new reign the first grouping of young revolutionary authors called themselves the *Jeunes-France*, or the *Bouz-
ingos*. Amongst them were Petrus Borel, the self-styled *Lycanthrope*;
Philothée O'Neddy; Gérard de Nerval, and Théophile Gautier. At
first they were under the leadership of Petrus Borel but, in a few
years, his influence waned, and he played no part in the Art for
Art's Sake Movement when it was established. The Bouzingo Movement marked the transition from official Romanticism to Art for Art's
Sake.

Gradually Louis-Philippe was accepted by the majority of the
country, and revolutionary doctrine was out of date. Eventually the
wild Bouzingo movement of Petrus Borel was replaced by the Art for
Art's Sake Movement of Théophile Gautier.

The ideals of this new movement were set out in the Preface to
Gautier's notorious novel, *Mademoiselle de Maupin*, which appeared in
1835, and became the manifesto of the new school. It was an attack
not so much against Romanticism, as it had been in its early days, as
against what it had become in the hands of the older writers, and particularly against their theory that art should have a moral or useful
purpose.

Mademoiselle de Maupin is one of the most famous works of the
nineteenth century—certainly one of the most notorious—with the
most widespread influence, and its Preface stands in the same relation

to the Art for Art's Sake School as the Preface to Hugo's play *Cromwell* stands to the Romantic Movement. It is there that Gautier declared: 'Les choses sont belles en proportion inverse de leur utilité. Il n'y a de vraiment beau que ce qui ne peut servir à rien. Tout ce qui est utile est laid.' He expressed contempt and horror for all the political and social theories of the humanitarians, especially for the theory of the importance of utility. 'A quoi sert ce livre?' he enquired ironically. 'Comment peut-on l'appliquer à la moralisation et au bien-être de la classe la plus nombreuse et la plus pauvre? Quoi! pas un mot des besoins de la société, rien de civilisant et de progressif? Comment! au lieu de faire la grande synthèse de l'humanité, peut-on faire des romans qui ne mènent à rien, qui ne font pas avancer la génération dans le chemin de l'avenir? Comment peut-on s'occuper de la forme et du style en présence de si graves intérêts?' He answers the question himself. 'Non imbécile et goitreux que vous êtes! un livre ne fait pas de la soupe, un roman n'est pas une paire de bottes, un sonnet n'est pas une seringue, un drame n'est pas un chemin de fer!'

In this Preface Gautier gave expression to his revolt against all accepted doctrines and principles. He attacked Christianity because it had given mankind sadness and anxiety, with a sense of sin and shame, and he repudiated Christ's sacrifice, claiming that He had not died for him. He attacked Romanticism on account of its false sentimentality, its excessive subjectivity, its lack of any sense of form, and its pasteboard and fancy-dress historical local colour. 'Encore du moyen âge!' he cried with irritation. 'Toujours du moyen âge! qui me délivrera du moyen âge, ce moyen âge qui n'est pas le moyen âge?—moyen âge de carton et de terre cuite qui n'a du moyen âge que le nom! . . . Comme ils m'ont gâté mon moyen âge si fin et si coloré! comme ils l'ont fait disparaître sous une couche de grossier badigeon. . . . Donc, à bas le moyen âge tel que nous l'ont fait les faiseurs! Le moyen âge ne répond à rien maintenant, nous voulons autre chose!'

The aim of Gautier and of most of the poets of the Art for Art's Sake Movement was to approximate to the plastic arts, and he regretted not being a painter or a sculptor, so as to be able to render, in the same way that a plastic artist might, the physical beauty of form and line, beauty which could be realized through the sense of sight. He saw poetry and sculpture as sister arts which could resist the attacks of time. In his *Salon* of 1845 he wrote: 'Le marbre et le vers sont deux matières également dures à travailler, mais les seules qui gardent éternellement la forme qu'on leur confie!' And, in his poem *L'Art*, added later to the collection *Émaux et Camées*, published in 1852, he said:

'Tout passe.—L'art robuste
Seul a l'éternité
Le buste
Survit à la cité.

Sculpte, lime, cisèle;
Que ton rêve flottant
Se scelle
Dans le bloc résistant!'

In the Preface to *Mademoiselle de Maupin*, Gautier crystallized, already in the eighteen-thirties, his conception of art. He never changed it, and expressed it again, in his first leading article, after he took over the editorship of *L'Artiste*, twenty years later, in 1856, when he repeated his theory that the poet must follow the methods of the plastic artist. 'Après avoir vu, notre plus grand plaisir a été de transporter dans notre art à nous, monuments, fresques, tableaux, statues, bas-reliefs, au risque de forcer la langue, de changer le dictionnaire en palette.' He emphasized again that art is an end in itself. 'L'art n'est pas le moyen, mais le but. Tout artiste qui se propose autre chose que le beau n'est pas un artiste. Nous n'avons jamais pu comprendre la séparation de l'idée et de la forme, pas plus que nous ne comprenons l'âme sans le corps. Une belle forme est une belle idée, car que serait-ce qu'une forme qui n'exprimerait rien?'

As far as *Mademoiselle de Maupin* itself is concerned, this work which became the artistic bible of a whole generation, one cannot claim that, as a novel, it is a success. Psychologically it is weak, and the most memorable passages are the descriptions and digressions on art—what French critics call *transpositions d'art*, that is, the rendering of a visual picture in words. The novel itself has no co-ordinated plan, or unity of style and treatment. Part of it is a projection of Gautier himself who, in the person of the hero, pours out a confession of his literary aims, and his philosophy of life and love. This part is written in the contemporary Romantic idiom. However, the central plot is drawn from a seventeenth-century tale, which had appeared in *L'Artiste* in 1830, but which was considered of topical interest at the time when—according to Houssaye —the relationship between George Sand and the actress Marie Dorval was at the height of its intensity.

The heroine's disguise leads to many misconceptions. D'Albert, the hero, fears that he has become an invert because he experiences love for someone he imagines to be a youth; his mistress Rosette is attracted by her, taking her for a man; and Mademoiselle de Maupin herself, the only person knowing all the facts, is in love with both of them.

As the novel ends, Mademoiselle de Maupin, after spending half the night with D'Albert—having disclosed her true sex to him—and the rest with Rosette, departs, leaving a letter of farewell for each of them, exhorting them to love one another for her sake since they had both loved her.

Such a story, with its frank treatment, which would certainly have been banned had it been published under the Second Empire, was considered very immoral and shocking, and it did undoubtedly '*épater le bourgeois*' at the time—as well as later.

Gautier carried out the theories laid down in the Preface to *Mademoiselle de Maupin* in his poetry, and especially in his best, and most famous, collection, *Émaux et Camées*, published in 1852, the poems of which are little pictures, on cameo or enamel, like those of a Renaissance craftsman.

Émaux et Camées, in spite of its limited and materialistic aim—perhaps even because of it—is one of the most perfect and successful poetic ventures of the nineteenth century, and fulfils admirably the ideals set forth in *L'Art*, one of its main poems, embodying the doctrine of Art for Art's Sake, the belief—the article of faith—that the poet must first and foremost be a good craftsman, and understand fully the resources of his art. He must not be—as the Romantic poets had been —an amateur singing of his private emotions and personal sufferings; he must not declare, as they had done, following Musset: 'Frappe-toi le coeur, c'est là qu'est le génie!' He must, before everything else, seek perfection of form, since form alone endures eternally, since perfection of form is stronger than time, stronger even than death.

Gautier had many followers in France before acquiring them in England, and it is from him that both Flaubert and Baudelaire learned their first lessons in the search for perfection in art. Baudelaire, a far greater poet than Gautier, turned to him with admiration, dedicating to him his *Fleurs du Mal*: 'Au Poète impeccable, au parfait magicien ès lettres françaises', and that, coming from Baudelaire, was high praise.

In England, as in France—though without revolution—there was restlessness, and growing exasperation against the materialistic values of the established writers. The Exhibition of 1851 marked the height of materialism and middle-class prosperity, but it rested on foundations of discontent and disillusionment, and there were already signs of change, when literature went in search of new ideals and turned to France to find them.

In England it is amongst the Pre-Raphaelites that the first manifestations of the Art for Art's Sake School are found. The first Brotherhood was formed in 1848, and they had much sympathy with French culture. Ford Madox Brown, the painter, who was associated with them, though he was not one of the founders, had lived and studied in France. In the French fashion, the Pre-Raphaelites founded a magazine in which to set forth their aesthetic aims. This was *The Germ*, which had two numbers, one published in December 1849 and the other in January 1850, but only a quarter of the copies printed were sold. Then, under the title *Art and Poetry, Being Thoughts towards Nature*, it published two further issues, but in March 1850 the enterprise was abandoned. Amongst those associated with the paper were the three Rossettis—Dante-Gabriel, William, and Christina—Ford Madox Brown, and Coventry Patmore. Rossetti contributed poetry, including *My Sister's Ship*, *Hand and Soul*, the first draft of *Sea Limits*, *The Carillon*, also his most famous poem *The Blessed Damozel*, and a number of sonnets describing various famous pictures. These poems remained unpublished in book form until 1870.

Rossetti, with his dual personality—the poet and the painter—would seem to be the true embodiment of the Art for Art's Sake artist as conceived by Gautier, its most perfect symbol. He also seemed nearer in inspiration than any other poet to the French Master. It is however difficult to claim that he owed much directly to French literature, for his brother William, when introducing his *Collected Poems*, declared that the only French poets whom he knew were Hugo and Musset. It may have been that his Italian blood produced in him a vein of poetry which was in harmony with the southern and classical inspiration of the Art for Art's Sake Movement in France.

The Pre-Raphaelite Brotherhood aroused a great deal of opposition and adverse criticism, and their contributions to the Royal Academy in 1850 were made the occasion for an onslaught. They were accused of being morbid, affected, and precious, as well as conceited. It was said that they did not know how to draw and that their subjects were indecent. *The Athenaeum* charged them with worshipping an art idol which had visible deformity as its main attribute. It was said that their affectation and trick was to defy and go counter to accepted principles of beauty and recognized axioms of good taste. The critics accused them of being a conspiracy to debauch the taste of the people of the time, and not only to corrupt their taste, but to undermine, as well, their Christian faith and their morals.

Ruskin eventually became one of the strongest of their opponents. In his *Modern Painters*, published between 1843 and 1860, he expressed the view that art and morality were one and the same thing. He was unfavourably impressed by French culture, especially by the Art for Art's Sake Movement, and he considered the country frivolous and immoral. Contrary to Gautier, he believed that art and morality should be closely allied, and that what was beautiful must also be moral—no beauty without moral principles. In his Oxford lectures he attacked the ideals of the Art for Art's Sake School which were beginning to infiltrate into England, and declared that it was to the moral part in each of us that beauty must address itself.

'The theoretic faculty,' he said in *Modern Painters*, 'is concerned with the moral perception and appreciation of ideas of beauty. And the error respecting it is the considering and calling it Aesthetic, thus degrading it to a mere operation of sense . . . so that arts which appeal to it sink into mere amusement and minister to morbid sensibilities.'

This is in complete opposition to the ideas of the Gautier School and those of the Pre-Raphaelites. Rossetti once remarked ironically: 'As Ruskin is only half-informed about Art, anything he says in favour of one's work is sure to be invaluable in a professional way.'

The Pre-Raphaelite Brotherhood expired in 1853, but it was resurrected temporarily in Oxford in 1856 by William Morris and Burne-Jones, when they were undergraduates at Exeter College. They invited the Brotherhood to come to Oxford, and were responsible for the frescoes in the Union Society Debating Hall. They founded *The Oxford and Cambridge Review Magazine* to propagate their theories of art. Rossetti, Ford Madox Brown, and William Morris were the chief contributors, and Rossetti published in it various poems, amongst them a revised version of *The Blessed Damozel*.

The English attitude towards France had been changing during the past decade. It had now become an accepted fact that she was capable of shining in the arts, in literature and learning, and it was now fashionable for those who had artistic aspirations to go there for instruction and inspiration, as well as for recreation. Paris seemed less materialistic than London, and it was possible to lead a very pleasant life there without much money. This was the hey-day of Bohemia and the Latin Quarter. With the development of national education, writers and artists were now emerging from all classes of society, even from the poorest, and a great many of them lived in the direst poverty while devoting themselves to art. This was the time of the 'Buveurs d'Eau', a society founded by the best known of the Bohemians, Murger, the author of *Scènes de la Vie de Bohème*. A faithful picture of this society and its habits was given by George du Maurier, who had been a student in the Latin Quarter, in his novel *Trilby*, published in 1894.

Whistler was one of the first painters to go from England to study in

Paris, and he became close friends with many of the famous painters of the day in France, with Delacroix, Fantin-Latour, and Legros. He used to know the Bohemians, and called them his 'no-shirt friends'. Later, when he came back to England—he had been in Paris during the eighteen-fifties and returned to London in 1859—he brought back with him Fantin-Latour and Legros, and was thus responsible for introducing a French atmosphere into English artistic life. Legros settled down in London, but Fantin-Latour hankered after Paris, and went back there later in company with Whistler. In 1863 he painted the *Hommage à Delacroix*, in which figure Whistler and Rossetti, as well as Baudelaire.

Whistler, who was, as well as a painter, a talented writer, shows in his *Gentle Art of Making Enemies* and his *Ten o'clock* that he had absorbed much of Baudelaire's aesthetic doctrine. In *Ten o'clock* he writes: 'Nature contains the elements, in colour and form, of all pictures, as the keyboard contains all the notes of all music.' This is what Baudelaire had said in his *Salon* of 1846. Whistler agreed with him in believing that what the artist made of these elements was superior to their natural state. Nature was, according to Baudelaire, only a collection of raw materials, which the artist must put in order, for Nature knows neither colour nor line. Whistler says:

> 'The artist is born to pick and choose, and group with science, the elements, that the result may be beautiful—as the musician gathers his notes and forms his chords until he brings forth from chaos glorious harmony. To say to the painter that Nature is to be taken as she is, is to say to the player that he may sit on the piano. That Nature is always right is an assertion as artistically untrue as it is one whose truth is usually taken for granted. Still seldom does Nature succeed in producing a picture. How little this is understood, and how dutifully the casual in Nature is accepted as sublime, may be gathered from the unlimited admiration daily produced by a very foolish sunset.'

Although Baudelaire was a poet of the Art for Art's Sake Movement, with his influence came a new trend into English literature in the eighteen-sixties, when Swinburne published his article on *Les Fleurs du Mal* in *The Spectator* in 1862, and his own collection of poems, *Poems and Ballads*, in 1866, which will be discussed in the following chapter. This current was more passionately attacked than that of Gautier, and considered more immoral, obscene, and dangerous. There was, with Gautier, something more open and happy, with no hint of decadence; it was what Henry James, in his *French Poets and Novelists*,

B

called his pagan bonhomie, and the unquestioning serenity of his enjoyment of the spectacle of nature and of art. This gave him a kind of
innocence which did not offend as much as the subtler and deeper
analysis of Baudelaire.

Nevertheless, Baudelaire claimed to belong to the Art for Art's Sake
group and called Gautier his master. He did not, however, bear much
resemblance to him—except in his worship of work well done, and his
high regard for the purest standards of art. Baudelaire reacted against
the excesses of the Romantic School as violently as did the other poets,
but in a different manner. He disliked the Romantic historical local
colour, with its tawdry fancy-dress, as much as did his contemporaries,
but, instead of escaping into the Hellenic revival of the middle of the
century, with its veneration for everything Greek, he advised, as a
change from the false historical attitude of the Romantics, the search
for elements of beauty in the modern world. At the end of his *Salon* for
1845, he said: 'Celui-là sera le *peintre*, le vrai peintre, qui saura arracher
à la vie actuelle son côté épique, et nous faire voir et comprendre
combien nous sommes grands et poétiques dans nos cravates et nos
bottes vernies'.

He disliked, as much as did the others, the convention of Romantic
love, of the rights of passion, the belief that it justifies everything, that all
love is pure. On the contrary, he showed that there were two forms of
love—one ideal, as exemplified in the cycle of the White Venus, and the
other sensual—which is lust rather than love—as shown in the cycle of
the Black Venus.

He too worshipped beauty, as did his fellow-poets, Gautier, Banville, and Leconte de Lisle, but his conception was very different from
theirs. They all preached the cult of beauty, the necessity of reproducing
it in their works, but they did not understand it as he did. For them there
existed beautiful subjects, and the function of the artist was to reproduce that beauty in their works. Baudelaire, however, at the dawn of
the development of photography, understood that, if faithfulness in
reproduction is the highest function of art, then the logical outcome
will be that photography will become the most perfect and ideal form
of art. He, on the contrary, did not consider that there could be such a
thing as a beautiful subject. Beauty consisted in what the artist brought
to the subject; beauty was the fire that sprang up when the artist was
moved by contemplation of any subject, and this radiance could come
from objects reputed ugly, and which, in fact, were ugly. 'Tu m'as donné
ta boue,' he cried, 'et j'en ai fait de l'or.' He did not say, as has so often
been claimed, that ugliness was beauty, but only that from ugliness he
could distil beauty.

He did not consider that material progress was an advance, but believed that true progress could only come from the diminution in the natural evil of man, from the disappearance of original sin. He was exceptional, at that time, in believing in the existence of Satan and of sin. He did not agree with Taine's cynical claim that vice and virtue did not exist as moral considerations, but were only two products, like vitriol and sugar, which are dissimilar, but neither better nor worse one than the other.

With a sense of sin came bitter remorse, and this prevented Baudelaire from attaining that pagan serenity which Henry James admired in Gautier. The portrayal of the evil in mankind persuaded many readers that he revelled in sin and vice, because he was aware of their fatal attraction and dangerous power of luring men to their destruction. This is what is usually called Baudelaire's Satanism, which at this time—and indeed until after the First World War—was generally considered the most characteristic aspect of his genius.

Yet he was the only writer in the middle of the nineteenth century who was preoccupied with spiritual values. He considered artistic creation as a spiritual activity and believed that inspiration came from contact with ultimate reality. This experience was the same for each artist whatever might be his means of expression; but each rendered it in his own particular artistic language—painting, music, sculpture, or poetry. This led him to the most fruitful of his artistic experiments, that of *correspondances*, of finding the earthly symbols for spiritual truth, and also the symbolical *correspondances* between one art and the other, in a desire to create one perfect unified art which would express them all at once. In *Richard Wagner et Tannhäuser à Paris* he writes:

'Ce qui serait vraiment surprenant, c'est que le son ne pût suggérer la couleur, que les couleurs ne pussent pas donner l'idée d'une mélodie, et que le son et la couleur fussent impropres à traduire les idées; les choses s'étant toujours exprimées par une analogie réciproque, depuis le jour où Dieu a proféré le monde comme une complexe et individuelle totalité.'

He conceived the possibility of a total art appealing to all the senses in one, or, as he himself says, in his poem *Tout Entière:*

'O métamorphose mystique
De tous mes sens fondus en un!
Son haleine fait la musique
Comme sa voix fait le parfum.'

As a spiritual being, Baudelaire realized that music, above all the other arts, had the power of rendering, of conveying, a transcendental experience, and his effects thus tended towards making poetry approximate to music in powers of expression and suggestion. This eventually became one of his most valuable contributions to French poetry.

Translations into English of Baudelaire's poetry began to appear shortly after his death in 1867. In 1869 *À une Charogne*, *Moesta et Errabunda*, and *Lesbos* were translated by Herne Shepherd. In 1870 fifteen poems were translated by Harry Curren in a collection of translations from the French entitled *Echoes from the French*. And, in 1871, a translation of *Examen de Minuit* appeared in the December number of *Dark Blue*. He was not, however, accepted and appreciated by the English in the same way as Gautier. Nevertheless, in spite of opposition, Saintsbury wrote in the October number of *The Fortnightly Review*, in 1875— the most intelligent article which had yet appeared in England concerning him—that 'it was not merely admiration of Baudelaire which was to be persuaded to English readers, but also imitation of him which, at least with equal earnestness, was to be urged on English writers'.

By 1870 French influence was strongly established in England, and poets were beginning to be inspired by French models. John Payne, who was at Balliol about 1860, devoted most of his life to a study of French literature. In 1871 he had the pleasure of meeting Mallarmé in London, a friendship sprang up between the two poets and a correspondence started between them. In 1873 Payne went over to Paris to discuss plans with Mallarmé for founding an international association of poets, and, in 1875, he invited him to come to London to stay with him.

Payne, who was much interested in the doctrine of the Art for Art's Sake Movement, translated Gautier's aesthetic essay entitled *Du Beau dans l'Art*, and also many poems from the French, of various periods from the earliest days to modern times—amongst them were the entire poetic works of Villon. He published these translations under the collective title *Flowers From France* in five volumes. Volume One was entitled *The Dawn* which included poems from the thirteenth and fourteenth centuries. Volume Two was called *The Renaissance*, and Volume Three *The Dark Ages*, comprising the seventeenth and eighteenth centuries, which he did not admire. Volumes Four and Five dealt with the period from the Revolution to Leconte de Lisle.

He published a collection of his own poems in 1877 entitled *Songs of Life and Death*, which is his most distinguished work, especially in his use of the ballad form, which he borrowed from Banville. These poems are inspired and influenced by his wide reading of French literature—

as can be seen by the variety of quotations from French poets, which he uses as epigraphs to his separate poems, passages from Aloysius Bertrand, Senancour, Baudelaire, and Lamennais. His poems recall Verlaine, or Baudelaire when he is not in his most tragic mood. His *Madrigal Triste* contains echoes of Baudelaire's *Invitation au Voyage*, which Payne transposes into his own milder idiom.

O'Shaughnessy also shows traces of French influence in his poetry, in his *Epic of Women*, published in 1870, in his *Lays of France* of 1872, and in his *Music and Moonlight* of 1874. *The Epic of Women* is written in the French epic tradition of the nineteenth century, with echoes of Victor Hugo and Leconte de Lisle. In *The Lays of France* he has adapted and paraphrased some of the verse tales of Marie de France. But his last collection, *Music and Moonlight*, is his most original work. He shows here that he realizes that art should be consciously composed and he devotes immense care to the technical execution and the symmetry of the verse. There is some mild Baudelairean influence when he paints beauty allied to evil, as in the poem addressed to a young murderess, and the one entitled *From Heaven and Hell*.

A critic, after reading these poems, wrote: 'Some day perhaps Mr. O'Shaughnessy will give us splendid poetry, showing a sense that woman's fairness is no such baneful thing when its influences are judged justly and widely.'

The English poets, at this time, did not borrow only their subject matter from their French counterparts, but they adopted, as well, some of their poetic forms. The Second Empire in France was a period of experimentation in technique, particularly in the minor forms which had been neglected since the advent of classicism—such forms as the ballad, lay, virelay and rondeau, which were being used, with great effect, by Banville.

Banville was the virtuoso in French poetry at this time, who performed with great facility and brilliance, and he became the model in England for all those who were making similar experiments. His *Petit Traité de Versification Française*, published in 1872, became well known in England and exercised a fruitful influence. He believed that, as far as his own country was concerned, the restrictions it had endured in verse had had an enervating effect for two centuries, while French poetry had become, he said, 'réduite en esclavage, tuée, embaumée et momifiée'.

Andrew Lang, in *Lays and Lyrics of Old France*, published in 1872, reproduced French metrical forms in English. The collection contains translations from the French, beginning with Charles d'Orléans, in the fifteenth century, and going as far as Victor Hugo. He also published, in 1881, twenty-two ballads entitled *Ballads in Blue China* which, again, owe much to Banville.

In 1877 Austin Dobson, whose mother was French, and who had been educated in France, brought out a collection of poems in old French forms, entitled *Proverbs in Porcelain*, and it includes a poem entitled *Ars Victrix* which is an adaptation—almost a translation—of Gautier's poem *L'Art*.

That same year, in 1877, Edmund Gosse, in the July number of *The Cornhill Magazine*, published an article entitled 'A Plea for Certain Exotic Forms of Verse'. It is in fact a summary of Banville's ideas, from his treatise on French verse, with some additions from Grammont's book on the same subject. He exhorted his fellow-countrymen to adopt some of the more exotic forms of French verse.

In 1878 Austin Dobson wrote an essay entitled 'Some Foreign Forms of Verse', which appeared in *Latter Day Lyrics* edited by W. D. Adams.

In 1887 Gleeson White made an anthology of various exotic poetic forms—*ballade, rondeaux, rondelais, chant royal, kyrielles, pantoums, redoublés, triolets, villanelles, virelais*, and so forth. It was prefaced by a long Introduction on poetic forms current in France, which made extensive use of Banville's *Petit Traité de Versification Française*.

In April 1891 Lionel Johnson, in *The Century Guild Hobby Horse*, published an essay entitled 'A Note upon the Practice and Theory of Verse at the Present Time Obtaining in France' in which he compared the practice of English verse unfavourably with that prevailing in France in matters of technique, saying that it was possible in English to find masterpieces—Shakespeare and Shakespearean—which produce their effect by a richness and splendour of imagination, but which have no perfection of detail, no careful excellence of language, considered by strict eyes. Verbal precision, he declared, was not within the strength of the English.

Of the French Symbolist poets he said: 'It is in the deliberate *science*, the practical science of these French poets, that their distinction lies. Each word is chosen, not for its own beauty or excellence; but as a painter chooses his scheme of colour, or the musician his key; just so do these poets choose what shall be the dominant and tone of their poems.'

It was on the model of the French system that J. A. Symonds composed a whole collection entitled *In the Key of Blue*, published in 1893.

The Art for Art's Sake Movement had by now gained a foothold in England, but it was fighting its way against severe opposition, not only from the ignorant and prejudiced, but also from the older masters as well. Hallam Tennyson, in the second volume of his *Memoir* of his father, quotes an unpublished poem from his pen, dated 1869, which declares that no movement should be called Art for Art's Sake, since such a conception is immoral; it should, on the contrary, be called Art for Art's—and Man's—Sake.

'Art for Art's Sake! Hail, truest Lord of Hell!
Hail Genius, Master of the Moral Will!
"The filthiest of all paintings painted well
Is mightier than the purest painted ill!"
Yea, mightier than the purest painted well,
So prone are we toward the broad way to Hell!'

3

SWINBURNE AND PATER

THE writers who exercised most influence in the propagation of the theories of Art for Art's Sake in England were Algernon Swinburne and Walter Pater. The former was the first imitator of Baudelaire's poetry; while the latter was more interested in his aesthetic doctrine, and brought the conception of the dandy to the University, in England, thus giving rise to a new generation of literary men, who were to become the authors and public of the nineties. Swinburne was the first Decadent in England, owing much to French example; while Pater was the first Aesthete, also much indebted to France.

It was not strange that Swinburne should feel sympathy for France, since he was partly French by blood. His grandfather, Sir John Swinburne, who was born in 1762 and died in his ninety-ninth year, was born and bred in France, being the son of a naturalized Frenchman who had married a Frenchwoman. He himself had been the friend of Mirabeau and, to the end of his days, remained, in appearance and manners, more like a Frenchman than an Englishman. Sir John spent his childhood, and his youth until he was twenty-five, in France, but then returned to England to inherit the family estates.

His second son, who became Admiral Swinburne, produced six children of whom the eldest, Algernon, the future poet, was born on 5 April 1837.

Algernon Swinburne entered Eton in 1852 and showed great gifts for languages, which was not astonishing considering the advantages he had enjoyed of hearing French spoken at home. From childhood he formed the habit of reading French and, while at school, he read *Notre-Dame de Paris* by Victor Hugo, which started his admiration for the French poet, who was to remain amongst his favourite authors. He also read his *Châtiments*, when it appeared in 1853, and he considered his deplorable play, *Le Roi s'amuse*, one of the greatest dramatic works in world literature. At Eton he won the Prince Consort Prize for French and Italian, and was honourably commended for his Greek verses.

After he left school he went up to Oxford in January 1856 and entered Balliol College. Soon after his arrival, a literary society was founded in the College called 'Old Mortality', which consisted of Swinburne himself, Grenfell, John Payne, James Bryce, T. H. Green, and later, but only after Swinburne had gone down, Walter Pater.

In Swinburne's second year Matthew Arnold arrived at Oxford as Professor of Poetry, and the young man who, at school, had enjoyed his *Tristram and Yseult* and *Sohrab and Rustum*, looked forward to his lectures, but he was disappointed and disillusioned. Arnold seemed to him unadventurous, and unaware of what was happening in contemporary literature in France, with his taste firmly set in the classical mould. Swinburne was much more attracted by the Pre-Raphaelite Brotherhood when, during his freshman year, they had come to Oxford on the invitation of William Morris and Burne-Jones. Swinburne made friends with them, remaining closely associated with them until they finally disbanded in 1862. He dedicated his *Poems and Ballads* to Burne-Jones when it appeared in 1866.

While he was an undergraduate, Swinburne read a great deal of French literature at the Taylor Institute library—Stendhal, Balzac, Dumas, Sand, Janin, Michelet, Choderlos de Laclos, and he seems, at this time, to have been particularly interested in Villon, whose *Ballade des Pendus* he began to translate. He also started a critical essay on the poet which he was never to finish—though later, in 1878, he was to publish a translation of *La Belle Heaulmière*. He read the first series of *La Légende des Siècles* by Victor Hugo when it appeared in 1859, and this increased his admiration for its author. He does not seem to have discovered Baudelaire, but it is not very likely that the Taylor Institute would provide its undergraduates with *Les Fleurs du Mal*, and moreover, since the book had been withdrawn from sale because of the poems banned at the trial in 1857, it was difficult to procure.

A milestone in Swinburne's life was his visit to Paris with his parents in 1858, when he immediately fell under the influence of modern French literature.

He returned to Oxford much changed. He was becoming bored with classical studies, but there was no Honours School of Modern Languages in Oxford at that time. He was rusticated in 1859, and it is not known whether he failed in his examinations, or whether he was sent down for other reasons. He returned to Balliol for the Trinity Term in 1860, and this may have been in order to sit for Schools, but he went down without taking them—or having failed in them—for he never took a degree.

In his final term he entered for the Newdigate Prize, with a poem entitled *The Death of Sir John Franklin*, but did not win it. There were some who thought that he had been unjustly passed over, and that it should have been awarded to him—he certainly thought so himself, and never forgave Oxford for this wrong.

Swinburne left Oxford in 1860 and went to London to take up the career of a man of letters. He got to know Monckton Milnes and Meredith, and renewed his acquaintanceship with Rossetti, Ford Madox Brown, and William Morris.

He was to have gone to France in the autumn of 1860, to join his family at Mentone, but the trip was postponed on account of the illness and death of his grandfather. However, they set out in December, and he remained in France until the early summer of 1861. This visit had an important effect on him, and he seemed to have matured in literary tastes on his return. Perhaps it was at this time that he read *Les Fleurs du Mal*, the second version of which had appeared in January 1861, while he was in France. It was certainly this edition that he knew, and not the banned one of 1857, which was given to him by Rossetti only in 1864. What is strange is that, despite his admiration for Baudelaire, he does not seem ever to have bought any of his works on his own account, for the only copies found in his library after his death were the volume given to him by Rossetti, and *Richard Wagner et Tannhäuser à Paris*, sent to him by its author with an inscription.

If he had not yet read Baudelaire, he had certainly read Gautier, at least *Mademoiselle de Maupin*, which he was to call, in *Notes on Some Pictures*, 'the most perfect and exquisite book of modern times'. Its influence is found in his next work, *The Chronicle of Tebaldeo Tebaldei*. This is the story of a page at the court of the Borgias, in the service of Cesare Borgia, but later transferred to Lucrezia, with whom he fell passionately in love. Like the hero of *Mademoiselle de Maupin*, he was a worshipper at the shrine of pure beauty and, inspired by the doctrine of Art for Art's Sake, he composed a discourse on ideal beauty, entitled *A Treatise of Noble Morals*. 'Beauty,' he said, 'is the beginning of all things, and the end of them is pleasure.' And again: 'Though we do much good, and though we become virtuous, notwithstanding to take pleasure, and to give it again, is better than all our goodness.' Beauty, for him, took the place of religion, and he exclaimed: 'A beautiful soft line drawn is more than a life saved; a pleasant perfume smelt is better than a soul redeemed.'

Lucrezia Borgia herself is of the same family as Mademoiselle de Maupin—and no more deeply studied, for we are given only external pictures of her, like those by some Venetian master. She is described lying naked on her bed, with 'nothing upon her, not a shred of silk or purple, but only the clothing of that adorable and supreme beauty of her flesh which God made her with for the delight of men'. This recalls many similar portraits in *Mademoiselle de Maupin*. 'Elle resta donc sans aucun voile, ses vêtements tombés lui faisant une espèce de socle, dans tout l'éclat diaphane de sa belle nudité, aux douces lueurs d'une lampe d'albâtre que d'Albert avait allumée.'

Tebaldeo Tebaldei is a rich, sensuous, and sensual chronicle which does credit to the talent of the young man, in his early twenties, who composed it.

In 1862 Swinburne returned to France, and it may only have been this time that he discovered *Les Fleurs du Mal*, for it is certainly then that he wrote the essay on Baudelaire which appeared on 6 September in *The Spectator*—Edmund Gosse claims that it was written in a Turkish bath in Paris—and it was the first article ever to appear on the poet in England. 'The writer believes that there is not one poem of *Les Fleurs du Mal*,' he wrote, 'which has not a vivid and distinct background of morality in it.' And, of *À une Charogne*, he said: 'Thus even of the loathsome bodily putrescence and decay he can make noble use, pluck out its meaning and secret, even its beauty in a way, from actual carrion.'

It is largely the Satanic, blasphemous, and violent aspect of Baudelaire which Swinburne admired at this time, and he saw him through Sade—indeed he quotes from the 'divine marquis' to set the tone of his essay, 'la vertu est une chose essentiellement stérile, impuissante, bornée, tandis que le vice fait germer et fleurir'.

He sent an offprint to Baudelaire, who was pleased and touched by it, and wrote to express his appreciation, but he entrusted the letter to his friend Nadar to deliver on his visit to England, who, however, failed to do so, and it came to light only many years after the poet's death.

That same year Swinburne also published in *The Spectator* five articles on *Les Misérables* by Victor Hugo, which seems excessively generous.

Emboldened by his contribution on Baudelaire to *The Spectator*, Swinburne tried to outdo this piece of daring, and to *épater le bourgeois* still more, by submitting reviews on two non-existent texts which he had invented—*Essays* by a certain Ernest Clouet, and *Poems* by an equally non-existent author. But so scabrous were the alleged quotations and the passages from Sade in support, that the editor refused to print them.

In 1863 Swinburne was back again in Paris with Whistler and Fantin-Latour—this was the year of the *Hommage à Delacroix* mentioned in the previous chapter—and, through them, he made the acquaintance of Manet, but it is strange that he should not have met Baudelaire, if indeed he did not meet him, considering that he is in the Fantin-Latour picture, as well as Whistler and Rossetti. Baudelaire was, however, constantly ill at this time, chronically worried on financial grounds, and also on the eve of his departure for Belgium.

On this occasion Swinburne visited the Louvre and was so much impressed by the sculptured *Hermaphrodite* he saw there that he composed a poem on the theme, in March 1865. This was one of the poems which aroused most violent opposition when it appeared in *Poems and Ballads* in 1866.

Between 1865 and 1866 Swinburne was working on *Lesbia Brandon*, again with the intention of shocking the conservative and puritanical public. It deals with sapphic love, and the heroine, Lesbia, symbolizes that ideal—her father even calls her half-male. She composes love poems in which she personally takes the male part, and Hubert, the hero, who seeks her hand, is introduced to her dressed as a woman. However, the novel did not run the certain risk of being banned, since it was published only after the Second World War, in 1952.

The inspiration of *Lesbia Brandon* is borrowed from a variety of French sources—from *Fragoletta* by Henri de Latouche, from *La Fille aux yeux d'or* by Balzac, and, most of all, from Gautier's *Mademoiselle de Maupin*.

The characters of the novel live entirely for art, in an aesthetic atmosphere, and they cultivate their sensations and sensibility. Even in her suicide Lesbia wishes to die in art and beauty, and she kills herself with eau-de-Cologne and an overdose of opium.

The sentiments expressed in the book are those of Art for Art's Sake and they suggest already the aestheticism of Oscar Wilde. 'I feel sometimes that Nature is a democrat. Beauty you see is an exception; and exception means rebellion against a rule, infringement of a law. That is why people who go in for beauty—poets and painters, and all the tail thrash of the arts—are all born aristocrats on the moral side. Nature I do think, if she had her own way, would grow nothing but turnips.'

On 2 May 1866, at the Royal Literary Fund Dinner, Swinburne replied for literature, and, in his speech, expressed his passion for Hugo and Baudelaire.

Poems and Ballads appeared in 1866, and it was the first expression of the influence of Baudelaire in England; also the most extreme manifestation of the doctrine of Art for Art's Sake.

Gautier and Baudelaire are the main influences found in the poems of the collection, but it is that of Baudelaire which aroused most opposition and disgust. In a sonnet Swinburne sings the praises of *Mademoiselle de Maupin*:

> 'This is the golden book of spirit and sense,
>> The holy writ of beauty; he that wrought
>> Made it with dreams and faultless words and thought
> That seeks and finds and loses in the dense
> Dim air of life that beauty's excellence
>> Wherewith love makes one hour of life distraught
>> And all hours after follow and find not aught.
> Here is that height of all love's eminence
> Where man may breathe but for a breathing-space
>> And feel his soul burn as an altar-fire
>> To the unknown God of unachieved desire,
> And from the middle mystery of the place
>> Watch lights that break, hear sounds as of a quire,
> But see not twice unveiled the veiled God's face.'

His direct influence is found in the visually descriptive poems such as *A Christmas Carol*, which Swinburne declares, in a note, was suggested by a drawing by Rossetti, but which equally recalls the carol from *Émaux et Camées* entitled *Noël*.

The strongest influence is however that of Baudelaire, and Swinburne follows him in abandoning the convention which insists that only what is agreeable to behold should be represented. He also followed him in depicting the pleasure which comes from suffering, and the boredom that ensues from the satiety of sin. In *Dolores* there is a passionate description of pain and pleasure intermingled. This poem recalls Baudelaire's *À une Madone*, with its linking of sin and sorrow. The poem is addressed to Notre-Dame des Sept Douleurs:

> 'Cold eyelids that hide like a jewel
>> Hard eyes that grow soft for an hour;
> The heavy white limbs, and the cruel
>> Red mouth like a venomous flower;
> When these are gone by with their glories
>> What shall rest of thee then, what remain,
> O mystic and sombre Dolores,
>> Our Lady of Pain?

Seven sorrows the priests give their Virgin;
    But thy sins, which are seventy times seven,
Seven ages would fail thee to purge in,
    And then they would haunt thee in heaven;
Fierce midnights and famishing morrows,
    And the loves that complete and control
All the joys of the flesh, all the sorrows
    That wear out the soul.'

There is the sensuality of Baudelaire's poems celebrating the Black Venus in *Laus Veneris* and the lesbianism of *Lesbos* and *Delphine et Hippolyte* in *Sapphics* and *Anactoria*, and the blasphemy of *La Révolte* in *The Leper* where Swinburne asks what he calls 'the old question, "will not God do right?" ' This recalls Baudelaire's outburst in *Le Reniement de Saint Pierre*: 'Saint Pierre a renié Jésus, il a bien fait!'

Shortly after *Poems and Ballads* was published, Swinburne heard the premature announcement of Baudelaire's death, and he composed his *Ave Atque Vale*, addressing him as brother—they were indeed brothers in their inspiration. This was published only in the second series of *Poems and Ballads* in 1878.

'Thou sawest, in thine old singing season, brother,
    Secrets and sorrows unbeheld by us:
    Fierce loves, and lovely leaf-buds poisonous,
Bare to thy subtler eye, but for none other,
    Blowing by night in some unbreathed-in clime;
    The hidden harvest of luxurious time,
Sin without shape, and pleasure without speech;
    And where strange dreams in a tumultuous sleep
    Make the shut eyes of stricken spirits weep;
And with each face thou sawest the shadow on each,
    Seeing as men sow men reap.'

Swinburne did not, unfortunately, follow Baudelaire in his belief that a lyric poem should be short, for his poems are too loosely constructed and would have gained from more concentration.

Poems and Ballads had an immediate *succès de scandale*. It burst, as Burdett says in *The Beardsley Period*, 'like a tidal wave upon the apparent security of the islanders'. There was a violent storm of protest against the book. *The Athenaeum* declared that Swinburne was unclean for the sake of uncleanness. He was abused in every way, and was even threatened with castration by a correspondent in Dublin. *The Pall Mall* attacked him in an article entitled 'Swinburne's Folly', describing his 'mean and miserable indecency', accusing him of being 'modern, artificial, and French', and ending: 'Here lies the moral sense of A. C. Swinburne.'

But it was an anonymous article in *The Saturday Review*, on 4 August 1866, which was most violent in its attack. John Morley—for it is now known that the article was his—talked of 'the lilies and languors of virtue' and 'the roses and raptures of vice' in Swinburne's poetry, and he described the 'unspeakable foulness of the whole book'. 'We are in the midst of fire and serpents, wine and ashes, blood and foam, and a hundred lurid horrors,' said the article. 'The bottomless pit encompasses us on one side, and the stews and bagnios on the other,' and it ended by calling the poet 'the libidinous laureate of a pack of satyrs'.

The protests were taken up by other papers as well. *The Times* was threatening to urge prosecution, and the publishers, frightened of suffering the fate of Baudelaire's publisher, when *Les Fleurs du Mal* was taken to the courts, withdrew the whole edition from sale. It was, however, bought up by another publisher, a man with a somewhat shady reputation, called Hotten, who republished it by merely changing its cover.

Swinburne then decided to reply and to defend himself. This he did, in an article entitled 'Notes on Poems and Reviews', in September 1866. This was his artistic credo, and he saw himself as a martyr, as Flaubert and Baudelaire had been, nine years before, at their trials. He showed that Baudelaire's poems were moral because they were beautiful, and, as Baudelaire had done before him, he protested against separate poems being torn out of their context, as an expression of personal opinions. He claimed that his book was a dramatic work and that 'no utterances of enjoyment or despair should be assumed to be their author's personal feelings or faith'. *Anactoria*, he said, was considered particularly horrible, yet all he had done was try to express the violence of feeling between two human beings, which hardens into rage and deepens into despair. In *Dolores* he had wanted to demonstrate how the use of violent delights leads to violent ends. He closed his defence—just as Baudelaire had done—by saying that if one listened to such criticism one would be able only to produce books that were consoling and fit solely for convent girls. He complained that everyone seemed to think that publishing a book was equivalent to thrusting it, with violence, into the hands of every mother and nurse in the kingdom, as fit and necessary food for female infancy. 'Let those read who will,' he said, 'and let those who will abstain from reading. No man wishes to force men's food down the throats of babes and sucklings. The verses analysed were written with no moral or immoral intent, but the upshot seems to me moral rather than immoral, if it needs be one or the other. Purity and prudery cannot keep house together. And if literature is not to deal with the full life of man, and the whole nature of things, let it be cast aside with the rods and the rattles of childhood.' He ended: 'When England has again a school of poetry as she had at least twice before, or as France has now, if such a day should ever rise or return, it will once more be remembered that the office of adult art is neither puerile or feminine, but virile; that its purity is not of the cloister or the harem; that all things are good in its sight, out of which good work can be produced.' These are the sentiments of Baudelaire, Flaubert, and Gautier; they are the theories of the Art for Art's Sake Movement. Swinburne returned to them again in his essay on Blake, published in 1868, when he vituperated against all moral teaching in art, saying that art exists for the sake of Art first of all. 'Art is at her peril if she tries to do good; she shall not try to do that under penalty of death and damnation. Her business is not to do good, but to be good on her own; all is well with her while she sticks to that. Art for Art's Sake first of all!'

The year of *Poems and Ballads* was an important one for Swinburne —probably the highest point in his career—and he was only twenty-nine. In 1867 an article in *The Westminster Review* declared that he might soon replace Tennyson as the most significant poet in England, and that English poetry would now draw inspiration from new springs.

The attacks, however, did not cease. In 1870 a certain Mortimer Collins described, in a work entitled *Two Plunges for a Pearl*, a man called Reginald Swynfen, who was obviously intended for Swinburne, 'built like a grass-hopper', whose poems deal with 'effeminate heroes and masculine heroines'. Next came an article entitled 'The Fleshly School of Poetry', in *The Contemporary Review*, in 1871, by Robert Buchanan, which caused a sensation. The immediate occasion of the article was the publication of Rossetti's collection of poems, *The House of Life*, in April that year. These were all the poems he had composed up to date, some of which had appeared in *The Germ* and *The Oxford and Cambridge Review* over fifteen years before, and some of which had been rescued from the coffin of his wife, Elizabeth Siddal, after they had lain buried with her for more than nine years. Swinburne had reviewed them enthusiastically in *The Fortnightly Review*, and William Morris in *The Academy*. However, more critics were unfavourable than favourable. Browning, writing to Isabella Blagdon, said that they 'were scented with poetry, like the trifles you take out of a cedar or sandalwood box; you know how I hate the effeminacy of his school!' Many readers took exception to the personal note of the book, especially its sensuality, and, above all, the poem entitled *Nuptial Sleep* roused protest. Tennyson called it 'the filthiest thing' he had ever read. Disapproval was so violent that Rossetti did not print it in the 1881 edition of his poems, and his brother omitted it from the *Collected Poems*. Evelyn Waugh, however, quotes the offensive passage in his *Rossetti*:

> 'At length their long kiss severed, with sweet smart,
>   And as the last slow, sudden drops are shed
>   From sparkling eaves when all the storm has fled,
> So singly flagged the pulses of each heart.
> Their bosoms sundered, with the opening start
>   Of married flowers to either side outspread
>   From the knit stem, yet still their mouths burnt red,
> Fawned on each other where they lay apart.'

Although no direct influence of French literature can be proved in Rossetti, it is the kind of poem associated more with France than with England.

Rossetti's poem was the occasion of Buchanan's article, but he gave more attention to Swinburne. He started with a general denunciation of the sexual depravity of the age, and showed how this depravity had come from France. He described the abnormal types of 'diseased lust and lustful disease' to be found there, and he likened the poets to a sort of 'demi-monde, not composed, like the one in France, of simple courtesans, but of men and women of indolent habits and aesthetic tastes, artists and literary persons'. In these, he said, are found 'that fever-cloud, generated first in Italy, and then blown westward, sucking up, on its way, all that was most unwholesome from the soil of France'. He added that it was a double misfortune for England to have this nuisance, but also to have it second-hand. 'This scrofulous school of literature had been distinguishing itself for many long years in Paris, but it reached its final and most tremendous development in Baudelaire.' After that, according to him, it had spread to England, and, 'encouraged by his tuition', Mr. Swinburne attempted to surpass Baudelaire, to excel 'even that frightful artist in the representation of abnormal types of diseased lust and lustful diseases'. He called him 'this Dandy of the brothel, this Brummel of the stews' and declared that his only known merit was the 'nasal appreciation of foul odours'. All the worst of Mr. Swinburne, he claimed, came from Baudelaire.

Swinburne was only amused by the attack, but Rossetti was bitterly hurt, and he answered in an article in *The Athenaeum*, in December 1871, called 'The Stealthy School of Criticism'.

The following year Buchanan renewed his attack in an article entitled 'The Fleshly School and Other Phenomena of the Day'. Swinburne bounded in with an answer, 'Under the Microscope', and Buchanan retorted with 'The Monkey and the Microscope'. Then, in 1875, an anonymous publication appeared under the title *Jonas Fisher: A Poem in Brown and White* which described the 'morbid immorality' of the new school. Swinburne jumped to the conclusion that here was Buchanan again at his tricks and he published, in *The Examiner*, his *Epitaph for a Slanderer*. But, in 1876, the author of *Jonas Fisher* took an action against *The Examiner* and was awarded one hundred and fifty pounds' damages—he was not Buchanan but the Earl of Southesk. Then Watts-Dunton came to the rescue of Rossetti and Swinburne, and wrote *The Octopus of the Golden Isles*—the octopus being Buchanan, and the golden isles the land of literature before his arrival.

Swinburne's next collection of poems—not counting *A Song of Italy*, published in 1867—was *Songs before Sunrise*, which appeared in 1871 and does not show any advance on the first book. There are still poems in the Art for Art's Sake and Baudelairean manner—such as *Hymn of Man*, and *Before the Crucifix*. The latter is of the same inspiration as Baudelaire's *À une Charogne*, and Swinburne is as much obsessed, as Baudelaire had been, by the physical aspect of death and decay—the physical death of Christ—but he is less profoundly spiritual, and his symbolism is less effectively worked out. He addresses Christ dying on the cross, 'God rotten to the bone' and 'carrion crucified', asking Him to contemplate the churches and the altars which have been erected in His honour, 'blood-blackened altars', and to reflect on what the priests have made of Him, saying:

> 'Come down, be done with, cease, give o'er;
> Hide thyself, strive not, be no more.'

Swinburne continued to be occupied with French literature, and he composed ten poems in French for *Le Tombeau de Gautier*. The poet had died in 1872, and this collection was to commemorate his death. Swinburne republished them later, with the obituary poem he had written for Baudelaire, and others inspired by France, in the second series of *Poems and Ballads* in 1878. He also included translations of Villon, and some other poems in French, which are of a high standard in achievement for a foreigner.

However, in 1879 Swinburne went to live at Putney with Watts-Dunton, and there ends his vital connection with literature.

The collection *Poems and Ballads*, in 1866, had played an important part in the battle against rampant philistinism in England, it had breached the battlements of Victorian respectability, and had introduced contemporary French literature. It crystallized one aspect of that literature, the Baudelairean, which was to last in Britain for more than half a century.

Swinburne was, later, to repudiate this early phase of his development for, in 1901, he wrote to W. Sharp to protest at his having included some of his Baudelairean poems in an anthology, saying: 'I never really had much in common with Baudelaire, though I still retain my early admiration for his genius at his best.'

This is not strictly true, and Swinburne's memory is playing him false, for, thirty-five years earlier, there had been no writer in England who possessed more in common with the French poet than he himself.

In 1871 Swinburne went to Oxford on a visit to see Jowett, who had kept, in spite of everything, a keen interest in him. At Balliol he met Taine, who was there to lecture, and he called on Walter Pater, of whom he had heard, though he had not known him when they were up together—their undergraduate days had overlapped by about one year.

They were very different in temperament and influence. Swinburne had been, in his most significant period, a figure of revolt, an iconoclast, arousing repulsion and hatred. He had started first and his importance was on the wane when Pater was just beginning. Pater, on the contrary, was no rebel, for he hated violence of all sorts. He wanted to formulate an aesthetic doctrine, to create a new way of life, but not to destroy. He wanted to raise a new altar on the ruins of the past. He did not favour the Satanic and rebellious aspect of Baudelaire, but preferred the Dandy and the Aesthete. He became the first Art for Art's Sake Dandy, the first academic aesthete, and he influenced a wider field than Swinburne through the teaching of the young.

He was of the same generation as Swinburne, being two years younger, born in August 1839. He was educated at King's School, Canterbury, where he was a King's Scholar, and went up to Oxford to the Queen's College, with an exhibition, in 1858. This was the time when Swinburne, John Addington Symonds, T. H. Green, and J. R. Green were at the university—a brilliant generation.

He too attended Arnold's lectures because, at school, he had enjoyed his *Scholar Gypsy* and his *Sohrab and Rustum*. At Oxford his chief interests lay in philosophy—particularly in German philosophy, which was fashionable at that time. He read the classics, but soon found that he was losing interest in them, and wanted to study only philosophy, particularly that branch which deals with aesthetics. He was much attracted by the doctrine of Art for Art's Sake—especially in Flaubert's theories of art—but he does not seem to have known much about Baudelaire—not his poetry at all events. He obtained a Second Class in his Final Schools in 1862 but, nevertheless, in 1864 he was appointed to a Fellowship at Brasenose College to teach philosophy. He enjoyed teaching, particularly discoursing on the subjects which interested him, and he liked influencing the young, but he had no taste for research.

As time went on he was becoming more and more drawn towards the aesthetic side of philosophy and literature. He was a close friend of John Payne, the poet and critic of French literature, who introduced him to French poetry. On the whole he was more interested in the past than in the present, more attracted by the classical aspect of the Art for Art's Sake Movement, as exemplified by Gautier and Leconte de Lisle, than by the contemporary as practised by Baudelaire, and his favourite period of culture was that of the Renaissance. He was, however, drifting along without any sense of direction, and it was only when he discovered the study of Winckelmann by Otto Jahn that he really found his vocation. This was a revelation to him and he immediately composed his essay on Winckelmann, which he published in *The Westminster Review* in 1867. Although Winckelmann had lived in the eighteenth century, Pater considered him, with his enquiring mind, his type of artistic appreciation, and his intention of reaching back to the root of the matter, as a figure typical of the Renaissance, and so, later, he included this essay amongst his studies of Renaissance figures.

Pater was very much moved by Winckelmann's view of art, and he seems to have cherished the ambition of becoming himself, for English literature and art, another Winckelmann. In 1869 he visited Italy for the first time—Florence, Ravenna, and Pisa—and saw the glory of the Renaissance on its own native soil. Hitherto, when he had travelled abroad, it had been to Germany, to Heidelberg University, for the purpose of philosophic study.

Between 1869 and 1872 Pater continued to study the Renaissance in various essays which he printed in *The Westminster Review*—essays on Pico della Mirandola, Luca della Robbia, Michelangelo as seen through his sonnets but not his plastic art, and a study of two early French lays, *Amis et Amile* and *Aucassin et Nicolette*, in which he saw, already, signs of the Renaissance. And, finally, there was the essay on Winckelmann. Undoubtedly the most famous of these essays was the one on Leonardo da Vinci, with its well-known passage describing La Gioconda, 'older than the rocks among which she sits', which Yeats included in his *Oxford Book of Modern English Poetry*, printing it as *vers libre*.

These essays on the Renaissance were reprinted in book form in 1873, under the title *The Renaissance, Studies in Art and Poetry*, with a 'Conclusion' which Pater omitted in 1877 from the second edition, because as he said on reprinting it later: 'I conceived it might possibly mislead some of these young men into whose hands it might fall.' These ideas formed, as it were, the gospel of Art for Art's Sake in England. They had all the more effect as they came *ex cathedra* from the University, and the ideas, which had been vaguely floating in the air, crystallized round it. It was an expression of his ideal of gracious living, but it led to misunderstanding and criticism as it was alleged that Pater was preaching free-thinking, and even atheism.

'To burn always with this hard, gemlike flame, to maintain this ecstasy, is success in life. . . . While all melts under our feet, we may well grasp at any exquisite passion, or any contribution to knowledge that seems by a lifted horizon to set the spirit free for a moment, or any stirring of the senses, strange dyes, strange colours, and curious odours, or work of the artist's hands, or the face of one's friend. Not to discriminate every moment some passionate attitude in those about us, and in the very brilliancy of their gifts some tragic dividing of forces on their ways, is, on this short day of frost and sun, to sleep before evening. With this sense of the splendour of our experience and of its awful brevity, gathering all we are into one desperate effort to see and touch, we shall hardly have time to make theories about the things we see and touch. What we have to do is to be for ever curiously testing new opinions and courting new impressions, never acquiescing in a facile orthodoxy of Comte, or of Hegel, or of our own. . . . The theory or idea or system which requires of us the sacrifice of any part of this experience, in consideration of some interest into which we cannot enter, or some abstract theory we have not identified with ourselves, or of what is only conventional, has no real claim upon us.'

In these Renaissance studies, although Pater undoubtedly owes something to Ruskin, he differs from him completely in his moral attitude. As befitted an admirer of the Art for Art's Sake doctrine, he considered that there should be no moral lesson in art, and that it was its own justification.

Although Pater did not appreciate the poetry of Baudelaire, he must have known his aesthetic doctrine as expressed in his criticism, for he shares many of his ideas. He too believed that music, at its most ex-quisite, expressed the essence of ultimate reality more perfectly than any other art, and he saw all art as aspiring towards the state of music, as he says in *The School of Giorgione*:

> 'It is the art of music which most completely realizes this artistic ideal, this perfect identification of matter and form. In its con-summate moments, the end is not distinct from the means, the form from the matter, the subject from the expression; they inhere in and completely saturate each other; and to it, therefore, to the condition of its perfect moment, all the arts may be supposed constantly to tend and aspire. In music, then, rather than in poetry, is to be found the true type or measure of perfected art. Therefore, although each art has its incommunicable element, its untranslatable order of im-pressions, its unique mode of reaching the "imaginative reason", yet the arts may be represented as continually struggling after the law or principle of music, to a condition which music alone completely realizes; and one of the chief functions of aesthetic criticism, dealing with the products of art, new or old, is to estimate the degree in which each of those products approaches, in this sense, to musical law.'

From Baudelaire also he drew his definition of beauty. Baudelaire had said, in his *Exposition Universelle*, in 1855, that there is always some-thing strange in beauty :

> 'Le Beau est toujours bizarre. Je ne veux pas dire qu'il soit volon-tairement, froidement, bizarre, car dans ce cas il serait un monstre sorti des rails de la vie. Je dis qu'il contient toujours un peu de bizar-rerie, de bizarrerie naïve, non voulue, inconsciente, et que c'est cette bizarrerie qui le fait être particulièrement le Beau!'

Pater wrote in *The Poetry of Michelangelo*:

> 'A certain strangeness, something of the blossoming of the aloe, is indeed an element in all true works of art: that they should excite or surprise us is indispensable. But that they shall give pleasure and exert a charm over us is indispensable too; and this strangeness must be sweet also—a lovely strangeness.'

His *Renaissance* created a sensation at the time—especially the

'Conclusion', which was considered profoundly immoral, and likely to lead to a life given over to purely sensuous and sensual enjoyment. Pater had immediately a large following amongst the undergraduate population at Oxford—this was the time when Oscar Wilde was at the University—and old-fashioned teachers, like Jowett, grew afraid as they saw the new generation of aesthetes which was arising, burning with 'this hard, gemlike flame' which Pater advocated, and prepared 'to maintain this ecstasy'.

Pater was now the model of the new aesthetes at Oxford, and his way of living and entertaining was copied by all those who wished to be considered up to date. When his friends came to dine with him he was most anxious that everything should be exactly as he wanted it, that everything should be properly appointed. He liked his table set with taste, and to see an orange strip down the middle of the white cloth, and plenty of flowers. He was in a fever of anxiety if he saw anything the slightest bit crooked, and the glass, which was rubbed until it gleamed, never quite reached his ideal.

Pater was now sufficiently notorious to be caricatured in *Punch*, and especially in a work entitled *The New Republic*, in 1877, by W. H. Mallock. Here Rose, the Pre-Raphaelite poet, with his 'soft lulling voice', is intended for Pater, who describes the chief aim of life as the consciousness of 'exquisite living' in a chamber decorated, as it were, for a beloved woman, with walls tinted with symphonies of subdued colours, and filled with flowers and strange scents.

Pater was bitterly hurt by what he considered this misunderstanding of his doctrine, and, the following year, in 1878, he began working on his *Marius the Epicurean*, which was to be the formulation and justification of his aesthetic ideal. It took him seven years to complete, and was published only in 1885.

In *Marius the Epicurean* he showed that his aim was not merely pleasure, but the fulness of life and 'insight' as conducting to that fulness—energy, variety, and choice of experience, including noble pain and sorrow. He emphasized that his doctrine was not 'the utterance of the jaded Epicurean' but 'of the strong young man in all the freshness of thought and feeling, fascinated by the notion of raising his life to the level of a daring theory, while in the first genial heat of existence, the beauty of the physical world strikes potently upon his wide-open, un-wearied senses'.

He advocated making life a perfect work of art, with deep feeling and experience of every sort, leading ultimately, in the case of Marius, to martyrdom and faith, but with the hope of further revelation some day, some ampler vision, which would explain 'this world's delightful shows, as the scattered fragments of a poetry, till then but half-understood, and might be taken up into the text of a lost epic, recovered at last. His soul then, having grown through all the years of experience, would be at its height, the house ready for the possible guest; the tablet of the mind white and smooth for whatever divine finger might choose to write there'.

Pater's aim was not attained, since most of his readers—amongst the young at all events—did not take to heart the exalted end, but accepted only the doctrine of aesthetic life, the cult of an élite.

In 1888 Pater published his article on style, which appeared in December in *The Fortnightly Review*, and was republished in *Appreciations* in 1889. This was the highest point of his critical career, when his reputation was highest, and when he was most sure of himself. That year he published the third edition of his *Renaissance* and he put back the 'Conclusion', which lack of self-confidence had made him omit from the second edition.

Of all the writers of the Art for Art's Sake Movement in France, it is probably Flaubert with whom Pater has most affinity, and from whom he borrows most. This is seen in the *Essay on Style*, where he follows his French master in his insistence on method, on perfection in prose writing. Like Flaubert, he considered that there should be a strict scheme, with the inevitability of an architectural plan, from which nothing could be taken, and to which nothing could be added, without endangering the whole construction. He declares in this *Essay on Style*:

> 'For the literary architecture, if it is to be rich and expressive, involves not only foresight of the end in the beginning, but also development and growth of design, in the process of execution. When this is not so it indicates, as Flaubert was aware, an original structure in thought not organically complete.'

He shows the ways to be adopted by the artist who must, as if it were poetry, work on his prose style in order to reach the desired effect. He advised, for this purpose, a close study of Flaubert's methods of composition, and especially a study of his correspondence—he was the first, in England, to realize the significance of these letters, and he had obviously profited much from their example himself, for he would have liked to do for English prose what Flaubert had done for French. His own style was most carefully composed, harmonized, and counterpointed, but the reader is conscious of effort, and Pater has not attained that air of effortless simplicity and austerity which, in Flaubert, was, nevertheless, the result of unceasing effort and labour. Pater understood this effort, without being able to reach the same results himself, and, in the *Essay on Style*, he says:

> 'If all things have their martyrs, Gustave Flaubert might perhaps rank as the martyr of literary style. As the exponent of truth that austerity (the beauty, the function of which in literature Flaubert understood so well) becomes not the correctness of purism, of the mere scholar, but a security against the otiose, a jealous exclusion of what does not really tell towards the pursuit of relief, of life and vigour in the portraiture of one's senses.'

Flaubert's style is ageless and has not dated with the passing of the years. Whereas, in Pater's prose, artifice is felt which, nowadays, gives it the old-fashioned appearance of a period piece.

In 1894 Pater was awarded an honorary degree by the University of Glasgow. This was the last public function of his life, for he died on 30 June that year when he was fifty-five years old.

Swinburne and Pater represent two aspects of the Art for Art's Sake Movement which are contradictory and complementary. Swinburne, at the time of his *Poems and Ballads*, represents the dark and troubled side, in opposition to accepted standards, which has affinity with the Satanic inspiration of Baudelaire. Whereas Pater's admiration for everything Hellenic brings him closer to Gautier than to Baudelaire. He disliked all violence, which he considered inartistic, and he thought that abnormal states of mind did not serve the purpose of art, which was to help us to forget the coarse and violent and to lead us towards the noble aspects of Nature. Although he was not so creatively gifted as Swinburne, his influence was more widespread and lasting, and he set the tone for literature and aesthetic criticism for a whole generation. The nineties would not have been possible without him.

4

REALISM

In the second half of the nineteenth century English literature did not draw only from the springs of the Art for Art's Sake Movement, but also from French Realism and Naturalism.

There had existed in France, since the late eighteen-forties, a realistic school of fiction, exemplified by Murger, Champfleury, Duranty, and Feydeau, who derive directly from Balzac. The link connecting them and Balzac lies in *La Bohème*, which arose, at first, as a manifestation of realism, though it eventually ripened into a late form of Romanticism in the *Scènes de la Vie de Bohème* by Murger.

La Bohème had exemplified, at first, the reaction against the prosaic ideals of the later Romantics by the Art for Art's Sake Movement. It had shown the same horror of everything that was bourgeois, and it arose at a time when the more progressive writers wished to separate themselves from the others, trying to prove that they did not belong to the same common herd. The reaction was first seen amongst the Dandies who tried to be different from others, in their clothes, their house-furnishings, and their behaviour. They were able to indulge their differences luxuriously, but they were followed by others who were often without the necessities of life, but who would not compromise with their ideals. They called themselves the Bohemians—in fact gypsies without hearth and home. They were sufficiently well established, even in Balzac's time, for him to devote a place to them in his *Comédie Humaine*, and he twice studied their milieu: in *Un Grand Homme de Province à Paris* in 1830, and in *Un Prince de la Bohème* in 1840. In the first he gives a picture of a group of nine young men of letters, all poor and struggling, all gifted with some talent, and all fervently devoted to art. The hero, Daniel d'Arthez, is the leader of the Bohemians, and symbolizes their noble attitude, even in the midst of poverty; whereas Daniel de Rubempré, the provincial in Paris, who gives his name to the novel, typifies the bourgeois climber, whose talents first draw him to the circle of young Bohemian writers, but whose materialistic ambitions eventually lead him towards fashionable society, and who becomes a successful journalist, the worst example of cheap journalism of the day. However, the most interesting part of the book is the description of the Bohemian milieu and the life of the young struggling writers.

In *Un Prince de la Bohème* it is not so much the struggle for life that is described but the *vie amoureuse*, the love life, of the Bohemian writers. Murger must have known this novel, for the love affairs of its hero, Rusticoli de la Palférine, are very like those of Marcel and Rodolphe, Mimi and Musette in his *Scènes de la Vie de Bohème*. The Bohemia painted by Balzac is very fantastic and exaggerated, not at all true to life, and it is only in the eighteen-forties that true Bohemia is found. As a result of the expansion in national education brought about by the Revolution of 1830, there was a new supply of writers, coming if not exactly from the very lowest class, certainly from the lowest middle-class—some did in fact come from the working-class, as did Murger and Champfleury.

Murger was the son of a poor concierge in a low part of Paris, who received a certain education which unfitted him for working-class employment, the only kind he could hope for, while he possessed neither sufficient intelligence nor culture for any other. His first compositions were poems in the debased Musset style current at that time, but he was living the kind of life from which he was to draw inspiration in his *Scènes de la Vie de Bohème*.

In 1842 Murger, with his friends Courbet, Champfleury, Nadar, and Dupont, founded a club, *Les Buveurs d'Eau*, so called because the members could afford nothing stronger than water, for they lived in the greatest poverty. Theirs was the kind of life which Verlaine was to lead towards the end of the century, when his only periods free from utter want were those he spent in hospital. 'Mes maladies ce sont mes rentes,' he used to say. Murger depicted this life in his two novels, *Scènes de la Vie de Bohème* and *Les Buveurs d'Eau*.

Champfleury encouraged Murger to notice the vivid scenes of everyday life and to make sketches from them. These were then published in the progressive literary paper, *Le Corsaire Satan*, between 1845 and 1848, and they were republished in book form in 1851. At that time it was considered a work of realism. However those who read it today, and enjoy it, are less struck by its realism than by its romanticism and sentimentality. In fact Murger's early romanticism found here its most complete and best expression—and, paradoxically, without this romanticism the book would probably have perished long ago. It is a picture of Bohemian life as people like to imagine it. In real life the Mimi of the novel was, in fact, more like the Sapho in Daudet's novel of the same name than like the heroine of *La Vie de Bohème*. Here she is, however, the eternal illusion, the symbol of a young man's dream of love, of first youthful love, and that is the everlasting appeal of the novel. The true picture of *La Bohème* is found in Champfleury's *Aventures de Mademoiselle Mariette*, which depicts the same people, but, being realistic and commonplace, it is now unread.

Murger represented the dying elements of Romanticism, and there is little true realism in his work.

However, when the revolution of 1848 broke out, it was evident that Realism had come to stay, and the elements of a school were apparent.

The painter Courbet was one of the important combatants in the Realist battle. For many years he had been struggling against what was called by the art critics 'le nu harmonieux', as exemplified in such figures as *La Source* by Ingres. He wanted to paint realistically, without false sentimentality and grace, and he used to sign his pictures 'Courbet sans idéal et sans religion'. He began to be known just after the revolution of 1848, and his various exhibitions show the progress and development of the Realist ideal, and opposition to it. In 1848 seven of his pictures were accepted by the Salon, amongst them *Un Après-midi à Ornans* and *Vendanges à Ornans*. They were not greatly admired, but did not arouse much excitement—*La Revue des Deux Mondes* merely called them trivial. Two years later three only of his pictures were accepted by the committee, and they were very unfavourably received. They were *Les Paysans de Flagny devant la Foire*, *Les Casseurs de Pierres* and *L'Enterrement à Ornans*—this last aroused most opposition for it was said that death and religion, instead of being made to arouse noble thoughts, were rendered ridiculous, and that the funeral was used solely as a pretext for the depiction of local types in idiotic costumes. The following year one picture only was accepted, *Les Demoiselles du Village*, which was considered merely vulgar. In 1853 *Les Baigneuses*, in which he had represented realistic female nudes, was refused with ignominy. The critics were indignant at what they called the 'nudités grosses' which, they said, were most repulsive. Patriotic articles were published in defence of French womanhood and beauty, protesting against these libellous lumps of flesh.

The Salon of 1855 exhibited no picture by Courbet. It was said that this was out of deference to Queen Victoria, who, with the Prince Consort, the Prince of Wales, and the Princess Royal, was visiting Paris for the first time, and that she might have disapproved of them— this might well have been true.

In protest Courbet held a private show of his paintings to which hundreds came to scoff and disapprove, but some to admire. His Introduction to the catalogue became the manifesto of the Realist School, for he had established several important conceptions: the right of the artist to choose whatever subject he wished to represent; his right to take a contemporary subject if he so desired; and his right to depict realistically contemporary life.

In 1855, with Courbet's private exhibition, the Realist battle was in full swing. In literature Champfleury, the friend and disciple of Courbet, took up the fight, and declared that his aim was to achieve in literature what Courbet had practised in painting, and he was thus always called 'the Courbet of literature'.

Champfleury's best novel is *Les Bourgeois de Molinchart*, in which he tells the story of adultery in a provincial town—the town of Laon, where he was born, and the local colour is well depicted. The plot is not of importance, but what is significant is the portrayal of the bourgeois milieu, and this shows some irony which recalls that of Flaubert—as for instance the scene of the Prize-Giving at the local school; that of an official banquet; and the meeting of the provincial Academy.

Flaubert was in the throes of writing *Madame Bovary* when Champfleury published *Les Bourgeois de Molinchart*, and he was anxious lest he should be forestalled in his treatment of provincial adultery but, when he read the novel, he realized how different was Champfleury's intention from his own. 'Il y a parité d'intention,' he said, 'plutôt que de sujet et de caractères.'

Les Bourgeois de Molinchart is the beginning of true realism in France, and it had an immediate and striking success, for ten thousand copies were sold in a very short time—many more than were to be sold of *Madame Bovary*.

With the appearance of this novel, Champfleury became the un-challenged leader of the Realist School, and, although he is never read today, he marks an important stage in the progress of realism in the novel, from Balzac to the Goncourt brothers. He is the chief exponent of realism in fiction before Flaubert, but there is all the world of differ-ence between what has been called his 'réalisme étriqué' and the imagi-native realism of Flaubert. Champfleury's aesthetic doctrine—if indeed it can be honoured with the title of aesthetic—forced him to describe only what he had seen with his own eyes, but the mediocrity of the kind of life that he had chosen to lead condemned him to see almost no-thing. He had, moreover, the mistaken theory that realism meant *terre-à-terre* triviality, and that is why his novels are now dead.

In 1856 Champfleury founded *La Gazette* to publicize his ideas, but it had only two numbers—which is the normal fate of such periodicals. He declared that the author should write only of what he had seen, and that no prejudices, moral or social, must be allowed to restrain him. 'Il ne faut pas s'interdire tel personnage,' he said, 'parce qu'il choquerait telle portion du public. Il faut tout montrer sans atténuation de politesse ou de prudence.' He admired great simplicity in art, and disapproved of descriptions, portraits, landscapes, and he insisted that little people were to be the sole subject of the novel.

Next, his friend Duranty, who had some means, founded another paper, *Le Réaliste*, with similar aims to those of *La Gazette*, but it also perished through lack of support. *Le Réaliste* distinguished itself by reviewing unfavourably *Madame Bovary* when it appeared in 1857, on the grounds that it contained far too many descriptions and that its style was laboured, too artistic—'trop artiste'.

By this time, with the general public, the word 'realism' had become a term of abuse and criticism. Both Flaubert and Baudelaire were accused of realism at their trials in 1857, as if it was a sign of moral obloquy. And, although Flaubert was finally acquitted—Baudelaire was less lucky—the judge permitted himself some moral strictures against the work itself.

'L'ouvrage déféré . . . mérite un blâme sévère, car la mission de la littérature doit être d'orner et de recréer l'esprit en élevant l'intelligence et en épurant les moeurs, plus encore que d'imprimer le dégoût du vice en offrant le tableau des désordres qui peuvent exister dans la société . . . Il n'est pas permis, sous prétexte de peinture de caractère on de couleur locale, de reproduire dans leurs écarts, les faits et les gestes des personnages . . . Un pareil système appliqué aux oeuvres de l'esprit . . . conduirait à un réalisme qui serait la négation du beau et du bon, et qui, enfantant des oeuvres offensantes pour les regards . . . commettrait de continuels outrages à la morale publique et aux bonnes moeurs.'

Art for Art's Sake and Realism became fused in the works of Flaubert, the Goncourt brothers and Huysmans. They are nearer to Gautier and Baudelaire—especially to the modern aspect of Baudelaire's work—than to the Realist School of Champfleury. Many of the ideas of Flaubert are the same as those of Baudelaire.

Like Baudelaire, Flaubert did not believe that there existed such a thing as a beautiful or ugly subject. 'Il n'y a ni beaux ni vilains sujets,' he wrote, 'le style étant à lui seul une manière de voir les choses.' Beauty, he thought, was centred in the vision of the artist, in what he himself brought to the subject. 'On peut écrire sur n'importe quoi aussi bien que sur quoi que ce soit,' he said.

Flaubert was the first novelist in France to believe that perfection was an essential attribute of fiction. Before him other writers may hav written well—as Mérimée did—but that was merely considered a personal idiosyncrasy, and no one thought it adverse criticism to declare that Balzac's style was clumsy and his planning confused.

Flaubert, however, did not believe that style consisted solely in fine language and harmonious periods. Vision was an essential part of style —as it was also with Baudelaire—and this entailed search until the one perfect and inevitable way of expressing the vision was attained. When the perfect expression was found, which fitted exactly, then contact occurred—as in the two parts of an electric fitting—and light, radiance, illuminated everything. In a letter of 12 December 1857—the year of the publication of *Madame Bovary*—he wrote 'la forme et l'idée c'est comme le corps et l'âme; pour moi c'est tout un; c'est inséparable, et je ne sais pas ce qui est l'un sans l'autre. Plus une idée est belle, plus la phrase est sonore, soyez-en-sûr. La précision de la pensée fait elle-même celle du mot.'

Style and vision were thus only two aspects of the same essence. Perfection of form in the novel did not only depend on inspiration and fine writing, but also on the harmony of all the parts, and on their inseparable relationship to one another. A novel, with him, was as strictly composed as any classical play, with the same sense of balance, and his scenario was as strict as any architectural plan, so that nothing could be altered without the whole edifice tottering to its ruin.

With this inevitability of style, it followed that each subject demanded its own special style, tailored and fitted for itself alone. The result was that he did not develop a personal style with his own hall-mark, which he used for all topics that he treated. In his *Trois Contes* he has gathered together, in one perfect nosegay, three separate styles, each one different, and each exactly suited to its subject.

In this he was in marked contrast with his fellow-members of the Art for Art's Sake Movement in fiction, the Goncourt brothers. Their aim was to be original and individual at all costs, to fashion a style which would be theirs alone, which all would recognize as theirs, even without their signature, and they applied this to all their novels. They wrote well for the sake of writing, and not for the sake of the organic whole of the novel. That is why passages from their books, fine in themselves, and admirable when met in extracts, are, critically speaking, 'hors d'œuvre', which do not belong inevitably and intrinsically to the structure of the work itself. They are exercises in noble writing; whereas Flaubert's style is clear and transparent as the purest water, through which the subject appears in its entirety, with no distortion.

This conception of impersonality of style was accompanied by complete objectivity on the part of the author towards the subject treated. While composing *Madame Bovary* Flaubert wrote, in a letter on 22 April 1854: 'Je ne veux pas considérer l'art comme un déversoir à passions, comme un pot de chambre!' He shared Baudelaire's disgust with the sentimental outpourings of Lamartine and Musset. The personal confession seemed to him immodest and egoistic, and he always declared that anyone was more interesting than Gustave Flaubert. He considered that the author should not express his own opinion of his characters, and that it ought no more to be possible to guess what he thought of them than what God thought of His own creations. The author must behave as the Almighty does, he must not take sides. Many readers have found this disconcerting and inhuman, for they like to get a lead, and to know definitely how the author feels about his characters; they like his intentions to be underlined, but he refuses to help them here. 'Un romancier n'a pas le *droit*,' he insists, and underlines it, 'de dire son avis sur les choses de ce monde! Il doit, dans sa création, imiter Dieu dans la sienne, c'est à dire faire et se taire.'

Flaubert considered that the novel should be based on scientific documentation, for this would ensure its remaining objective, and prevent the author from expressing his own feelings and prejudices. He did not mean that the novel should make use of the scientific jargon of the day, and journalistic scraps of information; it should not bring in scientific material as local colour, as so many of the other writers were in the habit of doing. The Goncourt brothers applied science in the same way as the Romantics did history, plastering it on the surface as local colour, with more concern for vividness of detail than for accuracy. 'Le roman doit être scientifique,' he said, 'c'est à dire rester dans les généralités probables. Il faut traiter l'âme humaine avec l'impersonnalité qu'on met dans les sciences physiques.'

Yet, in spite of his connection with Art for Art's Sake ideals and doctrine, in spite of his contempt for the Realist School and its aims, Flaubert, after the publication of *Madame Bovary*, was considered as the chief exponent of Realism in France, and it was on that score that he was either praised or blamed.

The public paid little attention to his lofty conception of art, and did not recognize the depth, originality, and novelty of his method of psychological analysis. What was remembered was that he had chosen for portrayal the vulgar adulteries of a stupid little provincial wife of the middle-class; and that he had described, with full scientific and realistic details, an operation for club-foot, and death from arsenical poisoning. What made this especially horrifying to the general reader was that the characters involved were ordinary people, in common-place settings, with whom he could identify himself—they were not particular or pathological cases, but universal, and thus true of all classes and of all times.

Madame Bovary was followed, between 1860 and 1870, by the novels of the Goncourt brothers.

Flaubert had chosen to depict universal characters, and, at the same time, characters who were unique individuals. The Goncourts followed the logical line of development from Balzac through the Realist School. Balzac had shown how characters are moulded and altered by the work which they perform, what was to be called 'la déformation profession-nelle'. The Goncourts showed how they are modified by their physical state, and they were the first novelists, in the history of French fiction, to analyse the pathological case. Their characters—Charles Demailly, Sœur Philomène, Renée Mauperin, Germinie Lacerteux, and Madame Gervaisais—are entirely conditioned psychologically by physical causes. This was very important for the development of the novel, and was to reach further heights in the twentieth century, when the patho-logical case was considered almost the only one worthy of analysis. In depicting such cases the Goncourts imagined that they were being scientific, and they declared: 'Le roman s'est imposé les études et les devoirs de la science.' They did not, however, understand science as did Flaubert, and they succeeded only in being sensational and up to date in superficial jargon. When he used scientific material, he did so from observation and universally, so that his deductions are as true today as when he made them. On the contrary, when they use it, they do so theoretically, and with contemporary speculations, so that when these are superseded, their psychological deductions become out of date and false, since they are based on faulty assumptions.

In other respects as well the Goncourts mark an important date in the development of the novel in France—especally in the growth of its realism. They were the first novelists to choose a heroine from the working-class—in *Germinie Lacerteux*, published in 1865. Zola, who owed much to them, said in his work *Les Romanciers Naturalistes*: '*Germinie Lacerteux* est une date. Le livre fait entrer le peuple dans le roman; pour la première fois, le héros en casquette et l'héroïne en bonnet de linge y sont étudiés par des écrivains d'observation et de style.' And the authors themselves said, in the Preface to their novel: 'Nous nous sommes demandé si ce qu'on appelle *les basses classes* n'avaient pas droit au roman; si ce monde sous un monde, le peuple,

C

devait rester sous le coup de l'interdit littéraire et des dédains d'auteurs qui ont fait jusqu'ici le silence sur l'âme et le cœur qu'il peut avoir.'

Germinie Lacerteux is the sordid account of a servant-girl in a respectable house, who, in her work, appears the model of propriety, but who carries on a secret life of vice with her evil genius Joupillon, whom she loves passionately and who is the cause of her downfall. Eventually, having sunk to the lowest degradations, she dies in hospital and is buried in a pauper's grave, with not even a wooden stake, with her number on it, to mark the place. This was to be the model for many other novels dealing with a similar theme.

Although the Goncourt brothers never reached the heights attained by Flaubert, they were more influential in the development of the novel, and they are in the direct line of succession from Balzac to Zola.

A novel by Zola, *Thérèse Raquin*, published in 1868, marks the next important date in the history of the realist novel, for, with it, Naturalism begins in France. After its publication Flaubert—and even the Goncourts—seemed timid and cautious. It tells the story of how Thérèse Raquin and her lover murder her husband, making it seem like a boating accident; but then are so overcome with remorse and horror at what they have done that she poisons herself and him, and they die in agony, in the presence of an old aunt who is completely paralysed and incapable of movement.

The novel had an immediate success, and a second edition was published within a few months, for which Zola wrote an important Preface, in which the word 'Naturalisme' was mentioned for the first time. This was really the manifesto of the new school, and Zola was its unquestioned leader.

Zola had been much interested in scientific reading since his youth, and particularly in the *Introduction à la Médecine Expérimentale* by Claude Bernard, published in 1865. He determined to follow the same method in fiction, and planned the series of the *Rougon-Macquart* novels, which was intended to study a family under the Second Empire, showing the differing effects of heredity and environment on its rise and fall. It had a more concentrated and rigid plan than that of Balzac's *Comédie Humaine*. Henry James said, in *Notes on Novelists with Some Other Notes*, published in 1914, that Zola had sacrificed to his huge plan, in something of the same way as Balzac had done to his, but that his work had been more nearly dried up than even Balzac's by the sacrifice.

Zola's plan was to study the effects of heredity in various sections of society, and to show how virtue and vice, carried through the stream of the blood, can develop in different ways. He wanted also to study social life during the Second Empire, in all its ramifications and classes, and thus to give a complete picture of society.

The first of the *Rougon-Macquart* novels, *La Fortune des Rougon*, was to have been published in 1870, but the Franco-Prussian War delayed it, and it appeared in 1871. The last of the series, *Le Docteur Pascal*, appeared in 1893, and there were finally twenty volumes in all, instead of the dozen originally planned.

The next important date, after *Thérèse Raquin*, was the publication, in 1877, of *L'Assommoir*, which portrayed, for the first time in fiction, working-class life in a working-class setting. *Germinie Lacerteux* had portrayed a couple from that class, but they had acted against the contrasting background of conventional bourgeois life. In *L'Assommoir* the whole texture of working-class life is depicted, and nothing else. Zola said that his intention had been to produce 'un roman qui aura pour cadre le monde ouvrier', and that he wished to show the tragic degeneration of the working-man under the influence of the public-house, and how he contaminated his wife with his own vice, and dragged her down with him into ruin.

With *Nana*, the following year, he showed, in the daughter of the woman in *L'Assommoir*, a girl sinking into the world of prostitution, and this is the first time that such a subject and milieu had been depicted in the novel, with complete outspokenness and frankness. In *Pot-Bouille*, two years later, he portrayed the bourgeois counterpart of *Nana*. His theory was that the education of women, at this time, led, in the case of the working-class girl, to prostitution, and, in the case of the girl from the middle-class, to adultery.

The Goncourts had studied, in each of their novels, a different layer of social life, as, for instance, the world of journalism and letters in *Charles Demailly*; the medical and hospital world in *Sœur Philomène*; and the world of art studios and exhibitions in *Manette Salomon*. Zola followed them in this method, and built up a different milieu for each novel. In *L'Assommoir* he shows us a low public-house and the absinthe-drinkers; in *Germinal* it is the mine world and the world of miners; *La Débâcle* is a picture of modern war; in *Au Bonheur des Dames* we are shown a large comprehensive store; and in *Le Ventre de Paris* it is Les Halles, the enormous and fantastic central market in Paris.

In all these investigations Zola imagined that he was being an experimental moralist who demonstrated, by experiment, the way in which the passions behaved in a social milieu, and he thought that, when he had made his diagnosis, treatment for the ailment would be possible. He was not aware that his method was not scientific, but imaginative, for he invented the theory and also created the evidence to prove it. Moreover, since he was fascinated by the sordid and gross side of life, he spent the largest part of his energies in depicting what occurs when men revert to the state of brutes. It is this aspect of his work which scandalized readers both in France and in England.

The Art for Art's Sake Movement from France had two channels of penetration into England—Swinburne and Pater—and Realism and Naturalism had also their ambassadors—Henry James and George Moore.

It is in the eighteen-eighties that the new conception of fiction spread from France to England, and this was the result of the reaction in the eighteen-seventies against the great Victorian novelists—Trollope, Dickens, Eliot, and Thackeray. All these novelists had, more or less, accepted the didactic conception of fiction. However, with the spread of the theories of Art for Art's Sake and Naturalism, this old-fashioned form of novel became distasteful to the more progressive writers.

Hitherto novels had been largely read by the middle-class as a means of recreation, and fiction was not highly considered at that time as a form of art. This was very different from the state of affairs then prevailing in France, through the efforts of Gautier, Flaubert, and the Goncourt brothers.

The novelists responsible for transforming fiction in England into a form of art were Henry James and George Moore.

Henry James spent most of 1875 and 1876 in Paris, and had developed an admiration for French literature, especially for Gautier—in this he resembled his predecessors, Swinburne and Pater.

In 1878 he published *French Poets and Novelists*, a collection of essays written during his visit to Paris. He examined a variety of themes and authors, amongst them Balzac, Gautier, Flaubert, Mérimée, and Baudelaire. They show wide reading and intellectual curiosity, though they are not particularly expert or perceptive, when it is remembered that he was thirty-five at the time. They are, however, a beginning, and they certainly opened up to English writers vistas into new realms of literary possibilities.

It was natural that James, as a future novelist, should be more interested in prose than in verse. He accepted the conventional view of the Satanic Baudelaire, whose poetry he did not like, and whom he considered 'an altogether inferior genius to Gautier'. In prose, his praise went to those who practised a carefully studied style, artists like Mérimée, Gautier, and Flaubert. He kept all his life a particular enthusiasm for Mérimée who was, he said, his first literary master, and there are many less worthy mentors.

At this time, although he admired his style, he did not appreciate Flaubert as a novelist, for he could find little of interest in *Madame Bovary*, and nothing at all in *L'Éducation Sentimentale*, which he thought 'massively and elaborately dreary', saying that reading it was like 'masticating sawdust and ashes'.

However, while he was in Paris he made the personal acquaintance of Flaubert and Goncourt, and became particularly interested in the former's theory of fiction, thinking that the English novel had much to learn from him. 'The English novel,' he said, 'has no air of having a theory, a conviction, a consciousness of itself behind it—of being the expression of an artistic faith.' He considered, on the contrary, that the French novelists 'had brought the theory of fiction to a remarkable completeness'. He learned from Flaubert and Maupassant to believe in the importance of form and style in a work of fiction—'there is no complete creation without style', he said. Although he recognized the prodigious effort of Zola, 'to whose solid and serious work no explorer of the capacity of the novel can allude without respect', he found his writings difficult to like on account of his absence of style and because he would not reconcile himself to 'absoluteness of taste'.

From the French novelists he learned to observe the detachment of the artist, to avoid turning literature into a vessel to contain the over-flow of his personal emotion. He learned also the necessity of a strong plan, an architectural plan such as Flaubert used. It is this sense of construction that he admired so much in dramatic literature, and which he would have liked to transpose into the novel. He said, in a review of Tennyson's *Queen Mary*, quoted in the Introduction to *The Art of Fiction and Other Essays*:

'The fine thing in a real drama is that, more than any other work of literary art, it needs a masterly structure. It needs to be shaped and fashioned and laid together, and this process makes demand upon an artist's rarest gifts. . . . To work successfully beneath a few grave, rigid laws is always a strong man's highest ideal of success.'

This ideal he found in Flaubert's conception of the novel, and he wished to transplant it to England.

Henry James was the first, in English literature, to formulate a theory of the novel as a form of art; this was in the essay entitled 'The Art of Fiction', written in 1884, but published only in *Partial Portraits* in 1888. This is significant in connection with the development of the novel in England away from the conception that moral teaching is

essential in fiction, and that literature should be either instructive or
amusing, and James declares:

> 'there is in many minds an impression that those artistic pre-
> occupations, the search for form, contribute to neither end, inter-
> fere indeed with both. . . . That I think represents the manner in
> which the latent thought of many people who read novels as an
> exercise in skipping, would explain itself if it were to become
> articulate. . . . It is therefore true that the conception of the novel
> as a superior form encounters not only negative but a positive in-
> difference.'

With regard to the reading of novels, he considered that the most
exquisite pleasure was to be obtained in recognizing the original work of
a true artist. 'Then, in a word, we can enjoy one of the most charming of
pleasures, we can estimate quality, we can apply the test of execution.
The execution belongs to the author alone; it is what is most personal
to him, and we measure him by that.'

He ends by stating that it is the first duty of the novelist to be as
complete as possible and to make a perfect work. However, he agreed
with Baudelaire in believing that the nature of the artist himself was
closely linked with his aesthetic doctrine, that there is a point at which
the moral sense and the artistic lie very near together. 'The deepest
quality of a work of art will always be the quality of the mind of the
producer. In proportion as that intelligence is fine will the novel, the
picture, the statue partake of the substance of beauty and truth. No
good novel will ever proceed from a superficial mind.'

As far as his own fiction was concerned, what James received from
the French novelists was the desire to penetrate deeply inside the
characters he was depicting, to reveal their motives rather than their
behaviour. That is the hair-splitting about hidden motives which
English readers too often accuse French novelists of practising.

More diverse in the propagation of French influence in England was
George Moore, who responded generally more spontaneously and sym-
pathetically to French culture and habits than did Henry James. He
went from Ireland to Paris in 1873 when he was twenty-one to study
painting, but soon discovered that he did not possess the true talent of
a painter. He became therefore interested in French literature, and, as
was natural in a former—or 'spoilt'—painter, he was first attracted to
Parnassian poetry, which in ideals is most closely linked with painting,
and to another 'unfrocked' painter, Théophile Gautier. *Mademoiselle
de Maupin* then became for him, what it had been, twenty years before,

for Swinburne, a revelation. It became, as he said, 'inexpressibly' part of himself. In *Confession of a Young Man*, he wrote:

'Never shall I open these books again, but were I to live for a thousand years, their power in my soul would remain unshaken. I am what they made me . . . I learned that the correction of form is the highest ideal, and I accepted the plain, simple conscience of the pagan world as the perfect solution of the problem that had vexed me so long! . . . I would have held down my thumbs in the Colosseum that a hundred gladiators might die and wash me free of my Christian soul with their blood.'

Gautier, before him, had asserted that Christ had not died for him.

Gautier was for Moore 'the highest peak of the literary mountain' and, of his writings, he said: 'Their power on my soul remains unshaken. I am what they have made me.'

Moore next discovered Baudelaire, who completed his conversion. Of *Les Fleurs du Mal* he wrote in *Confessions of a Young Man*:

'*Les Fleurs du Mal!* beautiful flowers, beautiful in sublime decay. What a great record is yours, and were Hell a reality how many souls would we find wreathed with your poisonous blossoms! O Baudelaire, and having tasted of your deadly delight, all hope of repentance is vain. Flowers, beautiful in your sublime decay, I press you to my lips . . . far from the rank Parisian garden where I gathered you.'

His first published work, a collection of poems entitled *Flowers of Passion*, is a pastiche—a parody almost—of Baudelaire's writings. It was published in 1878, when he was twenty-six, bound in black linen, embossed with a lyre and a skull in gold. Here are found what are, conventionally, termed the Baudelairean themes. The damned soul in *The Ballad of the Lost Soul*; disappointed and disillusioned love in *Love's Grave*; physical dissolution and decay in *The Corpse* and *Ode to a Dead Body*; and abnormal lust in *A Sapphic Dream*. There is also Baudelaire's habit of metaphorical comparison, such as 'Mon âme est un cimetière abhorré de la lune', in such lines as, in *Annie*, 'My heart is like a crystal filled with tears', and, in *Song*, 'My soul is like a house of doves'.

His second work, a further collection of poems entitled *Pagan Poems*, was published in 1881, and contains the same themes as the first. There are poems called *Spleen*, as in *Les Fleurs du Mal*; there are further poems about abnormality, such as *The Hermaphrodite*; poems of so-called Baudelairean passions, as in *The Portrait*:

'I am filled with carnivorous lust; like a tiger
I crouch and feed on my beautiful prey.'

There are poems in French, pastiches or parodies of Baudelaire, which are not wholly discreditable for a foreigner.

The two collections of poems rightly did not enjoy much success, with the result that Moore abandoned poetry, as he had given up painting, and turned his attention elsewhere.

In 1878 he had met Villiers de l'Isle Adam, who introduced him to Symbolism; soon afterwards he met Zola and Daudet, and was carried away with enthusiasm for Naturalist ideas—Symbolism was richer in its implications for poetry than for prose. In his *Confessions of a Young Man* he says: 'Now for a third time'—the first had been in connection with Art for Art's Sake, and the second with Symbolism—'I experienced the pain and joy of sudden and inward light. Naturalism, truth, the new art, above all the phrase, the new art, impressed me with a sudden light.'

Charles Morgan relates, in his *Epitaph on George Moore*, that Moore, in an anthology entitled *Pure Poetry*, described how his love of poetry began to wilt and how he had discovered the wonder of prose: 'Balzac opened a new world to me, a world of things, and in Balzac I found a poem so beautiful that I began to think that perhaps my love of poetry was not as dead as I thought it was.'

As in other matters as well, Gautier was here his guide and led him to Balzac and realism, as he had previously led him to Baudelaire. Gautier had mentioned Balzac in his Introduction to *Les Fleurs du Mal*, in the posthumous edition of 1868. This led Moore to read most of his novels. In his *Confessions of a Young Man* he says: 'Upon that rock I built my church, and his great and valid talent saved me from destruction, saved me from the shoaling waters of new aestheticism and the faint sickly surf of the Symbolists.'

Moore was now carried away with enthusiasm for a new art based on science, in opposition to the art of the old world, based on imagination; an art that should explain all things, and embrace modern life in its entirety, be, as it were, a new creed, a new civilization. This thought, he said, 'filled me with wonder, and I stood dumb before the vastness of the conception. In my fevered fancy, I saw a new race of writers that would arise, and, with the aid of the novel, would continue to more glorious and legitimate conclusions, the work that the prophets had begun.' It was then that he became interested in the novel as a form of art. 'The subjects are to hand,' he said, the 'formula alone is wanting.' He intended to follow Naturalism but, at the same time, he wished to preserve the high standards of writing introduced by the Art for Art's Sake Movement, and he reproached Zola with having no feeling for style.

Moore's *Confessions of a Young Man*, published in 1886, is more important for the relationship between English literature and France than his poetry. It is one of the first examples of deliberate and self-conscious English prose. Later he was often accused of writing too well and of being artificial. In his style he was much influenced by Huysmans in *À Rebours*, of which he says, in his *Confessions of a Young Man*: '*À Rebours*, that prodigious book, that beautiful mosaic. Huysmans is quite right, ideas are well enough until you are twenty, afterwards only words are bearable.' He used to say that he would like to have graven on his tomb: 'Here lies George Moore who considered the perfection of written speech as the only morality.'

The *Confessions of a Young Man* can be said to be the first stone—even the base—of the aesthetic movement in England. On bringing out a later edition, the author said, in the Preface: 'If I say that the end of the nineteenth century cannot brag of a more original book than the *Confessions of a Young Man*, I shall be deemed boastful and arrogant!' He is, however, right when he claims: 'The first eulogies written in England, I might say in any language, of Manet, Degas, Whistler, Monet, Pissarro, are in this book of *Confessions*, and whosoever reads will find himself unable to deny that time had vindicated all of them splendidly.'

George Moore now tried his hand at the novel, since painting and poetry had not proved his true element of self-expression. His first attempt, *A Modern Lover*, appeared in 1883. Some critics have claimed to find in it certain resemblances with Flaubert's *Éducation Sentimentale*, but this is too flattering to Moore, for it has none of the psychological analysis of the French masterpiece, and the characters are only abstractions. Neither does the novel possess the precise documentation of Zola, and cannot, as its author claimed, serve as a 'faithful reproduction of modern life'. However, Moore was familiar with the milieu of the studios, and the most valuable aspect of the novel is the portrayal of the life of young and struggling art students—in this it recalls *Manette Salomon* by the Goncourts.

Not surprisingly, it did not sell well, and cannot be considered a success, but Moore put a brave face on it, and tried to pretend that he was not disappointed. Writing to Zola, in September 1883, in a letter quoted by Hone in his *Life of George Moore*, he said: 'The fact that my novel has been successful may interest you; for I have already told you, I owe you everything. My book, alas, is not good, I know well, but it has succeeded. I was obliged to attenuate dreadfully, but what else could I do? I had to take a step and the step is taken!' The step was the introduction of the Naturalist novel from France into England. Moore persisted in his unfavourable opinion of his novel, for he refused to reprint it in his *Collected Works*.

His next novel, *A Mummer's Wife*, which appeared in 1885, is of much higher standard artistically and of greater interest. It is the first completely Naturalistic novel in English, and is nearer to the ideal of the Naturalist School than anything else that he was to write, with its portrayal of a certain way of life in cheap lodging-houses. In true realistic manner, he even went to live himself for a time in the same sordid surroundings in order to obtain his local colour. From the opening paragraph, the scene is set:

'In default of a screen, a gown and a red petticoat had been thrown over a clothes-horse, and these shaded the glare of the lamp from the eyes of the sick man. In the pale obscurity of the room, his bearded cheeks could be seen buried in a heap of tossed pillows. By his bedside sat a young woman. As she dozed, her face drooped until her features were hidden, and the lamp-light made the curious curves of a beautiful ear look like a piece of illuminated porcelain. Her hands lay upon her lap, her needle-work slipped from them; and as it fell to the ground she awoke.'

In the early part of the novel, Kate Ede, married to a sick husband whom she does not really love, but tends with great devotion, is closely modelled on Emma Bovary. She too liked to dream and to imagine herself in the person of the heroines in the stories which she read.

She eventually elopes with a seedy actor called Dick, who seems to her romantic, but, being fundamentally respectable and middle-class, she cannot grow accustomed to the loose morals of theatre life, and the infidelities of her lover. Moreover, she is tortured by remorse for having abandoned her sick husband, so that, in order to find oblivion, she takes to drink. Here Moore is remembering Zola's *L'Assommoir* and the deterioration which takes place in the character of Gervaise through her addiction to alcohol. Kate sinks down in a similar manner, changing, as did Gervaise, from a self-respecting and self-abnegating wife into a slatternly soak, a woman old before her time. In a powerful scene, worthy of Zola, she is described lying in a drunken stupor, un-mindful of the cries of her sick baby, who dies while its mother sleeps :

'The spirit diffused a grateful warmth through her, and she drank a second glass slowly, thinking of her child and her husband, and how good she intended to be to both of them, until ideas became broken, and she tumbled into bed, awaking Dick, who was soon asleep again, with Kate by his side watching a rim of light rising above a dark chimney stack and wondering what new shows must be preparing. Already the rim of light had become a crescent, and before her eyes closed in sleep, the full moon looked down through the window into the cradle, waking the sleeping child. But her cries were too weak; her mother lay in sleep beyond the reach of her wails. The little blankets were cast aside, and the struggle between life and death began . . . and a few minutes later little Kate, who had known of this world but a ray of moonlight, died—a glimpse of the moon was all that had been granted to her.'

Kate herself dies somewhat later, a typical drunkard's death, des-cribed with all the realistic detail of a similar scene in *L'Assommoir*. The novel ends on a cynical note, with Dick saying to his new love, as they sit in the room in which the corpse is growing cold, discussing a new play : 'Have you finished the second act, dear?'

A Mummer's Wife is one of the most successful of the Naturalistic novels in England, and it enjoyed a merited popularity. Moore, how-ever, did not want to remain imprisoned within one single style, and he was beginning, moreover, to realize the weakness, psychologically, of the Zola formula. In his next novel, *A Drama in Muslin*, published in 1886, he changed from the sordid surroundings of the mummer, and his wife, to the upper middle-class background of Dublin, with its Vice-regal court, its marriage slave-market, where young women, decked out for sale, awaited purchase by the highest bidder amongst the possible husbands—'poor muslin martyrs' he calls them.

Later, when publishing a revised edition, Moore was to say that it was a transition book, a link between two styles. It does, in fact, mark his passage from the Naturalism of *A Mummer's Wife* to the Symbolism of *The Lake*, and it contains far less of Zola's influence than did the previous novel, and more of the style of the *écrivains artistes* such as the Goncourts and Huysmans. The portrayal of the heroine owes much to Renée Mauperin, in the novel of that name by the former. Similarities between their pictorial style and his are to be found in *Manette Salomon*

which find an echo in such descriptive passages as the following from
A Drama in Muslin:

> 'At this moment men's voices were heard on the staircase. The
> ladies all looked up, the light defining the corner of a forehead, the
> outline of a nose and chin, bathing a neck in warm shadow, model-
> ling a shoulder with grey tints, sending a thousand rays flashing
> through the diamonds on the bosom, touching the finger-rings, and
> lastly dying away amid the folds of the dresses that trailed on the
> soft carpet.'

There are many more similar pictures in the description of the
official 'drawing-room' at Dublin Castle.

Huysmans is, however, the most powerful influence on this work,
especially *À Rebours*. The hero, Des Esseintes, possessed an 'orgue à
bouche' in which each of the various liqueurs represented a different
instrument, by means of which he could play symphonies and quartets
of taste. Moore uses similar *correspondances* in his descriptions of
the different materials bought for the court dresses of the young
ladies:

> 'Lengths of white silk clear as the notes of violins played in a
> minor key; white poplin falling in folds statuesque as the bass of a
> fugue by Bach; yards of ruby velvet rich as an air from Verdi played
> on the piano; tender green velvet, pastoral as hautboys heard be-
> neath trees in a fair Arcadian vale; blue turquoise faille fanciful as
> the tinkling of a guitar twanged by a Watteau shepherd; gold
> brocade sumptuous as organ tones swelling through the jewelled
> twilight of a nave; scarves and trains of midnight blue profound as
> the harmonic snoring of a bassoon, golden daffodils violent as the
> sound of a cornet. . . . Then, beautiful as a flower harvesting, the
> hues and harmonies of earth, ocean, and sky fell before the ravished
> eyes. The Surat silk, chaste, beautiful, delicious as that presentiment
> of shared happiness which fills a young girl's mind when her fancy
> awakens in the soft spring sunlight; the white faille with tulle and
> garlands of white lilac, delicate and only as sensuous as the first
> meeting of sweethearts, when the may is white in the air; trains of
> blue sapphire broché looped with blue ostrich feathers, seductive
> and artificial. . . . The beautiful silks hissed as they came through
> the hands of the assistants, cat-like the velvet foot-falls of the
> velvet fell.'

This description is also reminiscent of Baudelaire, and of certain passages from *Au Bonheur des Dames* by Zola.

Lord Drungory, with his aphorisms in French, is the near ancestor of the titled aesthete in the literature of the nineties. Such expressions of wit are: 'La beauté n'a jamais faim, elle se nourrit d'elle-même', or 'La femme est comme une ombre: si vous la suivez, elle vous fuit; si vous fuyez, elle vous poursuit'. Or again: 'L'âme du paysan se vautre dans la boue, comme la mienne se plaît dans la soie, dans le blanc paradis de votre corsage'.

Esther Waters, published in 1894, is undoubtedly Moore's finest novel, and good by any standards, however severe. It is also his most individual, and thus owes less to French models than the others. It may have been somewhat inspired by the *Germinie Lacerteux* of the Goncourts, being the story of a poor servant-girl, but the intention is very different. It is more human than any other of Moore's novels, and less composed according to a formula. Esther Waters herself is un-corrupted and healthy, and it is this goodness that is her salvation. There is in her something of the simple quality of Félicité in Flaubert's short story, *Un Cœur Simple*, and indeed when writing about it he describes it in similar terms to those used by Flaubert, when discussing his own story with George Sand. 'My next work,' wrote Moore in a letter quoted by Hone, 'will be more human. I shall bathe it in the simplest and most naïve emotions, which are the daily bread of humanity.' It ends on a tender and optimistic note, rare hitherto in his work. Esther, after much suffering and many tribulations to rear her illegitimate son, is rewarded, at the end, when he returns on leave, in uniform, and she is able to introduce him with pride to her mistress, realizing that her work has been good, and her sacrifices and suffering worthwhile.

Moore said that this time no one would be able to link his name with that of Zola and, citing the final passage as proof, he said: 'If I have a master it is Flaubert, this is pure Flaubert.'

Esther Waters became a best-seller and sold twenty-five thousand copies, but it was, unofficially, banned from the circulating libraries on account of a scene it contained describing childbirth.

Moore had introduced the Naturalist novel from France into England, and it began now to be accepted, in England as it was in France, that art must be free to deal with any subject, and that it need not be bound by conventional morality. This eventually led to difficulties, since it went counter to the 'Great Taboo'.

There had been growing, during the past twenty years, opposition in England to everything which came out of France. As early as October 1862 *The Quarterly Review* had expressed the opinion that:

'while Napoleon III embellished the streets of Paris, his era
enervated the minds of its inhabitants with a literature as filthy, as
frivolous and as false as ever sapped the morale of a nation. Such
works as *Madame Bovary*, dragging in their trail details of a medical
treatise on the nervous diseases of women, poisoned by the nasti-
ness of a prurient mind, are signs of the times amid which they
crawled out of the dunghill, their author's brain. Drowned in
beastly sinks of sensuality, France is only rescued by the vigorous
efforts of the faithful few.'

Twenty years later opposition was better organized and more active.
In 1880 a certain Henry Vizetelly, whose family had been connected
with printing for several generations, launched out into publishing—it
was he who brought out George Moore's *A Mummer's Wife* and *A Drama
in Muslin*. He had lived much in Paris and was interested in French
literature. He produced Sala's *Paris Herself Again*, which was very
successful, and he had printed translations of such novelists as Daudet,
Sand, Cherbuliez, Mérimée, in cheap editions, no one very daring, and
with little demand for them. Then one of his sons, who lived in Paris,
advised him to launch out into publication of translations of Zola's
novels, which were creating a sensation in France. It was thus that he
started with *Thérèse Raquin*, and went on to *La Curée* and *Pot-Bouille*,
with prefaces by George Moore. He also published translations of *Nana*
and *La Terre*.

However, in August 1888 *The Fortnightly Review*, in an article,
drew attention to Zola's habit of taking delight in wallowing in filth, and
then Mudie, of the circulating libraries, joined in, declaring that it was
high time to react against the corruption coming over from France, protesting that no example of pernicious literature would be issued through
his libraries, and he refused to circulate the novels of Zola or George
Moore.

Moore did not accept this attack without retaliating, and he threw
himself into the fray by replying with a pamphlet, in 1885, entitled
Literature at Nurse, or Circulating Morals, which was particularly
addressed to Mudie and the other circulating libraries. He declared that
when the libraries took it upon themselves to censor morals they were a
menace to human liberty, and that Mudie was trying to treat adult members of the public as if they were convent school girls. He said that it was
necessary to stop confusing art with morality, and trying to reconcile
them, since they were irreconcilable. The only worthy ideal for the
nineteenth century, he maintained, was a literature founded on the objective observation of all aspects of life. (This was the same kind of

attack that Swinburne and Rossetti had suffered twenty years before
in *The Fleshly School of Poetry*.)

However a society calling itself The National Vigilance Association
began to interest itself in the matter, and to canvass support for the
purpose of defending the public against the ravages of alleged immoral
literature. The result was that the question of 'pernicious literature' was
raised in the House of Commons at a debate on 9 May 1888, in which
the writings of Zola were described as the most diabolical ever written
by the pen of man, fit only for swine, and liable to turn the minds of
those who read them into cesspools.

In the meantime the Vigilants pursued their campaign. The press,
with few exceptions, endorsed their views, and Zola's works were
characterized as being of a 'dangerous lubricity' and their author as
wallowing in immorality.

The Government, encouraged by the press, took up the prosecution,
and Vizetelly was committed for trial. He was advised to plead guilty,
being assured by his friends that he would be acquitted. On George
Moore's suggestion, and with his help, he prepared, for his defence, an
anthology designed to show that, on the grounds alleged against Zola's
writings, the Bible, Shakespeare, and most of the English classics would
deserve to be suppressed. This was the same kind of defence that
Baudelaire, on the advice of Sainte-Beuve, had put forward at the trial
of his *Fleurs du Mal* in 1857, but it was no more successful in the case
of Vizetelly than it had been in Baudelaire's, for he was convicted and
fined one hundred pounds.

The following year the Vigilants, elated by their easy victory, returned to the attack, and Vizetelly was again charged, this time for
having issued in translation Zola's *Ventre de Paris*, *La Joie de Vivre*, *La
Faute de l'Abbé Mouret*, as well as Flaubert's *Madame Bovary*, and
Maupassant's *Bel Ami* and *Une Vie*.

Once more he pleaded guilty, and he was once more convicted, but,
this time, since he had no means to pay a fine, he was sentenced to three
months' imprisonment. One hundred and fifty writers, artists, and
public men drew up a petition and an appeal for his release. Amongst
the signatories were John Addington Symonds, George Moore, Edmund Gosse, Leslie Stephens, Thomas Hardy, Ouïda, Havelock Ellis,
Rider Haggard, and others, but it was of no avail.

The Vigilants were, however, unable to prevent the spread of the
ideas of the Naturalist School and there was a great blossoming in the
nineties in fiction, under the influence of France. There were such
novelists as Gissing, with his 'slice from life' realism, of the kind well
known in France—his *Nether World*, *Born in Exile* and, especially, his

Odd Women, which is a good novel in its own right, independently of any literary doctrine, describing the loneliness of unmarried women of the middle-class, in poor circumstances, with little or no education to enable them to obtain properly paid employment, carrying on their mean and furtive lives in cheap boarding-houses, low restaurants, and station tea-rooms.

There was also Crackanthorpe, who had learnt, in the school of Maupassant, how to tell a tale, and whose *Turn of the Wheel* has the vividness of detail which is to be found in the French Naturalistic short story.

The influence of French Naturalism persisted, in English fiction, substantially up to the end of the First World War, and is found, at the turn of the century, in the writings of Somerset Maugham and Arnold Bennett. The former's *Liza of Lambeth*, published in 1897, was written, as he himself admits, with the example of Maupassant before him; while Arnold Bennett recognized that he had been much influenced by those whom he called 'Flaubert & Cie'. He went over to France in 1900, and spent eight years there, keeping a Journal, as the Goncourts had done before him, and, like them, using it afterwards as the basis of his novels. In November 1903 he describes how, when dining at one of the Duval restaurants, and watching an elderly woman eating at the next table, he planned, with the example of *Une Vie* by Maupassant before him, to write her story. He first conceived his book as a short story, but, later, enlarged it, rendering it more complicated by duplicating the heroine, and it eventually became *The Old Wives' Tale*, published in 1908. He collected his material in the same way as did the Goncourts and Zola, and, like them, treated a special milieu. With him it was his own native scene, the Potteries, and he looked at it in the same way as the French had looked at theirs. He worked, in this manner, with *The Clayhanger Trilogy*—*Clayhanger* published in 1910, *Hilda Lessways* in 1911, and *These Twain* published in 1916. Also in separate novels such as *Anna of the Five Towns*, *The Card*, and *The Grand Babylon Hotel*.

Virginia Woolf quotes, in her *Writer's Diary*, on 2 December 1930, that Bennett once said to her that it was George Moore who, in *A Mummer's Wife*, had really shown him the Five Towns; had taught him what to see there. Moore, we have seen, especially in that novel, had closely modelled himself on the French Naturalists.

5

SYMBOLISM

THE Art for Art's Sake Movement in France corresponds to the Second Empire, and roughly ends with the defeat of the country in the Franco-Prussian War. Baudelaire died in 1867, Jules de Goncourt in 1870, and Gautier in 1872, although Banville lived on until 1891, and Leconte de Lisle until 1894. There is always, however, a time lag before a new movement begins after one has ended, and the Symbolist Movement did not start until the eighteen-eighties. That means that a period of some ten years separates the Art for Art's Sake and the Symbolist Movements. These were years of destruction when young writers imagined that literature hitherto had worshipped at the shrine of false gods, when their aim was to raze everything to the ground so that a totally new edifice could be erected. Those who wrote only in that decade—Lautréamont, Tristan Corbière, Charles Cros, Jean Richepin, and Arthur Rimbaud—were rebels and iconoclasts, dedicated wholly to destruction, and they were more violent in their revolt than any of those who succeeded them. They were not fully appreciated during the Symbolist Movement, and only came into their own in the next period of unrest, during and after the First World War, when their real originality was recognized. Their achievement will be studied later, with those with whom they have affinities.

As far as general literature is concerned, the Art for Art's Sake Movement, which, in 1866, developed into the Parnassian School, and became thus more rigid and regimented, continued through the eighteen-seventies, stifling the new original writers who were not banded together into a school.

In the eighteen-eighties, amongst those who had survived the troubled days of the seventies, there was a desire to create something constructive. It is then that the new movements arise, first the Decadent, which, eventually, developed into the Symbolist Movement.

Baudelaire still remained the most fruitful influence—his had been the only poetry during the Second Empire not concerned with external values and Positivism—and his relationship with the Symbolist Movement resembles that of Rousseau with the Romantic Movement; but Rousseau was no more the whole of Romanticism than Baudelaire is the whole of Symbolism. Both were the sauce with which all the dishes were served, and which flavoured everything. There were other influences as well, especially that of German Romanticism and of Wagner. The death of the composer in 1883 increased his interest, and the *Revue Wagnérienne* was founded in 1885, not merely to study his music, but also his aesthetic doctrine—his theory of total art. Wagnerism came to be considered as a complete philosophy of life, a complete metaphysical system, both aesthetic and moral.

Other influences were those of Verlaine and Mallarmé who, before the end of the Second Empire, had written poetry in advance of their age; Villiers de l'Isle Adam, who had shown no sympathy with Parnassian ideals; and Huysmans who, in his hero Des Esseintes, crystallized the ideal of the new literary figure of the early eighteen-eighties, the Decadent, the most characteristic personality of the time. The name was borrowed from Verlaine's poem where he exclaims: 'Je suis l'Empire à la fin de la Décadence.' The Decadent was a highly evolved human being, the final product of a dying civilization, with the charm of things on the point of fading. He was not a poet of the open air, like Corbière or Rimbaud; he was an aesthete, withdrawn, not into the ivory tower of Vigny, but into the parlour of Des Esseintes, with its candles, its lilies and its incense. He was interested only in the rarest forms of art, in the most sophisticated pleasures—in vice, the philistine bourgeois said. His prototype is seen later in the drawings of Beardsley. Caricatures of him began to appear in the press of France from 1883 onwards. He was very tall and thin, and always walked with a slouch, hollowing out his consumptive chest. His sombre eyes were made to appear still more dark and dissipated by their rim of mascara. He always dressed in the latest fashion and spent most of his income on clothes, which were very tight-fitting, and this increased the slimness of his silhouette. He normally sported a monocle, and carried a light cane, or a long stick—such as are seen in pictures of smart men under the Directoire. He wore one light-coloured glove, the other he always carried, leaving his right hand bare, to show his fingers covered with gemmed rings—rubies, sapphires, and emeralds. The Decadent always looked weary, and everywhere he passed he left a trail of scent, and it was rumoured that he indulged in hashish and opium. He enjoyed the reputation of practising every kind of vice, since virtue is a characteristic of the bourgeois.

The living model of the Decadent was Count Robert de Montesquiou, or rather he possessed to perfection the characteristics needed for the typical Decadent. He was the idol of the young aesthetes of his day, and scarcely veiled portraits of him are found in Proust and Gide, while he was especially the model for Des Esseintes, the hero of Huysmans' novel *À Rebours*, published in 1884. Whistler painted a full-length portrait of him in the pale mauve frock-coat with matching shirt, collar, and tie which he always affected while listening to Weber, since, he claimed, one should only wear mauve while listening to his music.

His literary counterpart, Des Esseintes, is one of the most famous characters in literature at the end of the nineteenth century.

He was the scion of an old and worn-out family, and both his parents had died, whilst he was very young, of aristocratic diseases. After a delicate and carefully nurtured childhood, he surrendered himself to a life of eccentric and aesthetic enjoyment, and he tried to outdo the other young men of his day in the extravagance of his behaviour. He used to wear suits of snow-white velvet, with a large nosegay of Parma violets tucked into the neck of his open shirt.

His rooms were hung with rich tapestries, crowded with works of art, and he used to change their style of decoration frequently according to the book he was reading, or the mood of the moment. He had a special hall constructed, on the model of a Gothic chapel, in which to receive his tailor, shirt-maker, and shoe-maker. Here they sat in oak stalls while he ascended into the pulpit, and preached a sermon on the proper cut of a suit, shirt, and shoes, threatening them with excommunication if they did not carry out his commands.

The rest of his behaviour was on a par with this. He gave once what he called a 'mourning' dinner. The dining-room was hung with black draperies, spangled with silver tears; it opened onto the garden where the grass was powdered with coal dust to make it black; and the fountains spouted streams of black ink into the air. The dinner was served on a black silk cloth, decorated with bunches of deep purple violets, and the burning candles were of black wax. An orchestra, hidden behind the black hangings, played dirges and funeral marches, while the guests were served by coal-black negresses, who were entirely naked, with food which was of a dark colour, served on china decorated in black.

Like Baudelaire, Des Esseintes professed to despise women and Nature. Women he considered merely as man's vice, his torturer, or the ornament of his house to grace his board. He despised everything that was natural and said that 'l'artifice était la marque distinctive du génie de l'homme'. He could not bear the platitudinous clichés concerning the beauties of Nature, and much preferred what was counterfeit. He ordered artificial scenery to be made, painted on screens, which could be wheeled in front of his windows, so that he could travel at will without leaving his own fire-side. He had artificial flowers made to suit his extravagant tastes and then, as the quintessence of aestheticism, by selection and cross-breeding, he evolved special forms of natural flowers which looked exactly as if they were artificial.

He had learnt his philosophy of life from Baudelaire:

'et là, près de ces confins où séjournaient les aberrations et les maladies, le tétanos mystique, la fièvre chaude de la luxure, les typhoïdes et les comitos du crime; il avait trouvé, couvant sous la morne cloche de l'Ennui, l'effrayant retour d'âge des sentiments et des idées. Il avait révélé la psychologie morbide de l'esprit qui a atteint l'octobre des sensations; montré la carie grandissante des impressions, alors que les enthousiasmes de la jeunesse sont taries, alors qu'il ne reste que l'aride souvenir des misères supportées.'

His most original piece of furniture was, as mentioned in the previous chapter, what he called his 'orgue à bouche'; which certainly was not a mouth-organ, but a collection of little barrels of liqueurs with taps attached to them, and these functioned in the same way as the stops of an organ. When he wished to play a tune on his 'organ', he used to pour, from the barrels, varying quantities from each tap. Each stop was labelled, as in an organ, 'flute' or 'horn' or 'heavenly voices', and so forth. Des Esseintes moved from one stop to another, playing a 'symphony' of tastes for himself. Each stop corresponded to a different liqueur, and each liqueur to a different instrument. Curaçao was the clarinet, Kümmel the oboe, Kirsch the trumpet, and so on. He also played string-quartets, with Old Brandy representing the fiddle, Rum the viola, and Bitters the 'cello. It is not recorded in the book what kind of hangover followed this musical orgy.

All this was an exaggeration—a parody almost—of the Baudelairean theory of *correspondances* between the different senses.

Des Esseintes was joined by a young disciple, a youth whom he had picked up one evening in a low bar, and whom he had chosen on account of his air of precocious depravity, so that he could train him for a career of vice. He spoiled him in every way, accustoming him to a life of indulgence, never allowing him to do anything for himself, yielding to his slightest whim. When the youth was eighteen, he gave him a season-ticket to a brothel, and then, after some months, he cut him off from all these pleasures. The young man, who could no longer do without them, and who felt capable of anything to recover them, was driven into delinquency and crime, and became an assassin.

À Rebours, more than any other work, helped to crystallize the conception of the Aesthete and the Decadent; more than any other work, it laid emphasis on the aesthetic aspect of vice, on the theory that vice is a nobler ornament of genius than virtue. This was the Aesthetic Ideal, which was taken very seriously by literary men, and it became The Tables of the Law for all those who wished to compete in advanced literary circles. Its moral aspect laid it open to attack as a very dangerous and corrupting influence.

Decadence eventually waned, and another aspect of aestheticism developed which did not take the form of self-indulgence in vice, and sensuous and sensual experience. There were those who, although they were disciples of Baudelaire, did not see why his theories should not be followed with a pure heart, and without sinking into the lowest depths of vice. These were the idealists, who worshipped only at the shrine of what was noblest and highest in art. They were often vaguely mystical and religious. They abhorred the commonplace and every manifestation of material life—indeed they had a fear of life and no interest in it; they withdrew from it and lived in a dreamland of their own, where no breath of modernity penetrated. They were, for the most part, delicate and consumptive poets, like Samain, who had not sufficient strength and energy for a life of vice. Their poetry breathes an atmosphere of closed rooms, with the blinds pulled down, by candle-light, in a mood of vague and aimless sadness. The season which they loved best was autumn, with the leaves falling fast, like their dreams, and rotting on the ground below. The hour of the day which they preferred was twilight, with its vague melancholy and the mystery of falling night. They felt sadness but not passion, and 'morne ennui' pervaded the whole landscape and their work. There was infinite weariness and lassitude in the air, as if the soul were dying. It was a mood to be reflected later in the music of Delius. One of the most characteristic collections of poems in this mood is *Serres Chaudes*—Hothouses—by Maeterlinck, published in 1889. He wrote, in the poem *Âme de Nuit*:

'Mon âme en est triste à la fin;
Elle est triste enfin d'être lasse,
Elle est lasse enfin d'être en vain,
Elle est triste et lasse à la fin
Et j'attends vos mains sur ma face.'

And, in *Serre d'Ennui*:

> 'O cet ennui bleu dans le cœur!
> Avec la vision meilleure,
> Dans le clair de lune qui pleure,
> De mes rêves bleus de langueur!'

The new movement began to consolidate itself and to crystallize. It was in 1886 that it first adopted the name of *Symbolisme*, and the honour of this christening—probably his most lasting claim to fame—must go to the Greek Papadiamantopulos, who wrote French poetry under the name of Jean Moréas. This was in his article, published on 18 September, in *Le Figaro*, in which he defined the aims of the movement suggesting its name, which emphasized its idealistic aspect at the expense of the decadent.

Le Symbolisme implied the search for the highest and noblest reality. The impossibility of expressing this vision directly was recognized, and it was shown that it could be suggested only through its earthly *correspondances*, through analogies or *symboles*. These were not the vision itself, but only its imperfect image or reflection. The *Symbole* thus became the most important element in poetry. It should not be confused—as has frequently been the case—with allegory. The *Symbole* was intended to suggest what could not be expressed adequately in words; whereas the allegory merely stated imaginatively what was perfectly capable of verbal expression. Critics thus mistakenly describe Vigny's poetry as symbolical, when it should be called allegorical. Many definitions of the *Symbole* were attempted, without much success, but the most satisfactory is that given by André Gide, in his *Traité du Narcisse*, published in 1891, at a time when he followed the movement:

> 'Les apparences sont imparfaites, elle balbutient les vérités qu'elles récèlent; le poète, à demi-mot, doit comprendre, puis redire ces vérités. . . . Le poète qui sait qu'il crée, devine à travers chaque chose, et une seule lui suffit, symbole, pour révéler son archétype; il sait que l'apparence n'est que le prétexte, un vêtement qui le dérobe, et où s'arrête l'oeil profane, mais qui nous montre qu'elle est là. Le poète pieux contemple, il se penche sur les symboles, et silencieux descend profondément au cœur des choses. Et quand il a perçu, visionnaire, l'Idée, l'intime Nombre harmonieux de son Être, qui soutient la forme imparfaite, il la saisit, puis, insoucieux de cette forme transitoire qui la revêtait dans le temps, il sait lui donner une

forme éternelle, sa forme véritable enfin, fatale . . . paradisiaque et cristalline.'

There were three living masters of the Movement—Baudelaire and Wagner were dead—Verlaine, Villiers de l'Isle Adam, and Mallarmé.

Verlaine was useful to the *Symbolistes* especially to attack Leconte de Lisle, who lay, like a dead weight, on poetry, holding it down and preventing any movement. During recent years Verlaine had come to the notice of the new poets, especially through his *Poètes Maudits*, published in 1884, in which he studied some of the latest writers, not yet well known; and also through his *Art Poétique*, which, although it had been composed thirteen years before, had been published only in *Jadis et Naguère*, in 1885, and was the first attempt at formulation of a new aesthetic. He declared that music was the most important element in poetry and asked for 'de la musique avant toute chose'. In his *Romances sans Paroles*, of which *Art Poétique* had been intended to form part, he had almost reached the evocative power of music, and succeeded in saying with words what music says with harmonies. He demanded that poetry should not be clear-cut and highly coloured, as it was in Leconte de Lisle's verse, but should have hazy contours, as in a *Nocturne* by Whistler. He liked to blur the lines of what he was describing—what French critics call *estomper* the outlines.'Rien de plus cher que la chanson grise', he said, and 'pas la couleur, rien que la nuance'. That was why he was happy in the mists of London, and was well inspired by them.

Verlaine was, eventually, to disappoint the *Symbolistes*, for he was no thinker, and metaphysical preoccupations played a very small part in his life. He spared himself, whenever possible, the fatigue of logical thought. His poetry differed greatly from that of the *Symbolistes*, in that he had no interest in the spiritual conceptions of the day. His best poetry, the poems which are remembered, are the expression of a sensation—sometimes vaguely religious, sometimes sensual—the sensations of a sensitive and childlike temperament, coupled with total sincerity and lack of self-consciousness. 'L'art, mes enfants,' he said, 'c'est d'être absolument soi-même.'

His most successful poems are little songs, 'Paysages Tristes' as he calls them, sad landscapes in autumn, or in the evening, when dusk comes on, and the rain is softly falling.

Verlaine liberated poetry from the too literal descriptions of the Parnassians. Only Baudelaire, before him, could have said:

> 'Le son du cor s'afflige vers les bois
> D'une douleur on veut croire orpheline.'

Only Verlaine himself could have written:

> 'L'ombre des arbres dans la rivière embrumée.'

Technically Verlaine did not invent anything, but he made the important discovery, which had far-reaching consequences, that poetry is really intended to be heard aloud, and not merely seen on the printed page. In his desire to escape from the rigid prosody of the Parnassians, he made use of the 'vers impair', that is, the line with the uneven number of syllables, giving it a flexibility and musicality it had not possessed in the hands of Sainte-Beuve who, in his *Poésies de Joseph Delorme*, published in 1828, had made use of it before him. His 'vers libéré' was liberated only on traditional lines, and he would never have gone as far as Rimbaud. He contented himself with using more flexibly what had already been freed before him. His most successful poems are those in short lines, but, when he used the Alexandrine, he has often achieved, what Victor Hugo, incorrectly, claimed to have done, 'désarticulé ce niais d'alexandrin'. With Verlaine there is no chance of slurring over the novelty of discarding the middle caesura, for he often places the sixth syllable of the line in the middle of a word, where no pause is possible.

Verlaine's influence with those who followed him was not so much in prosody as in the spirit and the power of evocation, and he managed to free words from their former obligation of expressing logical conceptions, for he used them as notes in music, or as shades of colour. His noblest achievement is in the little songs such as:

> 'Il pleure dans mon cœur
> Comme il pleut sur la ville.'

Or again:

> 'Le ciel est pardessus le toit
> Si bleu, si calme.'

It is this musical quality in Verlaine's poetry that made him so popular with the composers at the end of the nineteenth century, such as Debussy and Fauré, who set many of his poems to music.

Villiers de l'Isle Adam possessed most of the qualities valued by the Symbolists, especially idealism, with no admixture of decadence. Even in his lineage he represented the aristocratic ideal of the movement. One of his ancestors had been a Marshal in the fourteenth century, and another, in the fifteenth, had been the Grand Master of the Order of Saint John, who had received Malta from Charles V as the headquarters of his Order.

The most significant experience of Villiers de l'Isle Adam's life was when, at the age of twenty-three, in 1861, he met Baudelaire and Wagner, and both were to have a deep effect on him. At this time he was almost unique in appreciating the spiritual aspect of Baudelaire's genius and, later, he was perhaps the only one of the Symbolist masters to have any considerable knowledge of music, to understand, and even to perform himself, Wagner's music. Most of the others—Mallarmé included—did not really listen to music at all—not as a musician would —but merely enjoyed soaking in it, as in a warm, perfumed bath, allowing their imagination to play amongst the fantasies and dreams to which it gave rise in their minds, for there is no drug that induces such varied and pleasant dreams as music.

All Villiers de l'Isle Adam's work expresses disgust with the material world, and interest only in the ideal beyond this life. He was a Breton, a Celt, with his gaze fixed on the land of Tir-nan-Óg, the Isles of the Blest, beyond the setting sun. At the heart of his inspiration was belief in the sacrifice of the present for the sake of the ideal future. 'L'homme n'emporte dans la mort,' he said in *Axël*, 'que ce qu'il renonça de posséder dans la vie.'

Axël is Villiers de l'Isle Adam's most important work, and the one which had the largest impact on future literature. So important was it considered that Edmund Wilson, when studying imaginative literature between 1870 and 1930, calls the whole book *Axël's Castle*. It did not appear in its author's lifetime, but only posthumously, in 1890—he had died in 1889—though passages had already been printed, as early as 1872, in the short-lived literary review, *Renaissance Artistique et Littéraire*. It is based on the same central idea as most of his other works, the need for the sacrifice of the individual, in the physical sense, for the sake of the ideal.

Count Axël is a young man of beauty and talent, who inhabits a Wagnerian castle in the Black Forest, where he studies occult philosophy and the doctrine of the Rosicrucians, and he is preparing himself for the final revelation. In the castle lies hidden a large treasure, put there for safety when Napoleon's armies invaded the country. The existence of this secret hoard is known in the village, and a plot is hatched to murder the Count and to carry off the treasure. But the Count hears of this and he hides the treasure elsewhere, telling only his wife of its whereabouts, but she dies without divulging it to anyone.

Axël has a cousin, Kasper, who comes to the castle to see him, and mocks at his life of meditation. He tries to entice him away from the castle and to take the treasure with him. Axël, in long lyrical speeches, expresses contempt for Kasper's kind of life; he challenges him to a duel, and kills him.

In the meantime the secret of the treasure has been discovered in a Book of Hours belonging to Axël's mother, who had bequeathed it to a convent, where a young girl called Sara finds it. She goes to Axël's castle, begs him for shelter and, at dead of night, goes down to the secret cellar, the door of which she is able to open by pressing a hidden spring. Then, from behind a sliding panel, the treasure comes pouring forth, in a cascade of gold pieces, diamonds, rubies, and pearls.

Axël, however, has been watching her from the stairs, but she catches sight of him and, drawing a pistol from her pocket, fires at him, but only wounds him slightly. He seizes hold of her and wrenches the dagger out of her hand, with which she was about to stab him. They look into one another's eyes and fall in love immediately. She is a Rosicrucian also, and they embrace in ecstasy at having found one another. She begs him to flee with her, and describes the places they will visit together—Kashmir, Bengal, Sumatra, Japan, and many other exotic regions—the description of which takes ten whole pages without interruption, a prose poem of ten pages, which ends: 'Là-bas, tout nous appelle, Axël, mon unique maître, mon amour! La jeunesse, la liberté! le vertige de notre puissance! Et—qui sait, de grandes causes à défendre, tous les rêves à réaliser.' He answers, unexpectedly—but characteristically for Villiers de l'Isle Adam himself: 'À quoi bon les réaliser? Ils sont si beaux!'

When she says, in a lyrical passage, at further length: 'Axël, Axël! m'oublieras-tu déjà, pour des pensées divines? Viens, voici la terre! Viens vivre!' he answers: 'Vivre? Non.—Notre existence est remplie,— et sa coupe déborde. Quel sablier comptera les heures de cette nuit! L'avenir? Sara, crois en cette parole: nous venons de l'épuiser. Toutes les réalités, demain, que seraient-elles, en comparaison des mirages que nous venons de vivre? . . . Accepter désormais de vivre, ne serait plus qu'un sacrilège envers nous mêmes.' And he adds, the most famous sentence in the whole play: 'Vivre? Les serviteurs feront cela pour nous!'

He proposes then that they shall die together immediately, though she is anxious that they should at least enjoy one night of love together first, but he answers that this would only be an anticlimax after the joys they have experienced, even without physical possession. All these joys would be insignificant beside those which have been theirs, and would be unworthy to 'succéder à cette miraculeuse nuit nuptiale où, vierges encore, nous nous sommes cependant à jamais possédés'.

She tells him that she has, beneath the emerald of her ring, a deadly poison, and suggests that they should take it together. They find a golden goblet amongst the piled-up treasure, and they fill it with the poison. Then, after long rapturous talk together, they decide to share it, and Sara, as the woman, is given the last word: 'Maintenant, puisque l'infini seul n'est pas un mensonge, enlevons-nous, oublieux des autres paroles humaines en notre même Infini!'

They drink the potion together. The stage directions say:

'Les voici gisant, entrelacés, sur le sable de l'allée funéraire, échangeant sur leurs lèvres le souffle suprême. Puis ils demeurent immobiles, inanimés.

A présent, le soleil jaunit les marbres, les statues; le grésillement de la lampe et du flambeau se résout en fumée dans le rais lumineux qui flue obliquement du soupirail.—Une pièce d'or tombe, roule et sonne comme l'heure contre un sépulcre.—Et—troublant le silence du lieu terrible où deux êtres humains viennent ainsi de vouer eux-mêmes leurs âmes à l'exil du Ciel—on entend, du dehors, les murmures éloignés du vent dans le vaste des forêts, les vibrations d'éveil de l'espace, la houle des plaines, le bourdonnement de la Vie.'

On his death-bed Villiers de l'Isle Adam wished to alter the ending, to delete the suicide, which went counter to Christian principles, but he did not live long enough to mutilate it, which would have changed its emphasis completely, and have been false to the main conception of the work.

Axël became the model for the heroes of Symbolist literature at the end of the nineteenth century, and not only for France, but in England as well; while his castle became the escape and the refuge for all those whom the barbarities of the modern world wounded or offended—it was a more idealistic refuge than the ivory tower of Vigny, or the decadent parlour of Des Esseintes.

Mallarmé became the leader, the incarnation, of Le Symbolisme, round whom the movement crystallized. He was, in truth, 'le symbole du Symbolisme', though this, in fact, was said, far less correctly, of Laforgue. It was finally Mallarmé who justifies the movement and who became its most perfect exponent. He, more than any of the other poets, seemed to incarnate what the literary world—whether French or foreign—considered Symbolist. It was towards him that all men of letters gravitated as soon as they arrived in Paris, and his Tuesday literary evenings, at his home in La Rue de Rome—Les Mardis de la

Rue de Rome—became the most famous literary circle at the end of the nineteenth century.

In appearance there was nothing aesthetic or decadent about Mallarmé—although Verlaine included him amongst his *Poètes Maudits*. He was a short and somewhat stocky man, always dressed in sober black, as befitted a schoolmaster, for he was a teacher of English—though not a very distinguished or efficient one. The only sign of eccentricity he permitted himself was his Lavallière tie—not a very daring one in the eighteen-eighties when it was almost the badge of the man of letters.

He lived in a frugal and bourgeois manner; he kept no servant and it was he himself who, on Tuesday evenings, opened the door to his guests. They used to meet in the dining-room, where a china stove stood in one corner, a very ugly gas chandelier hung from the ceiling over a common table in the centre, round which the guests sat. The only cheer provided was a large bowl of tobacco from which they filled their pipes at intervals. However, on the walls hung what are now regarded as priceless works of art, but which, at that time, were not highly considered—a Monet, a Whistler, a Gauguin, and on a little console stood a Rodin.

In that room any Tuesday evening one might have met Henri de Régnier who, at twenty-eight, was already the author of *Poèmes Anciens et Romanesques*, and who with his monocle in his eye, his impeccable clothes, vied with Robert de Montesquiou as prince of dandies. There too came André Gide, very different from his later appearance, for he looked somewhat like the portrait of Liszt by Deveria, with his long moustache, his flowing locks, and his somewhat consumptive air—which in time disappeared—as became the begetter of *Les Cahiers d'André Walter*. There too were seen Pierre Louÿs, the author of *Les Chansons de Bilitis*, some of which had been exquisitely set to music by Debussy; the Americans, Vielé-Griffin and Stuart Merrill; the Belgians, beautiful Rodenbach, author of *Bruges la Morte*, and Verhaeren, somewhat like Vercingetorix, and never fully at ease in the aesthetic atmosphere of Symbolism; Whistler, Symons, George Moore, Yeats, and, of course, Oscar Wilde.

All those who describe the evenings in the Rue de Rome—there is a very good account of one of them in *Avowals* by George Moore, at which the work read must have been *Igitur* by Mallarmé, though it was not to be published, or known, until 1925—all who attended these evenings describe the extraordinary charm of the host, which was not merely due to his courteous manner but to the things which he expressed; yet none of them, afterwards, could ever repeat what it was that was so memorable in what he said, though none would admit failing to understand him. It is probable that they did in fact understand, in that deep and hidden region of their being, where comprehension does not entail the formulation of ideas. He was an 'illusioniste', a conjuror, who made them see the vision which his own eyes beheld—it was so also when he discussed his compositions. From long acquaintance with him they knew the way his mind worked and could understand, at the merest hint, what it was he wished to convey—just as amongst members of the same family sentences do not require to be finished since all know, at a word, what is intended. That is why Mallarmé's close acquaintances had no difficulty in understanding his poetry. But, now that his physical presence has disappeared, there is considerable doubt about what he intended to convey in many of his writings. But, just as with a difficult and unfamiliar piece of music, its comprehension depends on the skill of the artist who is interpreting it, so was it with Mallarmé when he read his poetry; he was the skilled interpreter and executant of his own writings. It must also have been thus in the case of the lecture he delivered at Oxford in 1893, *La Musique et les Lettres*, so difficult to interpret today when read in print, yet which was claimed to be understood by those who heard it at the time —probably with justification. Cazamian says, in his *History of French Literature*, that the fact that this lecture 'should have been patiently heard in 1894 at Oxford and Cambridge, speaks well for English courtesy'. It would be truer to say that it speaks well for Mallarmé's powers as an executant-virtuoso. The lecture was delivered by its author in French, but a translation, made by the Professor of History, York Powell, with the help of the poet, was afterwards read. Those who were present declared later that they had found the French easier to understand than the English—and this is comprehensible, for the latter lacked Mallarmé's personality, his interpretation and execution.

After the lecture there was a dinner in Christ Church in honour of Mallarmé, who found everything perfect—except the port, which had not agreed with him. The following day he went to Cambridge, to deliver the same lecture, but he did not go under the auspices of the University, as at Oxford, and tickets were sold for it. Tickets were five shillings each and there were twenty people present at the lecture. 'L'honneur est sauf!' Mallarmé remarked afterwards.

He carried away with him, from Oxford and Cambridge, a romantic view of the Fellows of Colleges, whom he saw as highly spiritual and evolved human-beings, the quintessence of the intellectual life of the country. In his article entitled 'Déplacement Avantageux' he wrote:

'Aujourd'hui choisissant à parfaire une impression de beauté, véritable-
ment la fleur, et le résultat ce sont les Fellows!'

In literary theory, Mallarmé continued further along the same path
which Baudelaire had trod, and he became the spokesman for the
aesthetic doctrine of the Symbolist Movement—it was these ideas which
were followed in France and abroad, rather than his actual poetry,
which was difficult to imitate.

The Symbolists believed, as Baudelaire had done, that artistic inspiration and execution were the result of a spiritual experience which
occurred in that region of the being where there is no separation into
different arts. The poet thus becomes a prophet. 'Il faut être voyant!'
Rimbaud said and, in Latin, the same word describes both prophet and
poet. Théodore de Wyzéwa said, in *Nos Maîtres*, 'créer l'œuvre d'art,
c'est être voyant, ou atteindre le vrai à travers la Maïa du Réel; c'est
être poète, ou s'efforcer de rendre l'infini par le fini, le monde émotion-
nel par le monde sensible; c'est être artiste, ou capable d'extérioriser
l'émotion ressentie au contact de l'invisible'. And Vanor wrote, in *L'Art
Symboliste*, describing the function of the poet: 'Un jour il dira aux
hommes le mot de Dieu et le secret de la Vie.'

The tragedy for Mallarmé was that, in an age when it was required
of the artist to be a visionary, his mystical powers did not equal his
poetic genius, and that he was never granted the ultimate vision. He
never entered the Inner Castle which Saint Teresa of Avila described,
and which certainly was Rimbaud's experience, when he wrote, in
Alchimie du Verbe, from *Une Saison en Enfer*: 'Enfin, ô bonheur, ô raison,
j'écartais du ciel l'azur, qui est du noir, et je vécus étincelle d'or de la
lumière *nature*.' It was this failure in Mallarmé which eventually induced
the sensation of sterility. The function of the artist, according to the
Symbolists, is to realize, to make concrete, that perfection of which we
have, here below, only the shadow. His function is to seek the ideal, and
to create a life more perfect than the one in this world, and then, as
Mallarmé says, 'musicalement se lève, idée même et suave, l'absente de
tous bouquets'. That is to say art brings into existence the perfect
platonic flower, which is not to be found in any earthly bouquet.

Then, since this spiritual experience is the same for all the arts, it
should be possible to create an art which would appeal to all the senses
at once, and unite them in one single art. As Rimbaud said in *Alchimie
du Verbe*: 'Je me flattai d'inventer un verbe poétique accessible, un
jour ou l'autre, à tous les sens.' Or, as Rodin said later, as reported by
Paul Gsell, in *L'Art*: 'Peinture, Sculpture, Littérature, Musique, sont
plus proches les unes des autres qu'on ne le croit généralement. Elles
expriment *toutes* les sentiments de l'âme humaine en face de la nature.

Il n'y a que les moyens d'expression qui varient.' That, as we have seen, is what Baudelaire also had believed.

Of the different elements making up this unified art, the Symbolists believed that music was more capable than the rest of expressing this spiritual quality which they all sought, and their aim was—as Valéry said—to 'reprendre à la musique leur bien'. That is, to take back from music the expressive powers which the other arts had allowed her to monopolize. All the arts thus tried, as far as possible, to approximate to music. This did not mean the mere copying of the harmonious sounds of music, to reproduce, as it were, programme music. What it meant was that poetry should be able to follow music in the power it possesses of evoking a state of mind—'un état d'âme', as they said. The artists envied music its language which was not merely used for the communication of ideas. Mallarmé wished his poems to possess, as music did, the faculty of multiple interpretation, the power of not being tied down to one single interpretation alone. Commentators, therefore, do his writings a disservice when they try to limit them to one interpretation alone— to one definitive meaning, as some of them claim. He tried, by every device in his power, to escape from the limiting characteristic of the French language—its clarity, its necessity to say something logical and precise. That is the quality which makes the language difficult to handle as an expressive instrument for poetry. The French are not less gifted than other races in poetry, but they possess a language which is handicapped, in comparison with English and German, as a means of exteriorizing a spiritual experience, since it possesses no overtones, no mystery. Mallarmé attained poetic ambiguity by omitting punctuation, by leaving it doubtful whether a word is a participle, a finite verb, an adjective, a noun, subject, or object. Philologists are for ever trying to parse his poetry, in order to interpret it, and give it final meaning. Yet he, deliberately, left it vague in order to permit the possibility of the multiple interpretation which music possesses, thinking that poetry thereby would gain in richness and depth.

Mallarmé also wished poetry to possess, as the religions did, its mystery into which it could withdraw and hide itself from the contamination of the vulgar herd. In *Hérésie Artistique* he wrote : 'Toute chose qui veut devenir sacrée s'enveloppe de mystère.' Mystery and obscurity are the protection of poetry from the idle curiosity of the masses.

Symbolist poetry is based on the assumption that the external world is not important—this was a reaction against the excessive materialism of the Parnassian Movement—that, in fact, it does not really exist until the artist has seen it significantly—this is an extension of Baudelaire's conception of beauty. There is thus no point in describing it minutely, all that should be done is to suggest the emotion which it awakens. As Mallarmé said in *Hérésie Artistique*: 'Peindre non la chose mais l'effet qu'elle produit.' Or as he declared later, in 1891 : 'Nommer un objet c'est supprimer les trois quarts de la jouissance d'un poème, qui est faite du bonheur de deviner peu à peu, le suggérer, voilà le rêve.'

The Symbolist poets realized the importance in life and art of the quality of mystery, and they tried to convey the sense of the deep and impenetrable darkness which surrounds man, the darkness whence he has come, and into which he will again eventually disappear. They wished not so much to render the atmosphere of this world as the soul's atmosphere, and to evoke this with beauty and compassion. This is found particularly in the work of Maeterlinck who, almost more than any of the Symbolists, affected English poetry. Most of his writings express awe and terror of the mystery of death, and suggest that man is warned by presentiments of the destiny that is lying in wait for him, if he can but learn to interpret these portents. The function of art, he believed, was to make these warnings clear, and he thought that this could only be achieved symbolically. His symbolism does not, however, owe anything to genuine supernatural effects, it is never a *deus ex machina*, and there is no supernatural intervention. The symbols are always capable of rational interpretation, and they are those that are met with every day but are not noticed, except by those who are particularly sensitive. For instance, in *La Princesse Maleine*, the ominous rustling at the door could, by a rational mind, be explained by the fact that the dog, at that moment, is scratching to be let in; the mysterious and regular tappings against the wall could be due to little Alain bouncing his ball as he plays outside. When the murderers come to assassinate Maleine, a lily falls off the window sill and is broken, and, when she is killed, the swans fly away from the lake, except one, which suddenly and mysteriously falls down dead. All these things are not supernatural in themselves, but the characters, in the play, see their symbolical significance, and it is intended that the audience should also, in a similar way, perceive the inherent symbolism in many ordinary and commonplace events that happen round them every day, and which they do not normally notice.

In *L'Intruse* Death is an invisible force that all the characters feel around them. A woman lies critically ill, the family sit in the next room, and talk together. Suddenly the nightingales, in the garden, stop singing and the swans fly away from the lake. The family is expecting a relative to arrive, and the members think it is her arrival which has disturbed the birds and frightened them away. Other warnings occur which are not noticed as especially strange: the sound of the scythe being sharpened in a nearby field; the noise of a door suddenly opening and which will not shut—it is as if someone were pushing against it from outside. Later it is known that Death has come while they were all talking together, and has taken the woman away.

Maeterlinck, in *Le Tragique Quotidien*, explained the symbolical significance which he sees in the simplest events of ordinary life when he says:

> 'Il m'est arrivé de croire qu'un vieillard assis dans son fauteuil, attendant simplement sous la lampe, écoutant sous sa conscience toutes les lois éternelles qui règnent autour de sa maison, interprétant sans le comprendre ce qu'il y a dans le silence des portes et des fenêtres et dans la petite voix de la lumière, subissant la présence de son âme et de sa destinée, inclinant un peu la tête, sans se douter que toutes les puissances de ce monde interviennent et veillent dans la chambre comme des servantes attentives. . . . Il m'est arrivé de croire que ce vieillard immobile vivait, en réalité, d'une vie plus profonde, plus humaine et plus générale que l'amant qui étrangle sa maîtresse, le capitaine qui remporte une victoire, ou l'époux qui venge son honneur.'

The Symbolist poets believed that the enveloping mystery of life expressed itself, in olden days, unconsciously, in folk-lore, which was a kind of racial symbolism. This explains why they made so much use of folk-lore in their writings, or gave their poetry its appearance, as we find in such poems as *Wieland le Forgeron* by Vielé-Griffin, *Mélusine* by Jean Moréas, *Polyphème* by Samain, and most of Maeterlinck's plays and poetry. His *Chansons*, which are composed on the model of folk-songs, had an influence, later, on the early Yeats:

> 'Et s'il revenait un jour,
> Que faut-il lui dire?
> —Dites-lui qu'on l'attendait
> Jusqu'à s'en mourir.
>
> Et s'il m'interroge encor
> Sans me reconnaître?
> —Parlez-lui comme une sœur,
> Il souffre peut-être.
>
> Et s'il me demande où vous êtes,
> Que faut-il lui répondre?
> —Donnez-lui mon anneau d'or
> Sans rien lui répondre.

D

Et s'il veut savoir pourquoi
La salle est déserte?
—Montrez-lui la lampe éteinte
Et la porte ouverte.

Et s'il m'interroge alors
Sur la dernière heure?
—Dites-lui que j'ai souri
De peur qu'il ne pleure.'

Later, countries like Ireland, with rising nationalism, found in the folk-lore of their own race the substance for their symbolism in poetry, and drew from it extensively. This explains the widespread influence which the Symbolist Movement exercised outside France, at the end of the nineteenth century.

As these new theories of poetry developed, it was felt that new forms were needed and, in the eighteen-eighties, there was more experimentation in prosody than at any other moment in French literary history. The most daring experiment was in trying to give more fluidity and musicality to traditional verse forms, through the invention of *vers libre*. Mallarmé had remained content with the verse which the Parnassians had used, and Verlaine's innovations were not of a revolutionary nature. But those who followed them desired more drastic changes. It is not easy to determine to whom credit should go for the revolution. It is certain that Rimbaud was the first ever to make use of *vers libre*, in two poems from *Les Illuminations* entitled *Marine* and *Mouvement*, composed in the early eighteen-seventies. However, they could have exercised no influence in connection with the invention of *vers libre*, since they were known only in 1886, when published in *La Vogue*, at a time when free verse had already been conceived. Apart from Rimbaud, there were several other claimants for priority— Gustave Kahn and Jules Laforgue, not to mention Marie Krisinska who, in certain lyrical poems, published between 1882 and 1885 in *Le Chat Noir*, claimed to be the first in the field, but most of the Symbolists would not admit that these were in verse at all. Eighteen-eighty-six is certainly the year in which *vers libre* was first known in France. In that year were published in *La Vogue* Rimbaud's poems in May; one by Gustave Kahn in June—and whether he obtained the idea from Rimbaud is not significant—and, in August, the first of Laforgue's poems in *vers libre*, *L'Hiver qui vient*. Nowadays it is universally considered that his are the most distinguished examples of *vers libre* in the Symbolist Movement, although those by Vielé-Griffin, Henri de Régnier, Jean

Moréas, and Verhaeren were more admired at the time—Remy de Gourmont called Vielé-Griffin 'le maître du vers libre'. Laforgue did not borrow the idea from a French poet—although he was greatly struck by Rimbaud's poems, when they appeared—but from Walt Whitman, and it was while translating *Leaves of Grass*, extracts of which appeared in June 1886, in *La Vogue*, that he conceived the plan of experimenting himself with this kind of poem.

The clearest definition of the theory of *vers libre* is that formulated by Gustave Kahn, in the Preface to the second edition of his *Palais Nomades*, in 1897, the first edition of which had appeared in 1887.

Symbolism, as an organized movement, was very short-lived, though its spirit pervaded literature right into the twentieth century. Its ideals were too lofty, too difficult to follow and to live up to, so that most writers fell by the wayside, or went to worship at other shrines. Moréas' manifesto in 1886 is generally taken as the date when Symbolism took over from Decadence—the fiftieth anniversary of the beginning of the Movement was celebrated in 1936—and the banquet given to Moréas, in 1891, to commemorate the publication of his *Pèlerin Passionné*, a symbolist work, is accepted as marking its end, for it was that year that he abandoned the ideals of Symbolism and founded the *École Romane*, with very different conceptions. This was a return to the Mediterranean inspiration of French culture, away from the Celtic and Scandinavian mists, a return to France's Graeco-Roman roots, to admiration for law, order, and balance, to the inspiration of the Renaissance of the sixteenth century, and to that earlier Renaissance of the twelfth century. Most of the poets followed Moréas—Henri de Régnier, Vielé-Griffin, Samain, and others—and they produced some of the most uninteresting poetry in the French language. One poet, however, did bring this *genre* to noble heights in the twentieth century, Paul Valéry.

Some of the northern poets—the Belgians in particular—having no classical traditions, and no roots on the shores of the Mediterranean, followed Verhaeren into descriptions of modern city life, modern industrial life, with its mechanical manifestations. Verhaeren treated all these aspects romantically—it was a new romanticism, and his influence spread all over Europe, from England, through Germany, right to the ends of Russia. As the new century opened, and up to the First World War, Verhaeren was considered the greatest poet in the world writing in French. His visits, in 1913, to England, Germany, and Russia were a triumphal progress.

The most original poet produced by the years of the Symbolist Movement was undoubtedly Jules Laforgue, who passed unnoticed in his true greatness. He was born in 1860 and so reached maturity just as the Symbolist Movement was beginning, and he died before it had ended, with his finest work as yet unpublished. He had been away from Paris, as Reader to the Empress Augusta of Prussia, during the largest part of his adult life, and so did not influence the progress of the Movement; and he returned to Paris only in 1886, to die the following year, at the early age of twenty-seven. In mood he is nearer to the Decadents than to the members of the Symbolist Movement, but in form he is nearer still to the iconoclastic poets of the eighteen-seventies in his use of imagery and language, to poets like Corbière, Cros, and Richepin, and he will find favour with the modern poets during, and after, the First World War.

Symbolism is the least French of all the literary movements of France, and this explains the appeal it had for foreigners of all nationalities, as varied as Stuart Merrill, Vielé-Griffin, Jean Moréas, and Verhaeren—not to mention Oscar Wilde and George Moore—all were received with open arms and assimilated, and did not stand out amongst the native writers. It was a movement that was international in its effects and its influence spread to all countries—Spain, Italy, Germany, Spanish America, Russia, Greece, the Balkans, and Ireland. It could be transplanted and grow in an alien soil, bringing forth new shoots, which were all a little different, but all sharing the same original root, and all bathed in the same poetic climate.

In particular it suited the English genius, for its idealism appealed to much that was fundamental in the English character. It fitted in admirably with Anglo-Catholicism, the Oxford Movement, the arty-crafty inspiration of William Morris, the devotion to the Italian Renaissance; and it presupposed a background of cultured leisure, security, and prosperity. It was, in every way, well suited to the British temperament, and it burst out in England during the nineties.

The more virile, realistic, and coarser atmosphere of Corbière, Rimbaud, and Laforgue awakened scarcely any ripple of influence at the time. In the following century, however, when the public had grown tired of Blessed Damozels, of knights *sans peur et sans reproche*, of rich hangings, of candles and incense; when it had grown weary of men with the weak appearance of Pre-Raphaelite Christs, and their faint air of secret—but probably only intellectual—debauch; when the Celtic twilights began to fade, then the poets longed for another atmosphere than that of stuffy rooms, or dim churches, or mist-enshrouded canals and lanes, and they turned to Corbière, Rimbaud, and Laforgue, prepared to appreciate their more direct and more virile inspiration.

6

THE YELLOW NINETIES

In the eighteen-nineties interest in French literature amongst English writers developed very rapidly. The way had been prepared, twenty years before, by Swinburne and Pater, and they were followed by others —especially by George Moore. However, as the influence of France spread, the exponents of the new art came more frequently into clash with the forces of philistinism. The middle-class had been growing more prosperous since the middle of the century, since the Exhibition of 1851, and their accumulated wealth added weight and force to their opposition to an art which did not support their ideal of goodness allied to riches.

After George Moore, the next writer significant in the propagation of the aesthetic ideal from France was Oscar Wilde, who did not doubt that it would ultimately prevail. 'The future belongs to the Dandies,' he said. 'It is the exquisites who are going to rule!' He became the perfect and supreme example of the aesthete in England. Like George Moore he was an Irishman; he was born in Dublin in October 1854, a few days before Arthur Rimbaud, and he was two years younger than George Moore. He seemed, however, very much more than that his junior, for he postponed his attainment of adult status by taking degrees at two universities. He obtained a First Class in Greek and Latin in Final Honour Moderations at Trinity College, Dublin, and also the Berkeley Gold Medal for Greek. After that he went up, as a young graduate of twenty, to Magdalen College, Oxford, with a Demyship. He obtained a First Class in Honour Moderations in Classics in 1876, and a First in Litterae Humaniores in 1878. At Oxford he made the acquaintance of Walter Pater, and fell forthwith under his sway. He read his *Renaissance* with passionate admiration, and spoke of it in terms very similar to those used by Swinburne about *Mademoiselle de Maupin*. 'It is my golden book! I never travel without it, but it is the very flower of decadence; the last trumpet should have sounded the moment it was written.'

Oscar Wilde, more fortunate than Swinburne, won the Newdigate Prize, in 1878, for his poem entitled *Ravenna*, and read a portion of it at the Encaenia in the Sheldonian Theatre, in June that year—his first taste of public fame and acclamation, and he enjoyed it.

Shortly after taking his degree he went to London to embark on the career of a man of letters. His first collection of poems appeared in 1881 when he was twenty-seven—the same year as Moore's *Pagan Poems*—resplendent in a white vellum parchment binding, with a cover device richly embossed in gold designed by himself. They are not very distinguished or original poems, and are very much influenced by the poets of the Art for Art's Sake Movement in France, by Baudelaire and Gautier in particular. Baudelaire's *L'Héautontimorouménos*, the self-torturer, is reflected in the following lines:

'Being ourselves the sowers and the seeds,
The night that covers and the lights that fade,
The spear that pierces and the side that bleeds,
The lips betraying and the life betrayed.'

Gautier's *Symphonie en Blanc Majeur*, from *Émaux et Camées*, is echoed in *A Symphony in Yellow*:

'An omnibus across the bridge
Crawls like a yellow butterfly,
And here and there, a passer-by
Shows like a little restless midge.

Big barges full of yellow hay,
Are moored against the shadowy wharf
And like a yellow silken scarf,
The thick fog hangs along the quay.

The yellow leaves begin to fade,
And flutter from the Temple elms;
And, at my feet, the pale green Thames
Lies like a rod of rippled jade.'

While *Harmony in the Gold Room* recalls Verlaine's poem, *Le Piano que baise une Main Frêle* from *Romances sans Paroles*.

Between 1881 and 1883 Oscar Wilde paid several visits to Paris, and met some of the well-known poets of the time. In 1882 he went to the United States to lecture and, even then, had already formed the habit of shocking those whom he met. When asked, at the customs examination, whether he had anything to declare, he answered : 'Nothing but my genius!' Everywhere he went, on this lecture tour, he was taken as the symbol of the Decadent—and this is interesting as it was two years before this figure became crystallized in France in the person of Des Esseintes.

Between 1880 and 1890 Oscar Wilde was training to be the aesthetic leader of English literature. Writing in *The Yellow Book*, in January 1895, Max Beerbohm said that, before Wilde, there had been poets and painters, but that no one, before him, had spoken of the quality of beauty :

'It would appear that it was to him that Art owed the great social vogue she enjoyed at this time. Peacock feathers and sunflowers glittered in every room, the curio shops were ransacked for furniture of Queen Anne's days, and men and women, fired with the fervid words of the young Oscar, threw their mahogany into the streets. A few smart women even dressed themselves in suave draperies and unheard of greens. Into whatever ballroom you went you would surely find, among the women in tiaras and fops and the distinguished foreigners, half a score of comely ragamuffins in velveteens, murmuring sonnets, posturing, waving their hands. The craze was called Aestheticism.'

At first Oscar Wilde followed very closely the poets of the Art for Art's Sake Movement, those who had been dead for many years now— Baudelaire and Gautier. In 1883 he wrote his first play, *The Duchess of Padua*; in 1885 another collection of verse entitled *The Harlot's House*, the name poem of which recalls Baudelaire. Next came, in 1888, a collection of short stories, *The Happy Prince and Other Tales*, and, in 1891, a further collection of tales, *The House of Pomegranates*. In these the influence of Flaubert is predominant, and Wilde wished to produce in English what the French novelist had achieved in his *Trois Contes*. In the second collection, *The Star Child* recalls *Saint Julien l'Hospitalier*, and *The Birthday of the Infanta* is reminiscent of the style of *Hérodias*. *The House of Pomegranates* is vastly superior to *The Happy Prince* and is, in fact, one of the most successful examples of Wilde's achievement in prose.

However, far more important than the poems or the short stories are the articles of aesthetic criticism, written between 1889 and 1890— though one of them, 'The Truth of Masks', had appeared under the title 'Shakespeare and Stage Costume' in 1885—and published under the title *Intentions* in 1891. 'Pen, Pencil and Poison' appeared in *The Fort-nightly Review* in 1889; 'The Decay of Lying' in 1889 and 'The Critic as Artist' in 1890—both in *The Nineteenth-Century Review*.

The ideas contained in these essays are largely borrowed from Baudelaire's aesthetic criticism, but Wilde has added a touch of blasé humour and flippancy, not present in the French author. They are the most extreme expression of the Art for Art's Sake doctrine, and Wilde declared that 'art never expresses anything but itself. All bad art comes from returning to life and Nature'. Like Gautier and Baudelaire, he raises art to the highest pinnacle, far higher than Nature, and he says: 'The more we study art, the less we care for Nature. What art really reveals is Nature's lack of design.' This is taken straight out of Baudelaire's *Salon* of 1846, as well as: 'There is no variety in Nature. It resides in the imagination, or fancy, of the man who looks at her. It is fortunate for us that Nature is so imperfect, as otherwise we should have had no art at all.' As for the imitation of Nature, he says: 'It is, on the contrary, Nature that copies art. A great artist invents a new type and life tries to copy it!'

'Nature is no great mother who has borne us. She is our creation. It is in our brain that she quickens to life. Things are because we see them, and what we see, and how we see it, depends on the arts that have influenced us. To look at a thing is very different from seeing a thing. One does not see anything until one sees its beauty. Then, and then only, does it come to existence. At present people see fogs, not because there are fogs, but because poets and painters have taught them the mysterious loveliness of such effects. There may have been fogs for centuries in London. But no one saw them, and so we do not know anything about them. They did not exist until Art invented them.'

Eighteen-ninety-one was an important year for Oscar Wilde for, as well as *The House of Pomegranates* and *Intentions*, he published *Lord Arthur Savile's Crime* and *The Picture of Dorian Gray*. As a story *Lord Arthur Savile's Crime* is not very interesting for the plot is weak and the characterization poor, but its style is brilliant, and it contains passages which resemble prose poems by Baudelaire from his *Spleen de Paris*— one might call them, perhaps, *Spleen de Londres*. One such describes Lord Arthur's walk, at dawn, through London :

'Where he went he hardly knew. He had a dim memory of wandering through a labyrinth of sordid houses, of being lost in a great web of sombre streets, and it was bright dawn when he found himself, at last, at Piccadilly Circus. As he strolled home towards Belgrave Square, he met the great waggons on their way to Covent Garden. The white-smocked carters, with their pleasant sunburnt faces and coarse curly hair, strode sturdily on, cracking their whips, and calling out now and then to each other; on the back of a huge grey horse, the leader of a jangling team, sat a chubby boy, with a bunch of primroses in his battered hat, keeping a tight hold of the mane with his little hands, and laughing; and the great pile of vegetables looked like masses of jade against the morning sky, like masses of green jade against the pink petal of some marvellous rose. Lord Arthur felt curiously affected, he could not tell why. There was something in the dawn's delicate loveliness that seemed to him inexpressibly pathetic, and he thought of all the days that break in beauty and that set in storm. It was now a London free from the sin of night and the smoke of day, a pallid ghost-like city, a desolate town of tombs.'

The Picture of Dorian Gray, which was inspired by *À Rebours*, became for England what Huysmans' novel had been for France, its aesthetic Bible, the book which gave the most perfect picture of the Decadent. There is no doubt that the 'yellow book' which leads Dorian Gray to perdition is *À Rebours*. 'Dorian Gray had been poisoned by a book' and, through it, he had learnt 'to look on evil simply as a mode through which he could realize his conception of the beautiful'. He procured from Paris no less than nine large-paper copies of the first edition, and had them bound in different colours, so that they might suit his various moods, and the changing fancies of a nature over which he seemed, at times, to have almost entirely lost control. The hero, the wonderful young Parisian, in whom the romantic and the scientific temperaments were so strangely blended, became to him a kind of 'prefiguring type of himself'. Indeed the whole book seemed to him to contain the story of his own life, written before he had lived it.

He proceeded then to make it true about his own life. Just as Des Esseintes had enjoyed his symphonies of perfume and taste, so did Dorian Gray in like manner:

'And so he would now study perfumes, and the secrets of their manufacture, distilling heavily-scented oils, and burning odorous gums from the East. He saw that there was no mood of the mind that had not its counterpart in the sensuous life, and set himself to discover their true relations.'

That is Baudelaire's theory of *correspondances*, and so is the following:

> 'What was there in frankincense that made one mystical, and in
> ambergris that stirred one's passions, and in violets that woke the
> memory of dead romances, and in musk that troubled the brain,
> and in champak that stained the imagination; and seeking often
> to elaborate a real psychology of perfumes, and to estimate the
> several influences of sweet-smelling roots, and scented pollen-laden
> flowers, or aromatic balms, and of dark and fragrant woods, of
> spikenard that sickens, of hovenia that makes men mad, and of
> aloes that are said to be able to expel melancholy from the soul?'

The Preface is composed of aphorisms borrowed from Flaubert's
correspondence. 'To reveal art and to conceal the artist is art's aim.' Or :
'There is no such thing as a moral or an immoral book. Books are
well written, or badly written. That is all.' Or again: 'No artist has
ethical sympathies. An ethical sympathy in an artist is an unpardon-
able mannerism of style.' Or, from Gautier: 'All art is useless.'

The Picture of Dorian Gray was very badly received by most of the
daily papers, and it was pronounced very immoral, for did the author
not say: 'The only way to get rid of a temptation is to give in to it.' The
Daily Chronicle wrote, on 13 April 1891, that the book had been
produced by 'the leprous literature of the French Decadents'. 'Leprous'
was the favourite term of abuse used against any literature coming
from France.

Salome, which appeared in 1893, was first written in French by
Oscar Wilde himself, but it was said to have been revised and corrected
by Vielé-Griffin. The subject, and some of the details, were taken from
Flaubert's *Hérodias* in *Trois Contes*, but the emphasis has been moved
from Herodias herself to Salome, the psychology has been made more
decadent and morbid—especially in the case of Herod—and the style
more luscious and unctuous.

The years from 1891 and 1895 were the most brilliant in Oscar
Wilde's life, and they marked the zenith of his literary and social career.
This fame was achieved largely on the stage, but the influence of the
French theatre is not very great on his plays. Then in 1895, in the midst
of success, came the bombshell of his trial, followed by his conviction
and imprisonment. This killed him as a writer. He wrote nothing more
except *De Profundis* and *The Ballad of Reading Gaol*, works in which
the inspiration of France is absent. He was then trying only to be himself, and not to shock public opinion or to outrage philistine suscepti-
bilities.

In the eighteen-nineties Arthur Symons was more responsible than any other writer for the propagation of French influence in England. Although, in his earlier days, he was, as everyone else, influenced by French Decadence, he eventually introduced the Symbolist Movement to his fellow-countrymen.

He was born in Wales in 1865 of Cornish parents, and so was a Celt, as were most of the writers who had affinities with French culture. He was privately educated and went up to Oxford, where he formed a friendship with Walter Pater, who was at the height of his popularity, and whom he so greatly admired that he dedicated to him his first book, a collection of poems, published in 1889, entitled *Days and Nights*. They are not very original and in 1906, when bringing out a collected edition of his verse, he preserved only nine poems from them. The most important influence found in this collection is that of Baudelaire—in such poems as *The Opium-Smoker*, *Satiety*, and *The Street-Singer*. In *The Opium-Smoker* occur these lines which recall Baudelaire's theory of *correspondances*:

> 'I am engulfed, and drown deliciously.
> Soft music like a perfume, and sweet light
> Golden with audible odours exquisite,
> Swathe me with cerements for eternity.
> Time is no more. I pause and yet I flee.
> A million ages wrap me round with night.'

In 1890 he went to Paris, and met Mallarmé at the 'Mardis' of the Rue de Rome. He writes of them in his *Symbolist Movement in Literature*:

> 'Invaluable, it seems to me, those Tuesdays must have been to the young men of two generations who have been making French literature; they were unique, certainly in the experience of the young Englishman who was always so cordially received there, with so flattering a cordiality. Here was a house in which art, literature, was the very atmosphere, a religious atmosphere; and the master of the house, in his just a little solemn simplicity, a priest. . . . Here, in this one literary house, literature was unknown as a trade. And, above all, the questions that were discussed were never, at least, in Mallarmé's treatment, in his guidance of them, other than essential questions, considerations of art in the abstract, of literature before it coagulates into a book, of life as its amusing and various web spins the stuff of art.'

In Paris Symons made the acquaintance of Verlaine, who was to be one of the most important influences on his poetry; and he read the works of Villiers de l'Isle Adam, but he was too late to meet him in person, since he had died the previous year.

In 1891, on his return to London, Symons, with some fellow poets, founded The Rhymers Club. The founders were W. B. Yeats, Rolleston and Lionel Johnson, Irishmen or of Irish stock; Symons and Ernest Rhys, Welshmen; John Davidson, a Scot; and Le Gallienne, in spite of his Gallic name an Englishman. Several other poets joined them later —Ernest Dowson, John Gray, and Wratislaw.

Walter Pater was their master and idol—Ernest Dowson, Lionel Johnson and Symons had known him as undergraduates at Oxford. Le Gallienne was to say later, in *The Romantic Nineties*, that Pater was to English literature what Flaubert had been to French literature, and that all the men of letters considered that *Marius the Epicurean* was the most beautiful book in the English language. Pater for them was the magician who had brought beauty back to earth, and had shown that the only wisdom was its pursuit.

The Rhymers Club succeeded in interesting a publisher in their cause, John Lane, who, in 1892, published *The First Book of the Rhymers Club*, in which most of the poets attached to the club were represented. The collection is very typical of the mood of the time, with its Decadence, and its fin de siècle pessimism.

That same year Symons published his second collection of verse, *Silhouettes*, where the most important influence is Verlaine, though traces of Baudelaire are still found in such poems as *Du Maquillage*, *Perfume*, and others. He follows Verlaine in his little songs like *Pastel*, *In Carnival*, and others of similar inspiration. He resembles him also in describing the London scene, as in the section entitled *City Nights*:

> 'The trains through the night of the town,
> Through a blackness broken in twain
> By the sudden finger of streets;
> Lights, red, yellow and brown,
> From curtain and window-pane,
> The flashing eyes of the streets.
>
> Night and the rush of the train,
> A cloud of smoke through the town,
> Scarring the life of the streets;
> And the leap of the heart again,
> Out into the night, and down
> The dazzling vista of the streets!'

Wratislaw, a follower of Symons, shows similar French affinities. His first collection, *Love's Memorial*, is only a parody of Baudelaire, but his *Caprices*, published in 1895, is of a higher quality. It borrows its title from Verlaine, and he is the chief influence on poems such as *A Moment*, *Silhouettes*, and *On the Embankment*:

> 'A mist on the darkened river
> Falls; in the rippled stream
> The yellow lights shake and quiver,
> The red lights quiver and gleam.
>
> For us in the maze of error,
> More weak than the wind-swept foam,
> The lights in the stream's dark mirror
> Seem lights of a perfect home.
>
> The tranquil river is going
> Down to the tranquil sea,
> And oh that its waves were flowing
> Silently over me!'

The Rhymers certainly fostered an interest in contemporary French literature, and one of their number, John Gray, translated many French poems in his collection entitled *Silverpoints*, published in 1893.

Symons, at this time, was a Decadent in inspiration and in 1893 he published an article entitled 'The Decadent Movement in Literature' which appeared in *Harper's Magazine* in November. There is nothing very original or new in it, as it consists of a boiling down of the aesthetic theories of Gautier, Baudelaire, and Huysmans—indeed his tastes in literature are exactly the same as those of Des Esseintes. The article was, however, important as being the clear statement, in English, of the French Decadent position.

The Second Book of the Rhymers Club appeared in 1894, and this was the final volume, for, shortly afterwards, the Club was disbanded.

The next group of writers, very similar to the first, was that associated with *The Yellow Book*, founded in 1894, and which further exemplified the Decadent ideals formulated by Symons. As Hubert Crackanthorpe said, in July 1894, in his article entitled 'Reticence in Literature': 'Decadence, decadence: you are all decadent nowadays!' And, in the same volume, Max Beerbohm wrote:

> 'There are signs that our English literature has reached that point when, like the literatures of all nations that have been, it must

fall at length into the hands of the decadents. Who knows but that artifice is in truth at our gates and that soon she may pass through our streets? Already the windows of Grub Street are crowded with watchful evil faces. They are ready, the men of Grub Street, to pelt her, as they have pelted all that came near her. Let them come down while there is still time, and hang their houses with colours, and strew the road with flowers. Will they not, for once, do homage to a new queen? By the time this letter appears, it may be too late!'

The ideal of *The Yellow Book* was that of Artifice and Artificiality, and Beerbohm wrote, in an article called 'In Defence of Cosmetics'—which recalls Baudelaire's *Du Maquillage*—in April 1894:

> 'For behold! The Victorian era comes to its end and the day of *sancta simplicitas* is quite ended. The old signs are here and the portents warn the seer of life that we are ripe for a new epoch of artifice. . . . Artifice is the strength of the world, and in that same mask of paint and powder, shadowed with vermeil tint and most trimly pencilled, is woman's strength.'

John Lane was the publisher of *The Yellow Book*, as he had been of *The Rhymers Club*, and its flaming yellow was intended as a kind of flag. Henry Harland was appointed editor, and the artistic direction was entrusted to Aubrey Beardsley, who had illustrated Oscar Wilde's *Salome* for the edition published by John Lane in 1894. These illustrations, which Wilde himself had not liked, had made Beardsley the most notorious draughtsman of the day.

The first volume of *The Yellow Book*, with its so-called immoral French influence, was severely criticized by most of the papers, and a poem by Symons which it contained, *Stella Maris*, shocked the public on account of its outspoken evocation of the physical aspect of love.

Decadence was now so well established in England that it was parodied by Robert Hichens in his *Green Carnation*, published in 1894, and which is a satire especially on *The Picture of Dorian Gray*. It is written in a style which is scarcely an exaggeration, and it preaches what was called 'the higher philosophy, the philosophy to be afraid of nothing, to dare to live as one wishes to live, not as the middle-class wish us to live; to have the courage of one's desires, instead of only the cowardice of other people's'. The hero, Esmé Amarinth, says: 'I am going to sit up all night with Reggie, saying mad scarlet things. The shadows of the lawns are violet, and the stars wash the spaces of the sky with primrose and crimson.' The sentiments which the novel expresses are an exaggeration of the ideals of Art for Art's Sake. 'Nothing that is beautiful can possibly be wrong' or again 'there is nothing in the world worth having except youth, youth with its perfect sins, sins with the dew upon them like red roses—youth with its purple passions and its wild and wonderful tears. To sin beautifully, as you sin, Reggie, and as I have sinned for years, is one of the most complicated of arts. . . . Sin has its technique, just as painting has its technique. Sin has its harmonies and its dissonances, as music has harmonies and dissonances.'

The trial of Oscar Wilde in 1895 finished *The Yellow Book*—and also Decadence—although it lingered on until April 1897.

While the fifth volume of *The Yellow Book* was in preparation, the trial started, and John Lane and Harland took especial precautions with this volume, but they were nervous on account of the impression which might be created, in the circumstances, by Beardsley's drawings, which had always been considered amongst the worst aspects of the Decadents. Suddenly William Watson, aided and abetted by Mrs. Humphry Ward and Alice Meynell, sent an ultimatum to the editors, declaring that, if Beardsley's drawings were not withdrawn from the volume in preparation, they would contribute nothing further to the periodical. Harland and Lane, frightened of what might happen, omitted the drawings from the issue, without consulting Beardsley. When he heard what had occurred he resigned from the paper, and Lane then decided to make a complete break with the Decadents, and henceforth to publish only works like those of William Watson and of Mrs. Humphry Ward.

There was sanctimonious satisfaction in some quarters at the result of Oscar Wilde's trial, and many talked of the need of purifying the atmosphere, now that the most pernicious influence had been removed, and was held safely under lock and key. When Symons published his *London Nights* in 1895, he was severely reprimanded for continuing the nefarious fashion from France. His *Stella Maris*, which was reprinted here, and other poems of similar inspiration—as for instance *Idealism*—were singled out for special condemnation:

> 'I know the woman has no soul, I know
> The woman has no possibilities
> Of soul or mind or heart, but merely is
> The master piece of flesh: well, be it so.
> It is her flesh that I adore; I go
> Thirstying afresh to drain her empty kiss;
> I know she cannot love: 'tis not for this
> I run to her embraces like a foe.'

This is debased Baudelaire, and so is *To One in Alienation*:

> 'As I lay on the stranger's bed,
>   And clasped the stranger-woman I had hired,
>   Desiring only memory dead
>   Of all that I had once desired;
>
>   It was then that I wholly knew
>   How wholly I had loved you, and, my friend,
>   While I am I, and you are you,
>   How I must love you to the end.'

Which is too near an echo of Baudelaire's poem:

> 'Une nuit que j'étais près d'une affreuse juive,
>   Comme au long d'un cadavre un cadavre étendu,
>   Je me pris à songer près de ce corps vendu
>   A la triste beauté dont mon désir se prive.'

Most of the former Decadents were now turning against the Movement—amongst them Lionel Johnson, Max Beerbohm, and Le Gallienne. The latter had indeed published, in his *English Poems*, an attack against the influence of France, in the poem addressed *To the Reader*:

> 'Art was a palace once, things great and fair
>   And strong and holy, found a temple there;
>   Now 'tis a lazar-house of leprous men!
>   O shall we hear an English song again!
>   Still English larks mount in the merry morn,
>   An English May still brings an English thorn,
>   Still English daisies up and down the grass,
>   Still English love for English lad and lass—
>   Yet youngsters blush to sing an English song.
>
>   Thou nightingale that for six hundred years
>   Sang to the world—O art thou husht at last!
>   For, not of thee this new voice in our ears,
>   Music of France that once was of the spheres;
>   And not of thee these strange green flowers that spring
>   From daisy roots and seem to bear a sting.'

The green flowers are the flowers of Decadence, the 'green carnation' of Robert Hichens' novel.

It looked indeed as if the Decadent Movement were over in England. Then *The Savoy* came along and, for a short time, gave it a new lease of life. This was founded by Leonard Smither in 1895, after John Lane had discarded the Decadents, and he appointed Arthur Symons as editor, who invited Beardsley to join the staff as arts director. The first number appeared in January 1896, but it was received by the critics with indifferent contempt and irony, and, by the third number, it had ceased arousing any interest at all. It lingered on until the end of the year, and finally expired through lack of funds. Symons wrote a valedictory article for its final number, entitled 'By Way of Epilogue', in which he complained that England was devoid of any interest in the arts.

The Savoy had lasted a bare year, and its aim had been to further interest in contemporary French literature, to discuss modern French poetry and its technique. It published articles on contemporary French poetry, with translations, and it dealt with further modern French poets, which the Rhymers and *The Yellow Book* group had not yet considered—poets such as Émile Verhaeren, the great poet of the Belgian renaissance in French literature.

The year 1896 saw, as well as *The Savoy*, the publication of the collected poems of Ernest Dowson, one of the most characteristic of the Decadent poets, and one whose interest in French literature was deepest, for he had lived a great deal in France, in Normandy, Brittany, and Paris, and it was his favourite country. He had a special fondness for the poetry of Verlaine which he followed closely, and he deals with the same climate and moods—the last days of autumn, twilight, the damp of dark woods, the fogs of London, and nostalgia for the past. In such a mood is *Amor Profanus*, which recalls Verlaine's *Colloque Sentimental*:

> 'Beyond the pale of memory,
> In some mysterious dusky grove,
> I dreamed we met when day was done,
> And marvelled at our ancient love.
>
> Met there by chance, long kept apart,
> We wandered through the darkling glades,
> And that old language of the heart
> We sought to speak; alas poor shades!'

This is a reflection of Verlaine's *Colloque Sentimental* from *Fêtes Galantes*:

> 'Dans le vieux parc solitaire et glacé
> Deux formes ont tout à l'heure passé.
>
> Dans le vieux parc solitaire et glacé
> Deux spectres ont évoqué le passé.'

Dowson also wrote a poem with the title *Chanson sans Paroles* which recalls Verlaine's *Romances sans Paroles*; there is also one called *Spleen*, reminiscent of Baudelaire's poems of the same name, in mood as well as title:

> 'I was not sorrowful, I could not weep,
> And all my memories were put to sleep.
>
> I watched the river grow more white and strange,
> All day till evening I watched it change.
>
> All day till evening I watched the rain
> Beat wearily upon the window pane.
>
> I was not sorrowful, but only tired
> Of everything that ever I desired.'

While *Ad Manus Puellae* must have been inspired by Gautier's *Études de Mains* from *Émaux et Camées*:

> 'I was always a lover of ladies' hands!
> Or ever mine heart came here to tryst,
>
> For the sake of your carved white hands' commands;
>   The tapering fingers, the dainty wrist;
>   The hands of a girl were what I kissed.
>
> I remember an hand like a fleur-de-lys
> When it slid from its silken sheath, her glove;
>
> With its odorous passing ambergris;
>   And that was the empty husk of a love.
>   Oh! how shall I kiss your hands enough?

> They are pale with the pallor of ivories;
> But they blush to the tips like a curved sea-shell;
>
> What treasure, in kingly treasuries,
>   Of gold, and spice for the thurible,
>   Is sweet as her hands to hoard and tell?'

And, finally, there is the Cynara poem, one of the best known and most characteristic poems of the Decadent Movement in England, a parable of the Movement, a symbol of the unattainable. It is written in the French metre, the Alexandrine:

> 'Last night, ah! yesternight, betwixt her lips and mine,
> There fell thy shade, Cynara, thy breath was shed
> Upon my soul betwixt the kisses and the wine;
> And I was desolate and sick of an old passion,
>   Yea I was desolate and bowed my head;
> I have been faithful to thee, Cynara, in my fashion.'

Ernest Dowson's collection of poems, and that of Lord Alfred Douglas—published in the same year, in Paris, with the text in both French and English—are the last poems of the Decadents in England, and the second edition of Symons' *London Nights*, published in 1897, marks the end of the Movement.

His next collections—*Amoris Victima* of 1897 and *Images of Good and Evil* of 1899—show a change towards a new inspiration, for they are far less in the Baudelairean mood.

The result of the change is seen in his next work, *The Symbolist Movement in Literature*, published in 1899. In the dedicatory epistle to Yeats he writes:

> 'I speak often in this book of Mysticism, and that I, of all people, should venture to speak, not quite as an outsider, of such things, will probably be a surprise to many. It will be no surprise to you, for you have seen me gradually finding my way, uncertainly but inevitably in that direction, which has always been to you your natural direction.'

There is more idealism here than in any of his previous works, and the influence of Villiers de l'Isle Adam and Maeterlinck have taken the place of that of Baudelaire. Discussing Decadence in the Introduction, Symons says:

'Meanwhile, something which is vaguely called Decadence had come into being. . . . It pleased young men in various countries to call themselves Decadents, with all the thrill of unsatisfied virtue masquerading as uncomprehended vice. . . . But a movement which in this sense might be called Decadent could but have been a straying aside from the main road of literature. Nothing, not even conventional virtue, is so provincial as conventional vice; and the desire to "bewilder the middle-class" is itself middle-class. The interlude, half a mock-interlude, of Decadence, diverted the attention of the critics while something more serious was in preparation. That something more serious has crystallized, for the time, under the form of Symbolism, in which art returns to the one pathway, leading through beautiful things to the eternal.'

The Decadents, on the whole, had been a doomed generation—as Yeats called them in his *Autobiographies*—and nearly all of them ended tragically. Most of them had delicate constitutions—it is hard to imagine a Decadent enjoying robust health—and generally their intemperate habits did not improve matters. Beardsley was a consumptive who died in penury in 1898; Dowson took hashish and also died in poverty in 1900; Lionel Johnson died an alcoholic in 1902; and John Davidson, after writing his *Testament* in 1908, committed suicide in 1909.

The new development in literature is seen in Symons' book on literary criticism, *The Symbolist Movement in Literature*. This is his most significant work, and the one which had most far-reaching influence on the coming generation. It is not that, intrinsically, it is very original, or that its ideas are profound or of permanent importance, but it is persuasive and was responsible for guiding many people towards French literature for the first time. It was Symbolism, and not Decadence, that Symons was now trying to further. In the Introduction he declares that Symbolism is

'an attempt to spiritualize literature, to evade the old bondage of rhetoric, the old bondage of exteriority. Description is banished that beautiful things may be evoked, magically; the regular beat of verse is broken in order that words may fly, upon subtler wings. Mystery is no longer feared, as the great mystery in whose midst we are islanded was feared by those to whom that unknown sea was only a great void. . . . Here then in this revolt against exteriority, against rhetoric, against a materialistic tradition; in this endeavour to disengage the ultimate essence, the soul, of whatever exists and can be realized by the consciousness; in this dutiful waiting upon every symbol by which the soul of things can be made visible; literature, bowed down by so many burdens, may at least attain liberty, and its authentic speech. In attaining this liberty, it accepts a heavier burden; for in speaking to us so intimately, so solemnly, as only religion had hitherto spoken to us, it becomes itself a kind of religion, with all the duties and responsibilities of the sacred ritual.'

This was a revelation to all those who read it. Eliot said later, in *The Criterion*, in January, 1930:

'I myself owe Mr. Symons a great debt. But for having read his book, I should not, in the year 1908, have heard of Laforgue and Rimbaud, I should probably not have begun to read Verlaine, and but for reading Verlaine, I should not have heard of Corbière. So the Symons book is one of those which affected the course of my life.'

Other poets owed it a similar debt.

The book is dedicated to W. B. Yeats, in the following terms:

'May I dedicate to you this book on the Symbolist movement in literature, both as an expression of a deep personal friendship and because you, more than anyone else, will sympathize with what I say in it, being yourself the chief representative of that movement in our country? . . . Your own Irish literary movement is one of its expressions; your own poetry belongs to it in the most intimate sense.'

Symons spoke truly, for the greatest poet of Symbolism—Symbolism as contrasted with Decadence—in the English language was certainly W. B. Yeats. He had no Decadence in his make-up, nor did he owe anything to Baudelaire—this was very rare at that time. There was a kind of austerity in his composition, a sort of Irish puritanism, which prevented him from indulging in such excesses. He was an idealist who had many affinities with the movement in literature which, emerging from Decadence, became Symbolism. Moreover, coming from a country with growing national feeling, he was able to perceive how the Symbolist doctrine could be used in connection with the folk-lore of his native land. He had been conscious of this possibility even before he had come into contact with the Symbolist poets in France, as he proved by his *Wanderings of Oisin*, which had appeared in 1889. However, in the second edition, published in 1895, after he had visited France, he revised the work to underline the significance of the racial symbolism.

Yeats was of the same generation as Symons, also born in 1865. Although he was born in Dublin, he lived his early life largely in the West of Ireland amongst what is called the 'gentry', even though they may have been poor, and the peasantry; knowing little of the middle-class struggle for life and position; in an atmosphere which had remained that of the eighteenth century. His father was a painter with a careless disregard of worldly success and stable position, and he did not mind moving his large family from Sligo to London, to Dublin, and back again to London. Yeats tells us, in his *Autobiographies*, that he had been brought up by his father not to think of the future, or any practical result. His father used to say: 'When I was young, the definition of a gentleman was a man not wholly occupied in getting on!'

Yeats started as an art student, and, as he tells us later in his *Autobiographies*, this was because neither his classics nor his mathematics were good enough for any examination, and he could not hope for an academic career. However, at the art school he became interested in France. 'No influence touched us but that of France,' he said in *Autobiographies*, 'where one or two of the older students had been already and all hoped to go.'

The most important influence of his early youth was that of the Fenian, O'Leary, and the debates of the Young Ireland Society, and he said later that all he had 'set his hand to since' arose from them.

In 1886 he read Hugo's *Shakespeare* and was delighted with the attack on critics which he found in it. 'I thought that one must write without care,' he said in *Autobiographies*, 'for that was of the coteries, but with a gusty energy that would put all straight if it came out of the heart.' Even in those days he was considering how he could escape from the English tradition, and produce something which was un-English, yet musical and colourful.

O'Leary had given him an interest in Irish legendary material, but some kind of other literary discipline he felt was needed before he would be able to give to the Irish subjects a mind sufficiently free from English influence to permit the fusion between style and matter. This he obtained, eventually, from France. He said later that it was years before he was able to rid himself of 'Shelley's Italian light'.

In 1887, when he was twenty, his first published piece of writing appeared, an article on Mangan in *The Irish Field*.

The same year the Yeats family migrated to London and W. B. became a Pre-Raphaelite, and much interested in William Morris. He

was an idealistic young man who was unmoved by the decadent
literature around him.

He was still much interested in France and he attended evening
classes in French in order to improve his knowledge of the language,
but, as he had no ear for musical sounds, his pronunciation remained
faulty. His sister Elizabeth recorded in her diary, on 8 January 1889,
after she herself had attended one class, a description of 'Willie's
intense way of saying his French, with his voice raised to telling directness, and every pronunciation wrong as usual!'

He continued reading folk-literature and said later, in *Essays*:

'I filled my mind with the popular beliefs of Ireland. I sought
some symbolical language reaching far into the past, and associated
with familiar names and conspicuous hills that might not be alone
amid the obscure impressions of the senses . . . or mourned the
richness or reality lost to Shelley's *Prometheus Unbound* because he
had not discovered in England his Caucasus.'

The result of his reading is seen in his *Wanderings of Oisin* of 1889,
and his *Lake Isle of Innisfree*, published in *The National Observer* in
1890.

The publication of *The Wanderings of Oisin* brought him into
relationship with the main poets of his generation, and it was a group of
them that founded The Rhymers Club in 1891, which has been mentioned earlier in this chapter. For a time he was on friendly terms with
Lionel Johnson but from whom eventually—as he records in his
Autobiographies—he was separated by 'a scruple of conscience', and
Arthur Symons replaced him in his intimate friendship. From Symons
he learned much of France, and he says: 'Arthur Symons, more than
any man, could slip, as it were, into the mind of another, and my
thoughts gained in richness and in clearness from his sympathy.' From
him he heard of French Symbolism, of Villiers de l'Isle Adam and of
Mallarmé. He read *Axël* with great labour, on account of language
difficulties, but imagined, nevertheless—or even because of this—that
here was the Sacred Book for which he had always longed. Writing in
United Ireland, on 15 October 1892, he said:

'The influence of France is every year more completely pervad-
ing English life. The influence of that school which calls itself, in the
words of its leader Verlaine, a school of the sunset, is now a dominat-
ing thing in many lives. "Poetry is an end in itself; it has nothing to

do with life, nothing to do with anything but the music of cadences and beauty of phrase." This is the new doctrine of letters.'

In a letter to his father, quoted by Hone in his biography, Yeats says:

'It is in dramatic lyrical expression that English poetry is most lacking as compared with French poetry. Villon always, and Ronsard at times, create marvellous drama out of their lives.'

It is then that he adapted, in his own poetic language, the sonnet by Ronsard, *Quand vous serez bien vieille* in 1893, in a poem entitled *When You are Old and Grey*, making of it something more profound than the original, in its spiritual implications. Ronsard's ending is that of a materialist:

'Je seray sous la terre, et, fantosme sans os,
Par les ombres myrteux je prendray mon repos:
Vous serez au fouyer une vieille accroupie,

Regrettant mon amour et vostre fier desdain.
Vivez, si m'en croyez, n'attendez à demain:
Cueillez dès aujourd'huy les roses de la vie.'

Whereas Yeats bears his readers, on spiritual wings, into the beyond:

'And bending down beside the glowing bars,
Murmur a little sadly, how Love fled
And paced upon the mountains overhead
And hid his face amid a crowd of stars.'

Yeats was now repudiating Arnold, when he said: 'I believe that all men will more and more reject the opinion that Poetry is "a criticism of life", and be more convinced that it is the revelation of a hidden life.'

The works which Yeats composed, while a member of The Rhymers Club, and which, already, show the influence of French ideas—obtained second-hand through Arthur Symons—were *Countess Kathleen* in 1892, *The Celtic Twilight* in 1893, and *The Land of Heart's Desire* in 1894. They all use folk themes as a form of Symbolism, as Maeterlinck was doing in French.

In February 1894 Yeats paid his first visit to Paris, because Maud

Gonne, with whom he had been devotedly in love for some years, was living there at the time. He accompanied her to a performance of *Axël* by Villiers de l'Isle Adam, and this was one of the most memorable experiences of his life. In his review of the play published in April 1894, in *The Bookman*, he declared that it would take a place in the hierarchy of his recollections 'with a night scene when the wind blew by a bed of roses, with a line or two from Homer, and with a Japanese picture of a crane flying through a blue sky'. This was the beginning of a real influence of French Symbolism on him, and *Axël* became his guide and his beacon in his doctrine of poetry. For him its moral was that 'the infinite alone is worth attaining, and the infinite is in possession of the dead'. He considered that 'seldom has utmost pessimism found a more magnificent expression'.

This was not a passing youthful craze, for, more than thirty years later, in an Introduction to an English translation, he said in 1925:

'It did not move me because I thought it a great masterpiece, but because it seemed part of a religious rite, the ceremony perhaps of some secret Order wherein my generation had been initiates. Even those strange sentences, so much in the manner of that time: "O, to veil you with my hair where you will breathe the spirit of red roses", did not seem so important as the symbols: the forest, the castle, the treasure, the lamp that had burnt before Solomon. Now that I have read it all again and recalled that first impression, I can see how those symbols became part of me, and for years to come dominated my imagination. I discover there is no escape, that I am still dominated. Is it only because I opened the book for the first time when I had a vivid sense of youth that I just see that tower room always, and hear always that thunder?'

He was never to forget it and, in 1928, when he gave *The Tower* as a title to one of his deepest and most moving collections of poems, he was probably as much inspired by the memory of the tower in Axël's castle, where the hero studied ancient manuscripts by lamplight, as by the round tower in Ireland, in which he had lived—it may even have inspired that choice of habitation.

In an essay, published in *Ideas of Good and Evil*, but written in 1895, entitled *The Autumn of the Body*, he says that, quite suddenly, he had lost all desire to describe outward things, and found that he took little pleasure in a book unless it was spiritual. He explains that he had not at first realized that the change was beyond his own mind, but later came to understand that 'writers are struggling all over Europe, though not often with a philosophic understanding of their struggle, against that picturesque and declamatory way of writing, against that "externality" which a time of scientific thought has brought to literature'.

In a desire to escape the materialism of some current literature which he deplored, he became interested in all manifestations of eastern philosophy and religion, which were fashionable in Paris at that time. He was much attracted by a curious occultist whom he met, who went by the name of Sâr Péladan. This man claimed to be an initiate, a descendant of an old Babylonian family of religious thinkers, from whom he had received the title 'Sâr', which meant High Priest. He was a follower of the nineteenth-century French 'magician' who went by the name of Éliphas Lévi, and who, in 1889, had revived the sect of Rosicrucians, and had given Péladan an important position in its hierarchy. Sâr Péladan also fulminated against the materialism of modern times, against the eclipse of what he called 'L'Idée', which had much in common with the idealism of Symbolism. He had written on the disappearance of idealism in his work entitled *Le Vice Suprême*, in 1884—the supreme vice being materialism.

Péladan claimed to be a prophet, a 'Mage', and in 1891 he published a text entitled *Comment on devient Mage*, which preached a return to standards of ideal beauty. It was intended to be the first in a series of works, the collective title of which was to be *L'Amphithéâtre des Sciences Mortes*. He planned also to compose a history to deal with the whole of civilization based on the study of the various racial myths, but he only completed two volumes of the project—*La Terre du Sphinx* and *La Terre d'Orphée*. He was typical of the mystical current of the eighteen-eighties in France, and was of the same spiritual family as Barbey d'Aurevilly, Villiers de l'Isle Adam, Huysmans, and Bloy. It is easy to see what appeal these ideas must have had for Yeats at this stage in his development.

Yeats' longing for escape from materialism led him to the fairylands, which were a characteristic feature of his writings at this time, to Tir-nan-Og, the Isles of the Blest, and they became for him a refuge, like the parlour of Des Esseintes, the Ivory Tower of Vigny, or the Castle of Axël. This inspired in him a contempt for life as lived by ordinary human-beings on earth, so that he could echo Axël's cry: 'As for living, our servants will do that for us!'

Nothing materialistic appealed to Yeats, and he admired love which does not seek consummation—this is seen in his love poetry, despite its passion—as Villiers de l'Isle Adam had described it in his plays *Elen* and *Axël*. He also admired the dream life and dream state, in which Maeterlinck's creations have their being. He thought as highly of

Maeterlinck as of Villiers de l'Isle Adam, and he was as much influenced by him. In *The Autumn of the Body* he said:

> 'Count Villiers de l'Isle Adam swept together, by what seemed a sudden energy, words behind which glimmered a spiritual and passionate mood, as the flame glimmers behind the dusky blue and red glass in an Eastern lamp; and created persons from whom has fallen even personal characteristics, except a thirst for that hour when all things shall pass like a cloud, and a pride like that of the Magi following their star over many mountains; while Maeterlinck has plucked away even this thirst and this pride and set before us faint souls, naked and pathetic shadows already half vapour and sighing to one another upon the border of the last abyss.'

After his meeting with the French Symbolists in person, Yeats was confirmed in his view of poetry as a spiritual activity, a means of obtaining a revelation of the hidden life—this was also Rimbaud's theory of *Le Voyant*—and as an escape from materialism. His ideas on artistic creation are set forth especially in the essays, written at various times during the next few years—*The Autumn of the Body*, *Symbolism in Poetry*, *Magic*, and *Moods*—all published later in *Ideas of Good and Evil*. They all re-echo the theories which by now had become well known in France during the Symbolist Movement, which had come largely from Baudelaire's aesthetic doctrine, and were based on the reaction against the materialism of the Parnassian poets. In *Symbolism in Poetry*, he writes:

> 'The scientific movement brought with it a literature which was always tending to lose itself in externalities of all kinds, in opinion, in declamation, in picturesque writing, in word painting, or in what Symons has called "an attempt to build with brick and mortar inside the covers of a book", and now writers have begun to dwell upon the element of evocation, of suggestion, upon what we call the symbolism of great writers.'

Later, defending the obscurity of poets such as Mallarmé, he said:

> 'The form of sincere poetry, unlike the form of popular poetry, may indeed sometimes be obscure, but it must have the perfections that escape analysis, the subtleties that have a new meaning every day, and it must have this whether it be but a little song made out

of a moment of dreamy indolence, or some great epic made out of
the dreams of one poet and of a hundred generations whose hands
were never weary of the sword.'

This, in other words, is Mallarmé's theory of the possibility of multiple
interpretation in a poem. Yeats adds, in the note to *Cap and Bells*, a
poem in *The Wind among the Reeds*: 'This poem has always meant a
great deal to me, though, as is the way with symbolic poems, it has not
always meant quite the same thing.'

Yeats' theory of Symbolism, as expressed in *Magic*, is very similar
to that of Baudelaire's *correspondances*. 'Symbols of all kinds,' he
says, 'for everything in heaven or earth has its own associations,
momentous or trivial, in the Great Memory.' He often mentions the
'Great Memory', by which he means ultimate reality, or God. In *Magic*,
he says, referring to visionary gifts, that they are 'the greatest of all
powers, whether they are used consciously by the masters of magic, or
half consciously by their successors, the poet, the musician, and the
artist'. He saw the poet—as did the French Symbolists—as the Seer,
who has taken the place of the former priest. In *The Autumn of the
Body* he says:

> 'The arts are, I believe, to take upon their shoulders the burdens
> that have fallen from the shoulders of the priests, and to lead us
> back upon our journey by filling our thoughts with the essence of
> things and not with the things. We are about to substitute once
> more the distillation of alchemy for the analyses of chemistry and
> for some other sciences; and certain of us are looking everywhere
> for the perfect alembic that no silver or golden drop may escape.'

In *Moods*, composed in 1895, he wrote:

> 'The only restraint that he'—that is, the artist—'can obey is the
> mysterious instinct that has made him an artist, and that teaches
> him to discover immortal moods in mortal desires, and undecaying
> hope in our trivial ambitions, a divine love in sexual passion.'

Yeats believed that the borders of our mind are for ever shifting,
that many minds can flow into one another, and create one single
mind. He thought that our memories are part of the Great Memory,
the memory of Nature herself; and that the Great Mind and the Great
Memory could be evoked by symbols. *Magic* ends:

'And surely, at whatever risk, we must cry out that imagination is always seeking to remake the world according to the impulses and patterns in that Great Mind, in that Great Memory? Can there be anything as important as to cry out that what we call romance, poetry, intellectual beauty, is only the signal the supreme Enchanter, or someone in His Councils, is speaking of what has been, and shall be again, in the consummation of time?'

Yeats came back to London to see his play, *The Land of Heart's Desire*, performed on the stage of the Avenue Theatre, but he returned to Paris again in 1896, and there he met Synge, who had been living over there for some years. This chance meeting brought about a radical change in Yeats' plans, and brought to maturity his conception of literature.

When he met Yeats in 1896 Synge had come very much under the influence of French literature, and he had no further plans but to continue to live in Paris, where he liked to be. He greatly admired the work of Maeterlinck, with which his own was to have much affinity—*The Riders to the Sea* has many resemblances with *L'Intruse*. But he also admired Racine, from whom he had learnt the advantage of selection and order—he was indeed planning to write a book about him, but Yeats dissuaded him from this project, persuading him to return to Ireland, where he considered lay his true source of inspiration. Yeats was coming more to the conclusion that he himself should use artistically the folk-lore of his native land, and he believed that, in Synge, he had discovered a kindred soul who would help him to further this project. He also thought that Synge was wasting his time in France, when what he needed, on the contrary, was to immerse himself in the atmosphere of Ireland. Later he was to write, in *The Municipal Gallery Revisited*, in *Last Poems*:

'John Synge, I and Augusta Gregory, thought
All that we did, all that we said or sang
Must come from contact with the soil, from that
Contact everything Antaeus-like grew strong.
We three alone in modern times had brought
Everything down to that sole test again,
Dream of the noble and the beggar-man.'

Synge used to say that he found richness only in certain elaborate books which are, he explained, 'far away from the common interests of life. Mallarmé and Huysmans produced such literature, but the writers who deal with the reality of life, Ibsen and Zola, confine themselves to the use of joyless and pallid words.'

He believed that folk drama might achieve his vision. 'In Ireland, where we still have a popular imagination,' he said, 'that is fiery and magnificent, and tender, the dramatist has a better chance.'

Nevertheless, although he returned to his own country and its exclusive inspiration, his stay in Paris had been profitable for him, for it is doubtful whether he would ever have written as he did if he had not come into contact with such writers as Mallarmé and Maeterlinck, whose method he was able to adapt to his own use. In *The Aran Islands*, for instance, there are many passages identical in mood with Maeterlinck:

> 'In this cry of pain the inner consciousness of the people seems to lay itself bare for an instant, and to reveal the mood of beings who feel their isolation in the face of a universe that wars upon them with wind and seas. They are usually silent, but in the presence of death all outward show of indifference or patience is forgotten, and they shriek with pitiable despair before the horror of the fate to which they all are doomed.'

In 1896, after the failure of *The Yellow Book* and *The Savoy*, Yeats went back to Ireland, taking Synge with him, and they brought to a country that was becoming conscious of itself as a culture separate from England, the lessons they had learnt in France.

In 1899 Yeats founded, in Dublin, the theatre which was to become the Abbey Theatre, a theatre dedicated to the production of Irish plays in the English language. Synge wrote six plays for the Abbey Theatre— *The Shadow of the Glen*, *The Riders to the Sea*, *The Well of Saints*, *The Tinker's Wedding*, and, most famous and notorious of all, *The Playboy of the Western World*; also the unfinished *Deirdre* which death prevented him from completing. Most of these plays were written under the influence of Maeterlinck. The main plays by Yeats produced at the Abbey Theatre—or its forerunner—were all Irish, but some heroic and some peasant. They were *Kathleen ni Houlihan* in 1902; *The Pot of Broth* in 1903; *On Baile's Strand* in 1904—which has a strong resemblance to *Axël*, for the hero becomes a monk in his search for union with the beyond; finally there was *Deirdre* in 1907.

It was after he settled in Dublin that Yeats composed the poetical works which carry out the theories of the Symbolist Movement—a collection of poems published in 1899 with the title *The Wind among the Reeds*; and a play, or rather a dramatic poem, *The Shadowy Waters*, the first version of which was written in 1900.

These works are the culmination, the full blossoming, of Yeats' Symbolist inspiration, for in his next work, *In the Seven Woods*, published in 1904, he was beginning to withdraw from that mood, to move towards real life, and to make use of a more commonplace vocabulary.

In *The Shadowy Waters* Yeats expressed the longing for the land beyond this world: Dectora says, as she hears the grey birds fly overhead: 'What are they? Unto what country do they fly?' And Forgael answers:

> 'To unimaginable happiness.
> They have been circling over our heads in the air,
> But now they have taken to the road
> We have to follow, for they are our pilots;
> And though they're but the colour of grey ash,
> They're crying out, could you but hear their words,
> "There is a country at the end of the world
> Where no child's born but to outlive the moon." '

The most Symbolist of Yeats' writings are contained in *The Wind among the Reeds*, in such poems as *The Poet pleads with the Elemental Powers*:

> 'The Powers whose name and shape no living creature knows
> Have pulled the Immortal Rose;
> And though the Seven Lights bowed in their dance and wept,
> The Polar Dragon slept,
> His heavy rings uncoiled from glimmering deep to deep:
> When will he wake from sleep?'

The poem, *He hears the Cry of the Sedge*, is thought by some critics to have been inspired by Mallarmé's sonnet, *M'introduire dans ton Histoire*, yet the two poems are very different in mood and inspiration, and their common use of the image of the 'axle' in connection with the stars is not sufficient to give them similarity. In fact the moving symbolism of Yeats brings him nearer to Rimbaud than to Mallarmé. However this may be, it is one of the loveliest poems in the collection.

> 'I wander by the edge
> Of this desolate lake
> Where wind cries in the sedge:
> *Until the axle break*

> *That keeps the stars in their round,*
> *And hands hurl in the deep*
> *The banners of East and West,*
> *And the girdle of light is unbound,*
> *Your breast will not lie by the breast*
> *Of your beloved in sleep.'*

In the meantime a change had come over England. The Boer War brought in a new kind of patriotism and a new spirit, which made it seem disloyal to dally with foreign influences and with aestheticism. What was now in fashion was the new imperial realism of Kipling. This was praised and taken as representing the new mood in England and its rebirth. Chesterton looked back to Merrie England of the past, to a time when the country was truly England. There was also the desire for social betterment, for progress, and a social conscience, as represented in the works of H. G. Wells. What was specifically English was now extolled, in such novelists as Galsworthy. All this had very little to do with France, and though French influence still lingered on, it was now in the background and not the forefront of literature.

The death of the old Queen furthermore brought out all that was most patriotic and conservative in the English, all that was even most jingoistic. Foreign influences had little chance of prevailing in such an atmosphere.

7

CONCLUSION

THE nineteenth century ended in 1914 with the beginning of the First World War, just as it had begun with the ending of the Napoleonic Wars in 1815. When the century started, France had been in a low and humiliated position, being despised by most other countries. When it ended she stood in the forefront of Europe in intellectual achievement. Although she had suffered a crushing defeat at the hands of the Prussians in 1870, she had recovered miraculously from that blow, and was in the vanguard, not only in intellectual and artistic matters, but in prosperity as well. To compensate for her lost provinces of Alsace and Lorraine, she had created a colonial Empire. She was admired and praised by all countries for, in art, music, and literature, her prestige stood as high as it had ever been during the course of her history. In painting she had the most interesting and fruitful school in Europe. Witness of this is the success of the Impressionist and Post-Impressionist Exhibition in London during the autumn of 1910, which was preceded by an exhibition of works by modern French painters in Brighton. The London exhibition was organized by a committee headed by Roger Fry, Clive Bell, Boris Anrep, and Robert Dell. Roger Fry's Introduction to the catalogue was the first essay on the Post-Impressionist Movement to be published in England. The exhibition, which was an immense success, showed works by the Impressionists, and also by Cézanne, Gauguin, Redon, Bonnard, Matisse, Rouault, Vlaminck, and others.

In music the composers of France ranked second to none in Europe. In literature she had one of the most interesting of her movements, which had spread all over the world, radically changing the climate of poetry wherever it passed. Her poets and novelists were models for the rest of Europe. Arnold Bennett wrote in his Journal on 11 January 1898:

'It seems to me that only within the last few years have we absorbed from France that passion for the artistic, shapely presentation of truth, and that feeling for words as words, which animated Flaubert, the de Goncourt (sic), and de (sic) Maupassant; and which is exactly described and defined in de Maupassant's introduction to the collected works of Flaubert. None of the (so-called) great masters of English nineteenth-century fiction had (if I am right) a deep artistic interest in form and treatment; they were absorbed in "subject".'

It is certainly from the French novel that writers of fiction in England—such as Henry James and George Moore—learned something about the novel as a work of art.

Connolly wrote in *Horizon*, in June 1945: 'When we compare Balzac and Flaubert to Dickens and Thackeray, Baudelaire to Tennyson, Sainte-Beuve to Hazlitt, we must lower our eyes! There is nothing to say! The Frenchmen are adults, beside them the English have not grown up.'

By the end of the nineteenth century Paris was considered the centre of civilization, and the place where happiness and fulfilment could most readily be found. France was beginning to have, in literature, art and music, a snob value, and cultivated people began to pride themselves on their appreciation and understanding of French ideals. It may still have been a sophisticated, an adult, taste—like caviar—but those who wished to be considered civilized and cultivated were obliged to make a parade of love and admiration for France. She was still seen as immoral and loose-living, but then too strict a sense of morality was considered a sign of philistinism!

It is illuminating to compare the position of France in Europe, in 1914, with what it was a century before. Much ground had been covered during these hundred years, and she had completely regained the prestige which she had enjoyed during the reign of Louis XIV, when all countries had followed her example, and had been influenced by her. The pro-German feeling which, on the whole, had prevailed during the reign of Queen Victoria, had much abated during the reign of Edward VII, who had been an ardent Francophile, and who had, indeed, been the creator of the Entente Cordiale in 1904. Since his early youth he had been in love with France, and had spent many of his happiest days on her shores. It had begun in 1855 when he had visited Paris with his parents during the Exhibition, and had fallen so much in love with the country that, boy of thirteen as he was, he had said to his host, the Emperor Napoleon III: 'You have a nice country! I would like to be your son!' Regretting, no doubt, that the land of France was no longer in the inheritance of the kings of England

At the end of the nineteenth century literature in England no longer possessed its fundamentally English character—in certain aspects at all events—any more than literature in France was typically French. In France this was due to the effect of the number of foreigners writing French, who coloured the literature from their own exotic palettes. In England it was probably due to the emergence of the Irish-born writers, and the manner of their emergence. There had been, in the past, Irish writers who had reached high places in English letters—Congreve, Sheridan, Goldsmith, Swift and many others. They had, however, been assimilated into the English tradition, and had made no claim to anything different for being Irish. At the end of the nineteenth century, on the contrary, the Irish-born writers had been more susceptible to French influences than their indigenous English counterparts, and they had thus tended to undermine the racial character of English literature. Moreover the Irish, observing in French poetry the revolt of the Belgian poets, who wrote in French, but were racially and nationally distinct from the French, they, in their turn, saw themselves as a separate racial group, with their own national pride and ideals to emphasize and express in the literature of the English language. This is an interesting manifestation in English letters during the last quarter of the nineteenth century, the flowering of the Irish writers, and they brought something alien and foreign to the literature of the English language. Having, like the Belgians, no national traditions of their own in modern literature, they were more ready than the indigenous English for new changes, more interested in them, and more susceptible to them, and they found, in French Symbolism, the ideal atmosphere in which to merge, without losing their own characteristics. It could be claimed, with verisimilitude, that it was the Irish-born writers who were largely responsible for the immense influence which French literature exercised on English letters at the end of the nineteenth century.

PART II

THE FRUIT

Between the Two World Wars

8

INTRODUCTION

THE First World War ended by leaving France morally, artistically, and intellectually in a supreme position on the continent of Europe, and her prestige was at its highest. Her conduct during the war had wiped out the accusation which had so often been levelled against her at the end of the previous century: of being a people sunk in moral decadence. This had been the undoubted opinion of a large section of the public, in spite of the high regard in which she had come to be held by the intellectuals and the aesthetes. France, during the war, had shown that she could fight against great odds, that she was capable of the highest sacrifice and devotion. She had given ample and moving proof of her courage in the Epic of Verdun.

England and France at the end of the war were closer to each other than they had ever been before. They had fought side by side; they had suffered and had died together. They had intermarried, had mingled their blood, and had grown together, as an old married couple. When the war was over, after their demobilization, Englishmen returned to France with their families, for they had learnt to appreciate the French philosophy of life, the way of life of the people, and they valued the *douceur de vivre* which they found there. They shared the opinion which Arthur Young had expressed in 1792, in his *Travels in France*, which was as true for the twentieth century :

'In the art of living the French have generally been esteemed by the rest of Europe to have made greatest proficiency, and their manners have accordingly been imitated and their customs more adopted than those of any other nation.'

In increasing numbers the English crossed the Channel to France, in search of intellectual delight, or more frivolous pleasure—and also for prestige, since it was important to have been to France. So all those who wished to be considered people of consequence had their eyes fixed on France, for she was the touchstone of the world artistically and intellectually, as well as the playground for the idle rich. There arose a new form of snobbery connected with liking and knowing France, with being appreciated there. Germany, Italy, Spain, and Russia had now faded out of the picture, for the time being, as important countries in Europe, culturally.

There were some pompous and portentous English admirers who, on landing on French soil, adopted an attitude as if entering a chapel; there were some who treated France as a temple and who, metaphorically, removed their shoes and hushed their voices as they penetrated into the sacred shrine, bowing low as if before the altar of the Holy of Holies. Charles Morgan wrote, in his *Ode to France*, composed in 1942:

> 'Thou art the wisdom, O France, within all knowledge,
> The salt of all delight. Who dies for thee
> Dies for mankind's perpetual redemption;
>   And none can live in thee
> That has not died the death of saints and lovers
> And been raised up, in hate and holiness,
> To beat down Satan under thy feet.'

All this was a great change from the attitude towards France in the previous century, which, at first, was one of contempt, and eventually became one of belief that those who had dealings with her were playing with fire, and being singed by it. The new attitude was no more realistic, but it was in the nature of a tribute. France was the country from which flowed all culture and enlightenment. Aldous Huxley, in *Chrome Yellow*, intending to give a satiric picture of post-war social life in the nineteen-twenties in England, makes one of the characters, Mary Bracegirdle, a cultural snob, whose aim was always to be in the vanguard of fashion, say that she knew 'that there were very very few first-rate things in the world, and that those were mostly French'.

No other country had so much prestige or influence as France had then. Lytton Strachey, the fashionable and intellectual critic, was soaked in her atmosphere, and many listened to him, modelling themselves on him.

It was not, however, only the older and well-known writers in France who influenced English literature after the war. There were others as well who had not been noticed earlier, and who now came to the fore.

In the years which immediately preceded the war optimism had been the keynote of literature, with belief in a rosy future, in the possibilities of man, in his perfectibility. This was in marked contrast with the pessimism of the last years of the nineteenth century. The authors who were most admired in France were such writers as Verhaeren, Duhamel, and Romains, who all believed in the brotherhood of man, in fraternity flowing out across frontiers, in the impossibility of war. This period between 1870 and 1914 was, after all, the longest period of peace France had known since the Revolution—perhaps even in the whole of her history—more than a generation of peace and prosperity, and there seemed no valid reason why it should ever cease. The war was a grievous blow to those optimistic writers, and they never really recovered from their shock. Verhaeren, in *Les Ailes Rouges de la Guerre*, burst out in abuse and anger against the Germans on whom he had counted, and who had disappointed him personally :

> 'Car c'est là ton crime immense, Allemagne,
> D'avoir tué atrocement
> L'idée
> Que se faisait pendant la paix,
> En notre temps,
> L'homme de l'homme.'

Verhaeren could not forgive Germany's action in having destroyed his belief in European fellowship and co-operation.

Nevertheless, even before the war, there had been portents of a coming change. The year 1913 is a significant one, for in that year were published several works which indicated in which channels literature would later flow—though this was not perceived at the time. These works were: *Le Grand Meaulnes* by Alain-Fournier, which became the model of the novel of adolescence, a characteristic feature of post-war literature; there was also *Les Caves du Vatican* by André Gide, the first of his 'disruptive' works; also *Barnabooth* by Valéry Larbaud, the first of the 'globe-trotting' novels; *Jean Barois* by Roger Martin du Gard, the first of the works expressing the *Angst* and guilt of the later period. Its author chose, as an epigraph, a quotation from Suarès, which said: 'La conscience malade, voilà le théâtre de la fatalité moderne.' This feeling of guilt and *Angst* was indeed at the root of all experience after the war. There was also published in 1913 *Alcools* by Apollinaire, which started a new technique in poetry. And, finally, most important of all, that year saw the birth of *Du Côté de chez Swann*, the first volume of Proust's *À la Recherche du Temps Perdu*, which was to dominate the novel during the first half of the century—and perhaps even beyond that, as time may show.

Nineteen-thirteen also saw the foundation of *Le Théâtre du Vieux Colombier*, by Jacques Copeau, which was to play so significant a part in the history of the French theatre in the twentieth century, and also in the theatre of Europe generally.

After the war French Symbolism still remained the strongest influence on poetry—indeed on literature in general—but it had become modified. *À Rebours* was put away with the candles and the incense, the lilies and the coffins. The poets moved out of the Celtic twilight, away from the fairylands. They no longer wanted the 'roses and rapture' of aesthetic vice, nor to allow their servants to live for them—the servants were fewer anyway, and now wanted to live their own lives for themselves. The strange and the rare no longer moved the poets, but only what was everyday—the 'quotidien', as Laforgue had called it. This was everywhere around them, stronger than ever, and not to be evaded. The day of the 'little man' was at hand, small and unglamorous, with his everyday emotions and prosaic ambitions; the commutor of the 'Croydon class', of Anna Wickham's moving poem in *The Man with a Hammer*, published in 1916:

> 'I married a man of the Croydon class
>   When I was twenty-two.
> And I vex him, and he bores me,
> Till we don't know what to do!
> It isn't good form for the Croydon class
> To say you love your wife,
> So I spend my days with the tradesmen's books
> And pray for the end of life!
>
> .   .   .
>
> I married a man of the Croydon class
>   When I was twenty-two.
> And I vex him, and he bores me,
> Till we don't know what to do!
> And as I sit in his ordered house,
> I feel I must sob or shriek,
> To force a man of the Croydon class
> To live, or to love, or to speak!'

Baudelaire was still an important influence, though it was no longer his Satanic aspect that was followed, but his modern realism. Writers now turned to the iconoclastic poets of the eighteen-seventies for inspiration, to those who had written then, but had not been fully appreciated or understood during Decadence or Symbolism; to

Tristan Corbière, Charles Cros, Lautréamont and Jean Richepin; and
to those later poets who resembled them, to Laurent Tailhade and Jules
Laforgue; and Laforgue's literary heir, Guillaume Apollinaire. The
irony of Laforgue which had stood out, like a sore thumb, as they say,
in the midst of the grave nobility of the other contemporary poets—he
was the only one to be gifted with irony—and his 'je m'en foutisme'
appealed to a generation which did not wish to take anything seriously
—itself least of all.

The irony of the post-war period was, however, accompanied by
pessimism, by a new 'mal du siècle', as Marcel Arland called it in *La
Nouvelle Revue Française* in February 1924. It was a 'mal du siècle'
with none of the melancholy, beauty, and nobility of Chateaubriand,
but with bitterness and a feeling of guilt which led to frustration and
even despair.

With so much of the flower of the country killed or maimed during
the war, youth was at a premium and idolized, and all the activities of
youth—as depicted by writers like Montherlant in such novels as
Olympiques, Le Paradis à l'Ombre des Épées, and *Les Onze devant la
Porte Dorée* which celebrates the wonder of football. Poets who had
perished young, like Laforgue, were worshipped, or those who, like
Rimbaud, had died in youth to literature. Rimbaud was also admired
as the rebel *à outrance*, a 'voyou', for that generation was indeed one of
'angry young men', who knew why they were angry, and they were
furious with their elders who had made the kind of world they had
inherited, and they were without scruples, discipline, or sentiment—
certainly without sentimentality. They are well represented by Radiguet,
who died before he was twenty, and who wrote one of the most characteristic novels of the early nineteen-twenties in *Diable au Corps*,
published in 1923, a few months before he died.

The new writers made fun of the poetic language and artistic
pretensions of their elders; mocked at Mallarmé's theory that poetry
should possess its own private language, raised above the common
usage of everyday life to protect its mysteries from the idle curiosity of
the masses. They took, as their examples, Corbière, Richepin, and
Laforgue, who had used the most common—and often the coarsest—
language. They believed that the rough slang of the trenches was better
able to reflect the cruder values of the post-war era than the more
polished diction of an earlier age.

This led to a change in descriptive style, in the choice of images and
metaphors, which were now intended to startle by their eccentricity and
originality, rather than move by their beauty. 'L'écriture devient une
peau,' Barbusse said, 'plutôt qu'un habillement.' Cocteau, in a poem,

wrote that the sea 'débouche bruyamment un Champagne qui mousse', and that 'la mer, de sa lente salive, imprègne le sol'. Morand described the sun rising 'après une rapide ablution', and said that 'encagé derrière les troncs d'arbres, le soleil disparut, betterave coupée'.

By the time hostilities had ended, the writers who were to be most eminent in the post-war period had reached middle-age. Claudel was already fifty, Gide forty-nine, while Valéry and Proust were forty-seven. Each of them was pre-eminent in his own field—Claudel in the theatre, Valéry in poetry, and Proust in the novel. It cannot be claimed that Gide excelled everyone else in any one literary *genre*, but, perhaps more than any of the others, his spirit permeated the whole of the intellectual climate in the years which followed the First World War. Claudel, Valéry, and Proust are more suitably studied in connection with the literary form in which each excelled; Gide, on the contrary, was less a model in any one literary form than element in the general spirit of the age, for there is definitely an atmosphere, in the post-war era, which can be called 'Gidism', just as there had been, at the beginning of the nineteenth century, a psychological climate which was called 'Rousseauism'. Although Gide may not have exercised widespread influence on literary technique, his novel, *Les Faux-Monnayeurs*, did serve as a model for Aldous Huxley when he wrote his *Point Counterpoint*. It would be truer to say that Gide was a ferment rather than a direct influence. Although he had many followers—especially many who found themselves in him—he did not have disciples—not at least in the sense in which one speaks of the disciples of Baudelaire, Flaubert, or Zola.

This ferment worked secretly and inwardly on many who had never even read his works—just as was also the case with Freud, and earlier with Rousseau. This influence had even more effect in the realm of morals than in aesthetics. The German critic, Curtius, described Gide as 'the voice of the European mind'; while Mauriac declared that Gide had helped the men of his generation to find their true vocation, and he said—while deprecating his influence—'On a l'impression que son œuvre a été pour notre génération une sorte de point de repère qui a permis à chacun de se situer.' Mauriac himself used Gide's influence in order to escape from his spell.

The interest of the general public in the works of Gide was slow to arrive. When his *Les Nourritures Terrestres* was published in 1897 it enjoyed no success whatsoever, and, in ten years, only five hundred copies were sold. There was a joke current in the offices of the publishers that they used to beg visitors to take a few of the 'Fruits' away with them, saying that they were a glut on the market, and would not keep much longer. Gide had his revenge twenty-five years later when this book became his most popular and influential work—especially in the nineteen-twenties.

His first book to reach popularity was *La Porte Étroite*, published in 1909, which was greatly admired and praised in literary circles, but it cannot be said to have made much impact otherwise. It was only after the war that it became evident that he was one of the most important forces in European culture. That was the time when the old answers to the old questions no longer satisfied anyone, and Gide's writings, which, a generation earlier, had asked precisely the same questions, came into their own, and were read by those looking for new guidance. In the nineteen-twenties there were few people, in any part of the world, who did not see their own problems reflected in him, and he seemed, middle-aged as he was by then, to be the spokesman for the whole generation. His works became, for anguished youth of the post-war world, the true expression of their *mal du siècle*. All through his life Gide had felt *Angst* and guilt, and it was this mood that commended itself to the young at that time.

In *Les Nourritures Terrestres* Gide addressed the young through Nathanaël, who is the symbol of youth, and that is why this book was so popular in the nineteen-twenties, that era particularly dedicated to youth. He takes them aside, at a moment when they are wearied from reading many books of the older generation, finding nothing in them on which their aspirations may feed, and he tells them that it is for them alone that he has written. But he advises them, when they have finished his book, to cast it behind them, to emancipate themselves from it, as well as from everything else. He says: 'Do not believe that your truth can be found by anyone else save by yourself alone', telling them to cultivate in themselves what is to be found in no one else. Each youth in the nineteen-twenties, reading this book, felt that it had been designed for himself alone, and many were turned into rebels—or were confirmed in their existing revolt. The irony was that, at the moment when this work—composed more than twenty years earlier—was having its greatest impact on the new generation, its author had emancipated himself from these anxieties, and had reached serenity. He had cast aside self-torture and a sense of guilt, he had turned his back on the past, and was determined to be moral in his own way.

In the works of his youth Gide had preached the need to escape from all the old conventions, the need to throw away old shibboleths, and to demolish the standards of the past. As a young man, when he had looked at civilization, he had been appalled by the pressure of outworn codes on the individual personality—the Church, society, the family, political theories—and he considered that, in his attempt to conform, the individual was obliged to develop an outward personality, a counterfeit personality. Discovery of our unacted desires, emancipation from the counterfeit personality, he thought, would bring freedom and fulfilment to the individual. It is the inner personality, beneath the counterfeit one, which he always tried to uncover; that inner reality where good and evil overlap as in a marriage of Heaven and Hell. In reaching that inner personality he stirs up its troubled depths, drags up from the thick overlying mud the hidden motives. This was for him the really fertile soil, the one which, in a state of Nature, is overrun by exuberant vegetation and which must be cleared before it can be cultivated. He considered that those who had first studied man's nature had done so only where it was most easily accessible, and that only very gradually did psychologists come to realize all the hidden possibilities in man. All the troubled, tortured, and distressed beings are those that interested Gide, because he believed that more could be expected from them, when the subterranean forces had been liberated and subdued, than from the complacent. So he studied cases of disconcerting behaviour, cases of apparent wrongdoing; he observed all the idiosyncrasies, the nervous tics, as signs that reveal hidden obsessions. Most of the characters in his writings have some maladjustment, or psychological flaw, which drives them to their doom, and often to the destruction of others as well. All this was the subject-matter for the post-war novel the whole world over. All this was the domain of the psychoanalyst, who is the shadow behind the modern novelist. In exploring these depths Gide brought in (what Victor Hugo had said of Baudelaire, after the publication of *Les Fleurs du Mal*)' *un frisson nouveau*', the breath of a new psychological climate.

Many accused Gide of undermining and destroying what had been built up, with so much labour, through thousands of years of tradition; of sweeping away all traditions. He was accused of debauching youth, of not taking into account the stored-up experience of the past, of squandering the accumulated spiritual capital of two thousand years of Christianity. It was said that, by plumbing the hidden depths of human nature, he had 'decomposed' the unity of man, and brought back the first state of incoherence which humanity, after long eras of growth, had managed to weld into some cohesion. Many thought that he was playing with fire, being tempted by the Devil, when he split up men again into the separate elements. It was said that modern man had already flirted too long with the forces of evil, and that the terrible chastisement which had followed was his agonizing despair and feeling of guilt.

Gide changed towards the end of his life, and came to value what had come from tradition, reaching the belief that culture needed, for its survival, a continuing and developing tradition. In his last creative work, *Thésée*, he shows how Theseus had returned from the maze only because he had never broken with his past, because he had clung firmly to his lifeline of tradition, symbolized by the thread which bound him to Ariadne.

Gide's influence persisted, without abating, during the rest of the first half of the twentieth century, and he relates, in the final volume of his *Journal*, which takes the events up to his eightieth year, in 1949, how a young man of twenty-two wrote to him for help, saying that he had struggled for five years against his influence, trying to do what he had advised his readers to do in *Les Nourritures Terrestres*—that is to say cast away his writings, and leave him behind—but he had been obliged to admit: 'I still live with everything you taught me. But I am thirsty. All young people are thirsty with me. A glimmer from you might indicate the direction to take—if there is a direction.' Gide answered him that the world would be saved, if indeed it could be saved, only by the unsubmissive. 'Without them it will be all up with our civilization,' he wrote in reply, 'the culture which we love, and which gave justification to our life on earth. The unsubmissive are the salt of the earth, and responsible for God.'

9

POETRY

JUST before the First World War a change came over poetry in France. The languors of Decadence and the idealism of Symbolism were equally incapable of appeal. The Symbolist Movement eventually failed because it was too much divorced from everyday life, because it concentrated too much on ultimate reality, and was too much occupied with artifice. Its poets had lived in a shut-in atmosphere, with drawn curtains, as if in a sick-room, or in one heavy with the smell of incense and wax candles. There were too many coffins in these heavily curtained and over-heated rooms, too many lilies and exotic flowers; there were too many symbolical gems and jewels; too many knights in gilded armour, too many golden-haired sexless princesses. Already, in the nineties, the movement had split into two parts. Some turned away with distaste from the barbarous North, from the Scandinavian mists and the Celtic twilights, to the South and the Mediterranean sun, and welcomed the new classical revival.

These poets were, firstly, Jean Moréas and his followers, the members of the *École Romane*—Ernest Raynaud, Maurice du Plessys, Raymond de la Tailhède, and Charles Maurras—but they soon attracted other poets as well, who had not felt completely at ease among the Symbolist ideals; some of these were Henri de Régnier, Vielé-Griffin, Albert Samain, Pierre Louÿs, and Charles Guérin. They realized that France lay between two climates. On one side she is bathed by the northern Atlantic; on the other by the southern Mediterranean; and they believed that she was truer to her destiny when she looked towards the south, and gave full play to what sprang from her Graeco-Roman roots. They looked back to the Renaissance of the sixteenth century, and to the abortive Renaissance of the twelfth century—particularly in Provence—and those early signs of the coming rebirth, which showed already in the fifteenth century, in the poetry of Charles d'Orléans. They cultivated the more sophisticated and artificial aspects of Symbolism, and their classicism was artificial too. They produced a watered-down form of classicism which was quite out of touch with the modern age.

The other group, largely poets from the North, escaped from Symbolism into the modern world of industry, and produced such poetry as Verhaeren wrote, which is most typical of this manner in the early twentieth century. Verhaeren had, in his temperament, too much of Flemish realism and materialism to remain long happy with Symbolism. He escaped into socialism, with a desire to serve humanity, and finally reached the full expression of joy in life. In this he was inspired by a broad uncritical optimism which seemed puerile to many. Very typical of his style is the poem from *La Multiple Splendeur*, entitled *Plus loin que les Gares le Soir*, which begins thus:

> 'L'ombre s'installe, avec brutalité;
> Mais les ciseaux de la lumière,
> Au long des quais, coupent l'obscurité,
> À coups menus, de reverbère en reverbère.
>
> Et le lent défilé des trains funèbres
> Commence, avec ses bruits de gonds
> Et l'entrechoquement brutal de ses wagons,
> Disparaissant—tels des cercueils —vers les ténèbres.'

This poem, a good example of its kind, is pure romanticism. Verhaeren had a romantic view of the products of industry, and he saw machines as if they were monsters from fairy tales or folk-lore. This attitude was not in sympathy with the views of the post-war period.

Valéry, the only true disciple of Mallarmé and his literary heir, when he reached his full stature as a poet between 1916 and 1922, was, in the early years of the century, sunk in his twenty years of silence. The poems of his first manner, written in the early nineties, do not differ greatly from those of other Symbolist poets of that era—except in being technically more proficient and skilful.

The poet most admired in France amongst the progressive writers, just before the First World War, was Jules Laforgue, then twenty years dead, and through him they reached his brother by affinity, Tristan Corbière, whose only collection of poems, *Les Amours Jaunes*, had been published in 1873, and who passed almost unnoticed amongst the Symbolists, except for mention by Verlaine in his *Poètes Maudits*, published in 1883.

Amongst the Symbolists Laforgue had passed for a Decadent and an Aesthete; it was not, however, that aspect of his talent which the twentieth century admired, but his modernity, and the qualities which made him different from the Symbolists.

He was born in 1860, thus reaching adult years when the Symbolist Movement began, and so he could not fail to be influenced by it. Nevertheless, as was shown in a previous chapter, he possessed many characteristics which were different, and it is these that gave him interest in the eyes of the twentieth century. He is the only poet during the Symbolist Movement gifted with a sense of humour, and he took nothing seriously—certainly not himself—whereas his fellow-poets took everything in deep earnest, and never allowed themselves to unbend.

It was not the ideal world which was the subject of Laforgue's poetry, but the everydayness of life, the 'quotidien'. He did not, on the other hand, appreciate the romantic realism of a Verhaeren, but wanted what was most trivial. This did not make him deny or repudiate Symbolism, for, on the contrary, he accepted its ideals, but twisted them and transposed them into something else. One of its chief aims was the approximation of its poetry to music. He accepted this, but conveyed, not the noble symphonic music of his fellow-poets, but what would be called today jazz, jiving, or rock-and-roll. It is not the full orchestra that is heard in his verse, but the barrel-organ, or the tinkling piano. He wished to evoke the characteristic cacophony of the modern town.

The Symbolists had believed in the deep meaning contained in folk-lore. Laforgue also accepted this, but treated it humorously in his *Les Moralités Légendaires*, giving a parody of Wagner's myth in *Lohengrin Fils de Parsival*, poking fun at the composer's stage effects in his ending; while in *Salomé* he mocks Flaubert, making the heroine drown herself, trying to get rid of the head of John the Baptist, of which she has grown tired, and the poet tells us that she perished because she tried to live 'dans le factice et non à la bonne franquette, à l'instar de chacun de nous'. *Les Moralités Légendaires* abounds in humorous anachronisms—John the Baptist wears glasses, and the characters discuss Napoleon and Jean-Jacques Rousseau; while in *Hamlet* they have fountain-pens and ink, and smoke cigarettes.

The Symbolists believed that the true quality of poetry was to be found in the little songs, on the model of folk-songs—such as are found in the poetry of Verlaine, Maeterlinck, and Rimbaud. Laforgue also used this form but treated satirically and with irony, as in *Complainte de cette Bonne Lune*:

'Dans l'giron
    Du Patron,
On y danse, on y danse,
    Dans l'giron
    Du Patron,
On y danse tout en rond.

—Là, voyons, Mam'zell' la lune,
Ne gardons pas ainsi rancune;
Entrez en danse, et vous aurez
Un collier de soleils dorés.'

In his descriptive poetry Laforgue has moved far away from the poetically evocative verse of the Symbolists and he produced something far more realistic and coarse, as in *Complainte d'un autre Dimanche*, where the proximity of the military hospital, Le Val-de-Grâce, conditions the nature of the imagery :

'C'était un très-au-vent d'octobre paysage,
Que découpe, aujourd'hui dimanche, la fenêtre,
Avec sa jalousie en travers, hors d'usage,
Où sèche, depuis quand! une paire de guêtres
Tachant de deux mals blancs ce glabre paysage.

Un couchant mal bâti suppurant du livide;
Le coin d'une buanderie aux tuiles sales;
En plein, le Val-de-Grâce, comme un qui préside;
Cinq arbres en proie à de mesquines rafales
Qui marbrent ce ciel crû de bandages livides.

Puis les squelettes de glycines aux ficelles,
En proie à des rafales encor plus mesquines!
O lendemains de noce! ô brides de dentelles!
Montrent-elles assez la corde, ces glycines
Recroquevillant leur agonie aux ficelles.

Ce fut un bien-au-vent d'octobre paysage.'

He liked to use a colloquial, inconsequent style, nearer to everyday speech than to normal poetic diction. As in a poem from *Derniers Vers*, which is also a good example of his *vers libre* :

'J'aurais passé ma vie le long des quais
À faillir m'embarquer
Dans de bien funestes histoires,
Tout cela pour l'amour
De mon cœur fou de la gloire d'amour.

Oh, qu'il sont pittoresques les trains manqués!

Oh, qu'ils sont "À bientôt! à bientôt!"
Les bateaux
Du bout de la jetée!
De la jetée charpentée
Contre la mer,
Comme ma chair
Contre l'amour.'

Laforgue, in inspiration and language, is nearer to the poets of the eighteen-seventies—to Charles Cros and Tristan Corbière—than to the poets of the eighteen-eighties. He claims to have known the writings of Corbière only at the end of his life, but it is generally believed today that this is not quite correct, and that he did, in fact, know *Les Amours Jaunes* earlier than he admitted.

Tristan Corbière was a Breton, born in 1845, who died when he was only thirty, two years after publishing his solitary collection of poems, *Les Amours Jaunes*. He lived most of his life amongst the rough fisherfolk in his native town of Roscoff, and he has immortalized them in the sections of his book entitled *Armor* and *Les Gens de Mer*, with a realism and a use of slang hitherto unknown in French poetry. He is the first true poet of the sea, and he pokes fun at Victor Hugo who, in his *Oceano Nox*, had asked poetically where they had gone, these sailors, 'qui sont partis pour des courses lointaines'. Corbière answers scornfully, and ironically, in *La Fin*:

'Eh bien, tous ces marins—matelots, capitaines,
Dans leur grand Océan à jamais engloutis,
Partis insoucieux pour leurs courses lointaines,
Sont morts—absolument comme ils étaient partis.

Allons! c'est leur métier; ils sont morts dans leurs bottes!
Leur *boujaron* au cœur, tout vifs dans leurs capotes . . .
Morts . . . Merci: la *Camarde* a pas le pied marin;

Qu'elle couche avec vous: c'est votre bonne-femme ...
—Eux, allons donc: Entiers! enlevés par la lame!
   Ou perdus dans un grain ...

Noyés?—Eh allons donc! Les *noyés* sont d'eau douce,
—Coulés! corps et biens! Et, jusqu'au petit mousse,
Le défi dans les yeux, dans les dents le juron!
À l'écume crachant une chique râlée,
Buvant sans hauts-de-cœur la *grand' tasse salée* ...
—Comme ils ont bu leur *boujaron.*—'

Hugo had said that no stone in the churchyard marked their last
resting-place, that nothing later remembered their passing. But
Corbière answers contemptuously:

'—Écoutez, écoutez la tourmente qui beugle! ...
C'est leur anniversaire.—Il revient bien souvent.—
O poète, gardez pour vous vos chants d'aveugle;
—Eux: le *De Profundis* que leur corne le vent.

—Qu'ils roulent infinis dans les espaces vierges!
   Qu'ils roulent verts et nus,
Sans clous et sans sapin, sans couvercle, sans cierges ...
—Laissez-les donc rouler, *terriens* parvenus!'

The most important aspect of his work, as far as the twentieth
century was concerned, was the use he made of the poem in the form of
a popular song, ten years before Laforgue, in such poems as the *Rondels*,
one of which is *Do, L'Enfant Do!*

'*Buena vespre!* Dors: Ton bout de cierge ...
On l'a posé là, puis on est parti.
Tu n'auras pas peur seul, pauvre petit?
C'est le chandelier de ton lit d'auberge.

Du fesse-cahier ne crains plus la verge,
Va! ... De t'éveiller point n'est si hardi.
Buena sera! Dors: Ton bout de cierge ...

Est mort.—Il n'est plus ici, de concierge:
Seuls, le vent du nord, le vent du midi
Viendront balancer un fil-de-la-Vierge.
Chut! Pour les pieds-plats, ton sol est maudit.
—*Buena noce!* Dors: Ton bout de cierge. ...'

There is a realism in the poetry of Corbière which is not to be found until the twentieth century, except in the writings of Laforgue, and a robustness which is found in no one else until after the turn of the century, until the writings of Apollinaire.

Just as Valéry was the heir of Mallarmé, so was Guillaume Apollinaire the heir of Corbière and Laforgue. He is also the most significant poet in France during the years which immediately preceded the First World War, the one whose influence was most widespread, and it was from him that sprang what was most vital in French poetry in the period between the two world wars.

Like many of the writers who were innovators in that disturbed period in French poetry, he was not French either by blood or birth, for he was the illegitimate son of a Polish noblewoman and of an unknown father. He was brought up in Italy, Monaco, and France, but his education had been French, and this international bastard eventually chose France as his country, and became a naturalized Frenchman. He also became one of the most typical poets of Paris.

Before the First World War Apollinaire played an important part in the literature and artistic life in Paris. He was the intimate friend of the advanced painters of the age, such as Picasso and Braque—the influence of his connection with painting is seen in his poetry.

As a young man Apollinaire's most striking characteristic was his exhibitionism, his desire to astonish at all costs. In L'Esprit Nouveau et les Poètes, the very last article that he wrote, and which was published posthumously in Le Mercure de France in December 1918, he said: 'Le nouveau est tout dans la surprise. C'est tout ce qu'il y a en lui de plus neuf et de plus vivant.'

Like many writers of his time, his favourite means of provoking surprise was to indulge in all sorts of grotesque tricks and hoaxes, like those of Jarry. Some of his poems were composed of what he called 'Poèmes Conversations'. He would sit at a table in a café, and put down, one after the other, odd fragments of sentences spoken by his friends, or overheard amongst strangers. These scraps of conversation had no link with one another, though certain over-zealous readers have tried, subtly, to show some hidden relationship, and to expound their meaning. However, the charm which they often contain comes from the clever manner in which he has contrived his mosaic out of the overheard scraps of conversation. This is very similar to what the Surrealists were to try in the nineteen-twenties.

Apollinaire arrived in Paris in 1898 and not long afterwards took the name of Guillaume Apollinaire, instead of Wilhelm Apollinaire

Kostrowitsky—he had the further Christian names of Albert-Wladimir-Alexandre.

At first he earned a precarious living by free-lance journalism, and by preparing erotic books for a publisher, for a series called *Bibliothèque des Curieux*. He carried on much research into erotica at the Bibliothèque Nationale, while preparing these books, and became an authority on Aretino and the Marquis de Sade.

It was Paul Léautaud who was responsible for the publication of his *Chanson du Mal Aimé* in the *Mercure de France* in 1909. That same year his prose work, *L'Hérésiarque*, appeared, which was considered for the Prix Goncourt, but did not win it.

In 1913 Apollinaire published his aesthetic manifesto, *L'Antitradition Futuriste*, based on consideration of the work of the Italian Futurist, Severini, which was the forerunner of the first number of Wyndham Lewis' *Blast*, which appeared the following year, and which will be discussed later.

Apollinaire was now at the head of the most advanced movement in literature in Paris and, in 1913, he published his first important collection of poems under the title *Alcools*, some of which were not surpassed in beauty and skill by his second collection, *Calligrammes*.

The poems contained in *Alcools* are of various inspirations. There are those, like *Chanson du Mal-Aimé* and *Le Voyageur*, in the personal, Romantic tradition, though the second has the moving quality of realism not present in such poets as Victor Hugo, of whom it has echoes—apart from the absence of punctuation:

'Ouvrez-moi cette porte où je frappe en pleurant

Tu regardais un banc de nuages descendre
Avec le paquebot orphelin vers les fièvres futures
Et de tous ces regrets de tous ces repentirs
    Te souviens-tu

Je m'en souviens je m'en souviens encore
Te souviens-tu du long orphelinat des gares
Nous traversâmes des villes qui tout le jour tournaient
Et vomissaient la nuit le soleil des journées
Ô matelots ô femmes sombres et vous mes compagnons
    Souvenez-vous en'

There are the song-like poems in the Verlaine tradition, such as *Pont Mirabeau* and *Automne Malade*:

> 'Sous le Pont Mirabeau coule la Seine
>   Et nos amours
> Faut-il qu'il m'en souvienne
> La joie venait toujours après la peine
>
>   Vienne la nuit sonne l'heure
>   Les jours s'en vont je demeure'

There are the poems celebrating Paris, such as *Vendémiaire*, which recall Baudelaire. And there is the modern inspiration, and unpoetic vocabulary, initiated by Corbière and Laforgue: 'C'est la lune qui cuit comme un œuf sur le plat.' Or, in *Zone*, 'l'avion se pose enfin sans refermer les ailes'. Or, in a nameless poem:

> 'Soirs de Paris ivres de gin
> Flambent de l'électricité
> Les tramways feux verts sur l'échine
> Musiquent au long des portées
> De rails leur folie de machines'

And there are striking, original metaphors, as in *Rhénane d'Automne*:

> 'Oh! je ne veux pas que tu sortes
> L'automne est plein de mains coupées
> Non non ce sont des feuilles mortes
> Ce sont les mains des chères mortes
> Ce sont des mains coupées'

Or in *Merlin et la Vieille Femme*:

> 'Le soleil ce jour-là s'étalait comme un ventre
> Maternel qui saignait lentement sur le ciel
> La lumière est ma mère ô lumière sanglante
> Les nuages coulaient comme un flux menstruel'

In *Alcools* Apollinaire has used many different kinds of versification —some traditional and some free—and he has dispensed with punctuation. The absence of punctuation does not serve any decided purpose, for there is no doubt where the pauses occur, and they have their natural and inherent punctuation. Absence of punctuation with Mallarmé serves an important purpose, for it was intended to permit the possibility of multiple interpretation of a poem. With Apollinaire one interpretation alone is possible.

The war provided Apollinaire with a new set of striking images, which he used in his next collection of poems, entitled *Calligrammes*. Extrovert as he was, he was one of those who enjoyed the war, and found in it a source of exaltation and vision, as well as a source of new images. 'Ah! Dieu que la guerre est jolie!' he said. He went through most of it, was severely wounded, and yet was unique in not reaching disillusionment. He found in it an extension of his pre-war use of metaphor. In *La Nuit d'Avril 1915* he wrote:

'Les obus miaulaient un amour à mourir
Un amour qui se meurt est plus doux que les autres
Ton souffle nage en fleuve où le sang va tarir
Les obus miaulaient
    Entends chanter les nôtres
Pourpre amour salué par ceux qui vont périr

Le printemps tout mouillé la veilleuse l'attaque
Il pleut mon âme il pleut mais il pleut des yeux morts'

In *Océan de Terre* he says of the bombing-planes, 'les avions pondent des œufs'; while in *Les Collines* he compared his youth and his future to two planes locked in mortal combat.

In prosody *Calligrammes* is more daring than *Alcools*, and the poet is more original in his experimentation. As well as making more frequent use of *vers libre*, he often achieved his modern effects by means of peculiar typographical arrangements. From Mallarmé he had learnt the importance of the appearance of the page in the total effect which the poem produced, and in its aesthetic enjoyment. Instead of printing the verse in straight lines suggesting uniformity, he tried to arrange them to suit the sentiments expressed, or those that they were intended to convey, so that, by their appearance on the page, they would call up the object which was depicted. The page then became the metaphor itself. The words were no longer intellectual metaphors, but the very thing. In this, Apollinaire may have been inspired by the phenomenal expansion of advertising at this time. He said:

'Une page doit, s'adressant au coup d'œil qui précède, et qui enveloppe le lecteur, faire pressentir, par une sorte d'intuition matérielle, par une harmonie entre les divers modes de perception, ou entre les différences de nos sens, ce qu'on va produire à l'intelligence.'

In one poem, for example, in order to convey the impression of the rain falling straight, he has made the letters look as if they had dripped from his pen, one by one, vertically, on to the page. In another, *La Petite Auto*, they are printed so as to represent a car, complete with body, wheels, and chauffeur. In yet another, entitled *Fumées*, they are arranged so as to form a pipe with smoke issuing from the bowl. While a very elaborate example, *La Colombe Poignardée et le Jet d'Eau*, has the shape of a dove and a fountain in play made from the words. The visual pattern of this poem—leaving its actual meaning aside, which is simple, simpler than that of the poems printed in an orthodox manner —is graceful and pleasing, but does not seem to need the actual words for its aesthetic enjoyment.

Whatever may be the final verdict on the intrinsic value of Apollinaire's work—his stock has shown a tendency to rise in recent years—he certainly opened the way to the most characteristic movement in French poetry between the two wars, that of *Surréalisme*. This started in 1916, in Zürich, as a movement called *Dada*, the name of which was chosen, by Tristan Tzara, at random. A review was founded entitled *Le Cabaret Voltaire*, and Tzara formulated the first manifesto of the movement.

Apollinaire was responsible for the importation of Dadaism into France, for it was he who, in 1917, brought the activities of the Zürich group to the attention of André Breton. Several reviews were founded in Paris, the most important of which, at this time, was *Nord-Sud*, which began in 1917, and connected with which were the future *Surréalistes*, André Breton, Philippe Soupault and Louis Aragon, who were later joined by Apollinaire, Max Jacob and Pierre Reverdy. It was from the Preface to Apollinaire's play, *Les Mamelles de Tirésias*, performed in 1917, but published only in 1918, that the French *Dada* group borrowed the name it eventually adopted, that of *Surréalisme*.

In England at the end of the nineteenth century, amongst the poets who had come under the influence of French ideals, the most outstanding was certainly Yeats. However, after he returned to Ireland in 1896, he was taken up in the Irish Literary Renaissance and was withdrawn from the general stream of English and European poetry. When others were turning towards present-day realism, his preoccupations still lay in magic and folk-lore, and a world of fantasy. He remained aristocratic and aloof when his fellow-poets were becoming plebeian and gregarious—there was not in the whole of his composition one single grain of the salt of vulgarity. When the others were becoming aware of the wonder and beauty of modern industrial towns, he continued to wander amongst the hills and lakes of his native land, and it would be difficult to imagine anyone less mechanically minded than he. There is no proof that he had any interest in the rough-and-tumble of contemporary ideals, or that he read any modern French literature. He was particularly cut off from France, which had once provided him with a rich soil for his development, and was out of touch with the new literary movements, both in France and in England.

There are, nevertheless, in *In The Seven Woods*, published in 1904, signs of disillusionment with the fairylands, and awareness of the shock of modern reality—though without accepting it—as in such poems as *The Folly of being comforted, The Old Men admiring themselves in the Water*, and *O Do Not Love Too Long*:

> 'Sweetheart, do not love too long:
> I loved long and long,
> And grew to be out of fashion
> Like an old song.'

Yeats now used a more simple and realistic vocabulary than in his youth. In 1906 he wrote, in *Essays*: 'I ask myself if my conception of my own art is altering; if there too I praise what I once derided.' In 1904, in a letter to George Russell which was published in July 1934 in *The Dublin Magazine*, he said, in the same year as he published *In The Seven Woods*:

> 'In my *Land of Heart's Desire*, and in some of my lyric verse at that time, there is an exaggeration of sentiment and sentimental beauty, which I have come to think unmanly. I have been fighting the prevailing decadence for years and have just got it underfoot in my own heart.'

This tendency became more marked in *The Green Helmet*, published in 1910. Then, in 1912, he made the acquaintance of Ezra Pound, and this brought him back into the general stream of European literature, but the finest flowers that this phase of his writings was to produce were to bloom only after the First World War.

In England, as in France, during the years which immediately preceded the First World War, there was a longing for something new in literature. The younger poets wished to escape from the stagnation of English poetry which, except for Yeats, was at a very low ebb when the Edwardian decade began. Literature continued to hide in the dank thickets of the nineties until the advent of the Imagists and the Vorticists just before the war. Ford Madox Hueffer, who was closely connected

with these new movements, was later to write in *Thus to revisit*, published in 1921, that, since *The Yellow Book*, there had been nothing new
in poetry until the Imagists and the Vorticists appeared.

The first attempt at change was made in 1908 when T. E. Hulme
founded The Poets' Club which met once a week to discuss literature,
and what measures should be adopted to improve English poetry.
Hulme was an admirer of French poetry, who looked to such poets as
Corbière and Laforgue as examples, and wished, on the model of
Laforgue, to introduce *vers libre* into English poetry. At the end of the
year he published a pamphlet entitled *Pour Noël*, to set forth his
aesthetic doctrine, and he printed in it his *Autumn*, which is, in fact, the
first Imagist poem—though not so called at that time—and which has
affinities with the writings of Laforgue:

> 'A touch of cold in the autumn night,
> I walked abroad
> And saw the ruddy moon lean over a hedge,
> I did not stop to speak, but nodded;
> And roundabout were the wistful stars
> With white faces like town children.'

During the years from 1908 to 1912 Hulme was the centre of a
shifting group of writers who aimed at bringing innovations into
English poetry, and he was later to be called the Father of Imagism.

Early in 1909 he met Flint and a new literary club was formed,
consisting of himself, Flint, Florence Farr, and others. Later in the
year Ezra Pound joined them—he had just published his *Personae*—
and he immediately took over the leadership of the poets who wanted
the renovation of English poetry. But the group's hold on life was
never very strong and, after lingering on for a year, it expired at the
end of 1910.

In 1912 a new development occurred when Hulme began seriously
to study French poetry, urged on by Flint and Fletcher, and, in August,
he published in *The Poetry Review* an article dealing with French
literature since 1880, in which he expressed the hope that English
poetry should, one day, possess similar freedom. That same year he
gave a lecture on poetry, and his thesis was the necessity of discovering
a new form of verse to give new life to poetry. He believed that each age
must produce its own particular form of verse to express itself, and that,
without this new form, there could only be progressive decay. He was
much impressed by the possibilities afforded to French poetry by the
discovery of *vers libre*, and he thought that the new language used by

certain French poets was a great advantage to poetry. There must be, he maintained, new metaphors to startle the reader out of his apathy and to rouse him from sleep.

Another important event in 1912 was the appointment of Pound as foreign correspondent to the American review, *Poetry*, and this forged a link between English and American poets. He sent to America the first Imagist poems—three by Aldington and three by H. D. In September and October that year he published articles on French poetry in *The New Age*, entitled 'Approach to Paris', in which he wrote in praise of Corbière and Laurent Tailhade, pointing out the advantages they had enjoyed in comparison with English poets. At the end of the year his *Riposte* appeared, with a preface in which he used the term Imagist for the first time, saying that '*Les Imagistes*' were the descendants of the forgotten school of 1909—he did not remember the one of 1908, probably because he was not connected with it himself—and that they had the future in their keeping. He invented the word 'Imagist' to designate the aesthetic principles of the new school. At the end of *Riposte* he printed all Hulme's poems—only five in number, making thirty-three lines in all, for Hulme seems to have shared Baudelaire's view concerning the most effective length of a poem, and his, in their concision and economy of detail, recall Rimbaud. One of these is *Above the Docks*, a poem of only four lines:

> 'Above the quiet dock at midnight,
> Tangled in the tall mast's corded height,
> Hangs the moon. What seemed so far away
> Is but a child's balloon, forgotten after play.'

The first real grouping of the Imagists occurred in London, in 1913. It consisted largely of expatriates from the United States, Ezra Pound, H. D., John Gould Fletcher and Robert Frost; and the English members were Hulme, Flint, and Aldington. In an article in *Poetry*, published in March 1913, Pound established what he considered were the aims and principles of the Imagist Movement. He advised his readers to fix their gaze on France and not on England. In a further article entitled 'Paris', and published in *Poetry* that year, he enlarged on the theory, saying that English poets should study Remy de Gourmont for rhythm, Tailhade for form, Régnier for simplicity of expression, Francis Jammes for human interest, and Corbière for intensity. It is strange that he should have admired Jammes and Régnier, who are sentimental and diffuse, in comparison with the poets who rank highest in his esteem. He considered Corbière as the most poignant poet since

Villon, and he also ranked Laforgue very high. He said: 'It seems to me that without familiarity with Laforgue, we cannot appreciate—i.e. determine the value of—certain positives and negatives in French poetry since 1880.' He thought that Laforgue was the most important technical innovator in modern poetry. Amongst critics he most admired Remy de Gourmont, and called him the 'critical consciousness of a generation'. He modelled his own criticism on Gourmont's *Problème du Style*, adopting the ideas as his own. He also learned much from Flaubert in the art of writing, and, in his *Mauberly I*, he says of himself:

> 'His true Penelope
> Was Flaubert
> And his tool
> The engraver's.'

In 1913 Pound collected together the poems of the various Imagist poets—Aldington, H. D., Amy Lowell, Ford Madox Hueffer, and himself. These poems were published in a collection in 1913, both in London and New York, under the title *Des Imagistes, an Anthology*. This is the first collection to be published of Imagist poetry. Very typical is Aldington's *Evening*:

> 'The chimneys, rank on rank,
> Cut the clear sky;
> The moon,
> With a rag of gauze about her loins
> Poses amongst them, an awkward Venus—
> And here am I looking wantonly at her
> Over the kitchen sink.'

The Imagists succeeded in securing their own review, *The Egoist*, the first number of which appeared on 1 January 1914. It adopted this name because the Imagists were extreme individualists.

The review had a strange genesis, since it was born of a paper called *The Freewoman, An Individual Review*. It had been founded by a Miss Shaw and a Miss Marsden, for the purpose of advancing women's causes. However, Ezra Pound, who had great powers of persuasion and persistence—and also needed a review—made the two ladies believe that they urgently required a strong literary page for their paper. Eventually an agreement was reached, and they were persuaded to appoint Aldington as Assistant Editor in charge of the literary aspect of the paper, while Miss Marsden was to remain as General Editor—Miss Shaw was only a figurehead—and the title of the paper was changed to *The Egoist, An Individual Review*. The first number, in January 1914, had articles dealing with Tailhade and Péguy, and also with the Théâtre du Vieux Colombier, which had been founded in 1913 by Copeau. It also published extracts from *Les Chants de Maldoror* by Lautréamont, which, at that time, was almost totally unknown even in France, and the first complete edition was only to be published there in 1920.

In April and May 1914 Hulme gave a series of lectures on modern poetry, followed by discussions, and they dealt with the Imagist ideals, and their connection with French poetry. These discussions on poetry became a weekly institution, and they were attended by Pound, Squire, Middleton Murry, Epstein, and Gaudier-Brzeska; Rupert Brooke came occasionally, though they did not deal with the form of poetry favoured by him.

In June 1914 *The Egoist* was joined by a companion-in-arms, the review *Blast*, founded and edited by Wyndham Lewis, on the model of Apollinaire's *Antitradition Futuriste*, which had appeared the previous year. *Blast* was also interested in the theories of the Italian Futurist, Severini. Unfortunately, as a result of the war, it had only two numbers, one in June 1914 and the other in July 1915. Its main contributors were Ford Madox Hueffer, Pound, Eliot, Epstein, and Gaudier-Brzeska, and its ideals were very similar to those of *The Egoist*—in the second number there is a poem entitled *Respectful Homage to M. Laurent Tailhade*.

In 1914 the American poet, Amy Lowell, who had been associated with the Imagists since 1912, came over to England. She was a woman of independent means, and she came to London to arrange for the publication of several anthologies of Imagist verse. On 17 July she gave an Imagist dinner, to which came, amongst others, Aldington, H. D., Fletcher, Flint, Ford Madox Hueffer, and Pound. While she was in London she chose amongst them six official Imagist poets to be represented in her anthologies—Aldington, H. D., Fletcher, Flint, D. H. Lawrence—a strange addition—and herself. Pound, who never liked playing second fiddle to anyone else, refused to be associated with the venture. She signed a contract with the chosen six for three anthologies to be published at yearly intervals.

When the war came, in August 1914, she returned to the United States, but did not abandon her project for the anthologies. The first appeared in 1915, the second in 1916, and the third and final one in 1917. The first had a long Preface which laid down the principles of

Imagism, and the ideas were largely borrowed from Pound and Hulme.
They were very much opposed to Romanticism—and that was why they
admired Flaubert—and Hulme considered that the nineteenth century
had seen the culmination of the romantic spirit which, according to
him, was a pernicious drug. In *Speculations* he said:

> 'The awful result of Romanticism is that, accustomed to this
> strange light, you can never live without it. Its effect on you is that
> of a drug. We shall not get any new efflorescence of verse until we
> get a new technique, and a new convention to turn ourselves loose
> in. Romanticism, like a pot of treacle poured over a dinner-table, is
> spilt religion.'

The rules of Imagism, as set out in the Preface to the 1915 anthology,
insisted that poetry should use the language of common speech, and
employ the exact word—not merely the nearly exact. It must create
new rhythms, as the expression of new moods, and not copy old
rhythms, which merely echo old moods. The Preface did not insist on
vers libre although it declared that the individuality of the poet could
best express itself in free verse. It insisted especially on the poet's
complete liberty in the choice of subject, and on the artistic value of the
depiction of modern life, but modern life seen as it is and not as the
poet has been taught to see it. Finally it advised concentration as the
essence of real poetry—that is why the poems of the Imagists are
usually very short and concise.

With the last anthology of Imagist poetry in 1917, the movement
is at an end. Amy Lowell then wrote, in *Tendencies in Modern American
Poetry*:

> 'There will be no more volumes of *Some Imagist Poets*. The
> collection has done its work. Those three little books are the
> nucleus of the school; its spreading out, its amplifications, must be
> sought in the published work of the individual members of the
> group.'

The Egoist did not, however, come to an end then, but lasted for six
further years. During its first year it had appeared fortnightly, then,
after January 1915, it became a monthly publication. In 1917 Aldington
went to the war, and thus relinquished the editorship. Eliot undertook
the task, and occupied the chair until the review came to an end in
December 1919—but, during its last year, it had appeared only five
times. The principal contributors all through its life had been the

Imagists, but not merely the six chosen by Amy Lowell. Pound, Eliot, and Aldington were the most frequent contributors, but there were also contributions by James Joyce, Storm Jameson, and Wyndham Lewis. Joyce's *Portrait of the Artist as a Young Man* was serialized in it, and it would also have published his *Ulysses* if a printer could have been found to undertake the task, but all refused on account of its obscenity of language.

The Imagists also wrote for *The Little Review*. In February 1915 Aldington published in it his article entitled 'The Case of French Poetry'. This was an answer to an attack on the value of French literature by Edward Shanks. Aldington declared that if his opinion were the same as that of Shanks, he would not fight in the war on the side of the Allies, or he would fight for Germany. He maintained that French poetry 'was the first of our age in fertility, in scope and in charm in general'.

In 1918, in the February number of *The Little Review*, there appeared an article by Ezra Pound in praise of Corbière, Rimbaud, and Laforgue. Indeed this number is almost an anthology of modern French poetry, for it printed two of Laforgue's Pierrot poems, and several of his *Complaintes*; five poems by Rimbaud, two by Henri de Régnier, one by Verhaeren, one by Vielé-Griffin, and there were also poems by Vildrac, Moréas, and Jules Romains. It was a very comprehensive anthology. In the July number that year *The Little Review* published translations from Rimbaud's *Illuminations*.

The Imagist School was the most important group of poetry in the years preceding and during the First World War. Eliot, writing in July 1937, declared, in *The Criterion*: 'The accomplishment of the Imagist Movement seems to have been critical rather than creative, and as criticism very important.' Its work of criticism was to import the influence of France. It did also produce one important poet in Pound, who transcended the limits of the movement.

By the time the First World War broke out the realist example of Corbière and Laforgue was well established in England, and thenceforth it was adopted by many who were not directly influenced by French poetry. Those who, like Wilfred Owen, were able to adapt the mood to their personal war experience, were the poets to be most influential when peace came. Yeats, however, was to call the poetry of Owen 'all blood, dirt and sucked sugar-stick'—but he did not like coarse and brutal realism.

Wilfred Owen had visited France before the war as a private tutor in Bordeaux, and there he met Laurent Tailhade, whom the Imagists greatly admired, and Owen had shown him his own poetry, receiving encouragement and advice from him. He remained in Bordeaux from

F

1913 to 1915, then he returned to England, joined the Artists Rifles, and was killed in France a week before the Armistice in 1918.

Owen's poetry has the directness and realism which are found in Corbière, Rimbaud, or Laforgue, and which is very different from the soft sentimentalities of Rupert Brooke. *Dulce et Decorum* does not depict the noble aspect of war, and it possesses the bitter irony to be found in Corbière, as do many other of his poems inspired by the life in the trenches:

'Bent double, like old beggars under sacks,
    Knock-kneed, coughing like hags, we cursed through sludge,
Till on the haunting flares we turned our backs,
    And towards our distant rest began to trudge.
We marched asleep. Many had lost their boots,
    But limped on, blood-shod. All went lame, all blind;
Drunk with fatigue; deaf even to the hoots
    Of gas-shells dropping softly behind.'

This recalls Corbière's poem *La Pastorale de Conlie* in *Les Amours Jaunes*:

'À ceux-là qui tombaient bayant à la bataille,
    Ramas de vermine sans nom,
Espérant le premier qui vint crier: Canaille!
    Au canon, la chair à canon . . .

—Allons donc: l'abattoir!—Bestiaux galeux qu'on rosse,
    On nous fournit aux Prussiens;
Et, nous voyant rouler-plat sous les coups de crosse,
    Des Français aboyaient—Bons chiens!'

As the war ended, the poet in England who best represented the new ideals in poetry was T. S. Eliot, the editor of *The Egoist*. He was far nearer in sympathy to the new age than Yeats, for he was in the centre of the revolutionary group, at a time when Yeats was still gazing at wild swans at Coole. Eliot, at this time, was a far more disturbing influence on the young than Yeats, and those who grew up after the First World War will never forget the impact which *The Waste Land* made on them when it appeared in 1922.

Eliot, like the poets of the Imagist group with whom he had been associated, was profoundly affected by French literature. At Harvard he had studied under Irving Babbitt, though he cannot have obtained much illumination from that retrograde and unenterprising critic. But, between 1907 and 1908, he read Baudelaire—as he said later—'with great impact'. In June 1944, writing in *La France Libre*, he said that if he had not discovered Baudelaire and all his descendants, he would never have been able to write.

In 1908, when he was twenty, he read the book which of almost all others had most effect on him, *The Symbolist Movement in Literature*, by Arthur Symons, and this opened for him a world of which Babbitt had given him no suspicion, for he was led to Corbière, Rimbaud, and Laforgue. Before reading Symons' book, he had not greatly liked the poetry of Symbolism, which he had known only through the anthology of Van Bever and Léautaud, which had concentrated very strongly on the more sentimental poets of the movement, such as Samain, Régnier, and Guérin. He never cared for the decadent side of Symbolism and, in 1917, he wrote on 19 May, in *The New Statesman*: 'Time has left us many things, but amongst those it has taken away, we hope to count *À Rebours*.'

Now, through Symons, he discovered Corbière and Laforgue, and they became his masters, giving him a new conception of poetry. At this time they were nearer his preoccupations than Baudelaire. Many years later, writing in *Purpose*, in July 1940, he declared that 'the kind of poetry I needed, to teach me the use of my own voice, did not exist in England at all, and was only to be found in France'. He found particular stimulus in Laforgue because he expressed, even more than Corbière or Baudelaire, the problems of his own age, and he renewed poetry since he had understood modern man. 'Laforgue and Corbière were,' he said, 'masters more than any English poets of their time.'

In 1910 Eliot went to Paris and, as he said in *La France Libre* in June 1944, it was no accident that had brought him there, since France, for several years, had represented for him the soul of poetry. He attended lectures at the Sorbonne; he met Alain-Fournier, who made him read Claudel and Gide, and who also introduced him to his brother-in-law, Rivière; he went to hear Bergson at the Collège de France.

After Paris Eliot returned to Harvard before going to Oxford for a year, and finally arrived in London as the Imagist Movement was getting into its stride. He heard of Remy de Gourmont, and this had an influence on his critical writings, for Eliot was to become equally eminent in criticism as in poetry. Gourmont was very useful to those who were trying to shake off earlier influences, and Pound used to call him a purge, or a cleansing force. From his *Problème du Style*, Eliot learned the importance of style and diction, and he wrote in

The Egoist, in May 1918 : 'Every writer who does not help to develop the language is to that extent to which he is now read, a positive agent of deterioration.' In the Preface to *The Sacred Wood* he acknowledged his debt to Gourmont, saying:

> 'I was much helped and much stimulated by the critical writings of Remy de Gourmont. I acknowledge that influence and am grateful for it; and I by no means disown it by having passed on to another problem not touched upon in this book; that of the relation of poetry to the spiritual and social life of its time.'

This was written at the time when he was becoming interested in the moral aspect of Baudelaire's work.

Through Gourmont Eliot came into contact with Flaubert's ideas on art and literature. In 'Lettre d'Angleterre', in *La Nouvelle Revue Française,* in November 1923, he declared that Gourmont had made him study Flaubert 'lequel fut un maître à la fois d'art et de pensée'. Many of Eliot's aesthetic ideas came from Flaubert. The latter had protested against Romantic subjectivity, and thought that there should be complete detachment on the part of the author, that literature should not be a 'déversoir' for personal emotion. In *The Sacred Wood* Eliot said: 'Poetry is not an overflow of emotion. Poetry is not the turning loose of emotion, but an escape from emotion; it is not the expression of personality, but an escape from it.' And, in *After Strange Gods*, he declared:

> 'What is disastrous is that the writer should deliberately give rein to his individuality; that he should cultivate his difference from others; and that his readers should cherish the author of genius not in spite of his deviations from the inherited wisdom of the race, but because of them.'

This is very different from the cult of personality of the Romantics. Again, in *After Strange Gods*, he writes: 'The cult of emotion seems to me a symptom of decadence; it is a cardinal point of faith in a romantic age to believe that there is something admirable in violent emotion for its own sake.'

Flaubert believed that each subject should possess its own style, not that each author should have an individual style stamped with his own hall-mark; he believed that writing should be like clear water, which revealed but did not distort what was being described. Eliot says something very similar when he writes:

'that art which I have long aimed at, in writing poetry, is to write poetry which should be essentially poetry, with nothing poetic about it, poetry standing naked to its bare bones, a poetry so transparent that we should not see the poetry but that which we are meant to see through the poetry. Poetry so transparent that in reading it we are intent on what the poem *points at*, and not on the poetry, this seems to me the thing to try for.'

In 1917 Eliot's first collection of poems, *Prufrock and other Observations*, burst upon the public and began—as Edith Sitwell was to say—'a new reign in poetry'. The writer with whom Eliot has most affinity in these poems is Laforgue, and echoes of his voice are heard in most of the poems—in *Conversation Galante*, in *Portrait of a Lady*, in *The Love Song of J. Alfred Prufrock*, and in *La Figlia che piange*. Eliot borrowed from Laforgue his obsession with the squalor and decay of a modern industrial town, all the trivial detail which we find in *Preludes* and in *Rhapsody on a Windy Night*, all the boredom, and sense of frustration, the weariness and self-doubt of modern man. But there is similarity also with Apollinaire in this predilection for dirty sordid alleys, with unemptied dustbins. We have seen that Apollinaire in this has also affinity with Laforgue, and so Eliot would not have needed to go for it any further than Laforgue. Nevertheless the opening of *The Love Song of J. Alfred Prufrock* is nearer, in imagery, to Apollinaire than to Laforgue, when it says:

'Let us go then, you and I,
  When the evening is spread out against the sky
  Like a patient etherised upon a table.'

The imagery and rhythm of *Rhapsody on a Windy Night* are reminiscent of the poems in *vers libres*, in *Derniers Vers* by Laforgue, as, for instance, *L'Hiver qui vient*:

'Mais, lainages, caoutchoucs, pharmacie, rêve,
  Rideaux écartés du haut des balcons des grèves,
  Devant l'océan de toitures des faubourgs,
  Lampes, estampes, thé, petits-fours,
  Serez-vous pas mes seules amours!
  (oh! et puis, est-ce que tu connais, outre les pianos,
  Le sobre et vespéral mystère hebdomadaire
  Des statistiques sanitaires
  Dans les journaux?)

Non, non! c'est la saison et la planète falote!
Que l'autan, que l'autan,
Effiloche les savates que le Temps se tricote!
C'est la saison, oh déchirements! c'est la saison!
Tous les ans, tous les ans,
J'essaierai en chœur d'en donner la note.'

In these first poems Eliot borrowed much from Laforgue—in his Introduction to Ezra Pound's *Selected Poems* he declared that his own free verse was 'directly drawn from a study of Laforgue'. However, what he took he made into something new, which was entirely his. In *The Sacred Wood* he said:

'Immature poets imitate; mature poets steal; bad poets deface what they take, and good poets make it into something better, or at least something different. The good poet welds his theft into a whole of feeling which is unique, utterly different from that from which it was torn; the bad poet throws it into something which has no cohesion.'

That was indeed what he did with his own borrowings from Laforgue.

In his second collection, *Poems*, published in 1920, the influence of Corbière is more prominent than that of Laforgue—especially in the poems written in French. The title of one poem, *Mélange Adultère de tout*, is taken from Corbière's epitaph for himself, *Epitaphe pour Tristan-Joachim-Édouard Corbière Philosophe*; *Le Directeur* is also written in the Corbière style, and *Lune de Miel* has affinities with his *Veder Napoli*.

In *The Waste Land*, published in 1922, the main influence is now that of Baudelaire. Although he was one of the first French poets whom he had read, he did not draw on him for inspiration until now, when his own inspiration was growing in depth and he was becoming attracted by the religious aspect of the French poet, his spirituality and his revulsion against the sins of the flesh. It was the elevation in Baudelaire which Eliot admired, his way of raising the everyday into something majestic, with absence of the deliberately trivial note found in Laforgue. In *Selected Essays* he says of Baudelaire:

'It is not merely in the use of imagery of common life, not merely in the use of the imagery of the sordid life of a great metropolis, but in the elevation of such imagery to the *first intensity* —presenting it as it is, and yet making it represent something much more than itself—that Baudelaire has created a mode of release and expression for other men.'

Eliot was the first person in England to have appreciated the spiritual aspect of Baudelaire's work—at that time it was rarely noticed even in France. In 1922, in his essay on the French poet, entitled 'The Lesson of Baudelaire', published in *Tyro*, he wrote:

'All first-rate poetry is occupied with morality. That is the lesson of Baudelaire. As for (English) verse of the present time, the lack of curiosity in technical matters of the academic poets of today is only an indication of their lack of curiosity in moral matters.'

It was from Baudelaire that he now learned to escape from reality, the sordid reality, which had hitherto been an obsession with him, and which seemed to him now so vain. In *The Waste Land* he progressed to that 'expansion of reality' which he admired in Baudelaire, as well as in Dante. He wanted now to escape from destruction and the desolation of the waste lands. In 1922 he was awarded by *The Dial*—the New York magazine—their poetry prize for his *Waste Land*, and became the most significant poet in the English language of his day. In the same year he was appointed editor of *The Criterion*, which was modelled on *La Nouvelle Revue Française*, founded in France by Gide and his associates in 1909, and he now had a paper in which to propagate his own views of literature.

In 1925, in his *Hollow Men*, he described a dying civilization of hollow and stuffed men, with their headpieces filled with straw:

'Shape without form, shade without colour,
Paralysed force, gesture without emotion.'

They symbolize the old world ending 'not with a bang, but with a whimper'.

Eliot was gradually emerging from despair, and he was eventually to find himself in his form of Christianity. His moral progress was very similar to that of Baudelaire, who moved from Satanism and revolt to belief in moral values, and who, at the end, found peace in Catholicism.

In France Paul Valéry, on his return to literature, after his twenty years of silence, with *La Jeune Parque*, in 1917, was the most considerable poet in the period between the two world wars. However, although English poets admired him—he was very much a poet's poet—translated him and quoted him, he had no followers in England any

more than he had a school in France. He was completely out of sympathy with the largest group of poets in France after the First World
War, the Surrealists, whom he considered barbarous. He was a classi-
cist, who admired intellectual discipline and self-control, who valued
what man had made of himself, and not what he was by accident, or
subconsciously. In the Preface to Cohen's commentary on his *Cimetière Marin*, he declared: 'Je n'aime que le travail. Le spontané, même
excellent, même séduisant, ne me semble jamais assez bien.' He had a
horror of the revelations of the subconscious, or of the use of dreams,
and in *Variété* he says: 'La véritable condition d'un véritable poète est
ce qu'il y a de plus distinct de l'état de rêve.' And, protesting against the
automatic writing of the Surrealists, he said, in *Lettre sur Mullarmé*:

> 'S'abandonner à l'inspiration, aux forces cachées, c'est jouer
> à la pêche miraculeuse ... J'aimerais infiniment mieux écrire en toute
> conscience, et dans une certaine lucidité quelquechose de faible,
> que d'enfanter, à la faveur d'une transe, et hors de moi-même, un
> chef d'œuvre d'entre les plus beaux.'

He was interested in poetic creation as an intellectual exercise, as
an artistic game of chess, and he would have liked to have been able to
use a technique like that of music, devoid of emotion. Indeed his poems
are studied, line by line, like a musical score. He would have liked to
have lived in a world of pure musical sounds. In *Mémoires d'un Poème*
he says:

> 'J'avoue que je me sens parfois au cœur une morsure de l'envie
> quand je me représente ce musicien savant aux prises avec l'im-
> mense page aux vingt portées, distribuant sur ce champ réglé son
> calcul des temps et des formes. . . . Son action me semble divine.'

This form of art, unfortunately, he said, was denied to poets as, on
the whole, the public insisted on a specific meaning being given to each
poem. In *La Nouvelle Revue Française*, he wrote in February 1930:

> 'Mes vers ont le sens qu'on leur prête. C'est une erreur contraire
> à la nature de la poésie, et qui lui serait mortelle, que de prétendre
> qu'à tout poème correspond un sens véritable, unique et conforme
> ou identique à quelque pensée de l'auteur.'

This obscurity of interpretation has been the characteristic which has
attracted to Valéry academic critics in every country. But it has dimin-

ished his influence on others, and his appeal to them. But he did not ask to appeal to a large audience, and he was satisfied to be appreciated and understood by a small number of scientific specialists with similar interests. This meant that he could receive admiration and appreciation for his noble and perfect compositions in the art of poetry, but not the flattering sympathy of disciples or imitation. He was too classical and logically intellectual to have much impact on English poets, and Yeats did not appreciate him, considering him inhuman and cold.

The most characteristic school of poetry in the nineteen-twenties in France was that of the Surrealists. It expressed, as no other movement could, the restlessness, the uncertainty of values, the lack of discipline of the time. Surrealism was a revolt against everything, against nationality, against society, against intellectual and moral values—it was a revolt against art itself. The writers of the movement claimed that, before anything new could be created, all previous standards had to be destroyed and swept away—all dogmas and beliefs. It was a desperate, and despairing, effort to escape from what had previously been regarded as the law of life; it was an attempt to create a new life and a new law. They reached the general negations of everything. 'L'homme n'est rien,' they said. 'Tout se vaut! Rien ne vaut! Vouloir distinguer le vrai du faux dénote une outrecuidance ridicule.'

As they freed themselves from standards of art and morality, so too they wished to free themselves from the ordinary limitations of the material world as they saw it. Like the painters of the time, they freed themselves from the necessity of depicting known objects at all, for they considered that conventional minds had stabilized subjects in a fixed manner.

The Surrealist Movement developed out of *Dada*, which we saw reached Paris in 1917 from Zürich, where it had started with Tristan Tzara after the war.

Strictly speaking, Surrealism is not an aesthetic movement at all, and the poets very rarely discuss beauty. They were psychologists rather than artists, who wished to get at the real quality in man, and, to achieve this, they considered that all the control of reason should be removed. They tried to reach truth, as Rimbaud had done, through the 'dérèglement de tous les sens'. They went further than he had gone, and Breton and Eluard imitated the external symptoms of dementia praecox, hoping thereby to acquire, for artistic purposes, the subconscious outlook of a lunatic. In this way, they thought, the last vestiges of reasonable control would be obliterated. In their joint work, *L'Immaculée Conception*, they gave a record of their experiences in this field.

They considered that dreams were a valuable indication of hidden verities, and they tried to reach what Gérard de Nerval had called 'un état supernaturaliste'. André Breton, in his *Vases Communicants*, studies the connection between Surrealism and dreams, claiming that since dreams are part of the life of man, they should be capable of objective analysis. Dreams led them to the subconscious, and they aimed at exploring the hidden depths of man, where lurk the obsessions. They were much interested in the theories of Freud, and this explains the pornographic nature of much of their writing. They believed that, in the fantasies of the unconscious, in spite of their incoherence, lay real wisdom and truth, and, as they wrote, they allowed the images to flow without restraint or direction. In the *Manifeste du Surréalisme*, as translated by David Gascoyne, Breton says:

> 'Surrealism is a pure psychic automatism, by which it is intended to express, verbally, in writing, or by other means, the real process of thought and thought's dictation, in the absence of all control exercised by the reason and outside all aesthetic or moral preoccupations. Surrealism rests on the belief in the superior reality of certain forms of association neglected hitherto; in the omnipotence of the dream, and in the disinterested play of thought.'

André Breton advised poets to write, without any preconceived subject, at random, the first things that come into their minds, and not reread or correct their work. The eccentric texts thus obtained, he claimed, might bring the elements of a fragmentary answer to the great questions which moralists and thinkers have been asking since the beginning of time.

The Surrealists had various methods of attaining this fortuitous association of images which seemed to them revealing. Tristan Tzara used to say:

> 'Take a newspaper, take a pair of scissors, choose any article in the paper. Cut it out, then cut out each of the words. Jumble them up in a bag, then tumble them out and group them in sentences as they come out, and that will be a poem.'

They also invented a game which was called *Exquisite Corpses* after a sentence produced at one of the performances. A certain number of players sit round a table and pass round a sheet of paper. Each player in turn writes a word of a sentence, according to a set of rules—noun, adjective, and so forth. He passes the sheet to his neighbour, who continues the process, without looking at what he has written. It is like the game of consequences. When the sentences are finished they are read out, and the results thus obtained were supposed to be revealing. The following are frequently quoted. 'The winged vapour seduces the locked bird.' 'The Senegal oyster will eat up the tricolour bread.' 'The anaemic little girl makes the polished mannequin blush.'

In October 1924 André Breton published his *Manifeste du Surréalisme*, which set forth the aims of the movement. These were based on revolt in every manner, but they were more *anti* everything than *pro* anything. They were anti-bourgeois, anti-literature, anti-moral, anti-religious, and anti-patriotic. Their positive attitude was that they were —in the modern expression—*engagés* socially. The time had come, Eluard said in *Poetic Evidence*, 'for poets to proclaim their right and duty to maintain that they were deeply involved in the life of other men, in communal interests'. They considered that all the ivory towers must be razed to the ground—that explains why so many of the Surrealists became Communists.

The authors whom they most read and admired were Freud, on account of his exploration of the unconscious; the Marquis de Sade, because they considered that he had liberated the force of love; Rimbaud on account of his spirit of revolt, and his incapacity for submission; Lautréamont, whose *Chants de Maldoror* they were responsible for making accessible to the public, in a complete edition in 1920, on account of his blasphemous abuse of the Almighty, because his work was the epic of modern disillusioned man, and because of the inconsequence of his juxtaposition of images. A description of his which they were fond of quoting was: 'Il est beau comme la rencontre fortuite, sur une table de dissection, d'une machine à coudre et d'un parapluie.' And finally Charles Cros, on account of the liberties which he had taken with language, and whose *Coffret de Santal*, published in 1873, seemed to them the first Surrealist text.

The Surrealists used a free technique, and most of their poems are in free verse, or in a free form of prose poem, but neither possessed any formal structure—the subconscious cannot be expected to count syllables or follow a recurring pattern. With such ideals it is very easy to cheat, since all artistic and intellectual effort is derided, and on account of the theory of the linking of incompatibles; it is easy, with such a theory, to string together images that are startlingly original or eccentric, but which express nothing at all.

After reading much of this kind of verse it becomes clear that in such poetry—as in all others as well—it is only those who are, by

nature, gifted with powers of imagination, taste, and talent for writing—
as well as experience in the art—whose unconscious mind is worthy of
investigation. The plants that spring up in this strange soil only produce rare blooms when these are carefully tended as soon as they reach
the surface, the light of day. Only poets who have learnt their trade can
make a valuable use of their discoveries in their unconscious. Only true
poets, like Eluard, born and trained poets, can transcend the obstacles
which such a method imposes on the artist. Eluard was certainly the
most gifted and skilful of all the Surrealist poets—the outstanding poet
writing in France in the nineteen-thirties. His *Capitale de la Douleur*
and his *Vie Immédiate* are amongst the most beautiful collections of
verse at that time. His vision of human destiny, drawn from his conception of universal existence, owes much to his Surrealist practices,
but he was able to make of them works of art.

In 1936 Surrealism crossed the Channel and arrived in England—
though it was well known before that—through the works on the movement by Herbert Read and David Gascoyne published that year, and
through the exhibition held in London.

Gascoyne is the only English poet in whom a definite influence of
Surrealism can be traced—in him it was deliberate and he knew intimately the French poets and their writings—but many others were
unconsciously subjected to it, and have affinities with it.

As the undisciplined twenties moved towards their close the
younger poets in England, as those in France, were becoming more
engagés than they had been at the time of the Imagists. Eliot's *Ash
Wednesday*, published in 1930, marks an important step in his spiritual
progress. In that poem, as in those which followed it, the influence of
France is less obvious than it had been hitherto, and he was turning for
inspiration towards the English Metaphysical poets. He still owed
something to Baudelaire, especially to his spiritual ideas; he owed something also to the philosophy of Maritain, and his *Four Quartets* will
have some affinity with Mallarmé in their withdrawal from vulgar
reality. He now believed, as Baudelaire had done, in the value of
specific inspiration and did not agree with the Surrealists in considering that 'tout se vaut'. He remained completely untouched by the
Surrealist influence. In *Selected Essays* he said: 'The suggestiveness of
true poetry . . . is the aura round a bright clear centre. You cannot have
the aura alone.' His taste in French poetry had also somewhat changed,
and his next interest, Saint-John Perse, whose *Anabase* he translated in
1930, is in another poetic world from Corbière or Laforgue, with his
rich, exotic and unrealistic imagery. In the Introduction which he wrote
for Chiari's *Contemporary French Poets*, Eliot declared: 'Saint-John

Perse will prove to have been a greater influence on Anglo-American verse than is yet recognized.' He does not, however, state on which poets he sees this influence.

Yeats reached the pinnacle of his achievement in *The Tower*, published in 1928, and in *The Winding Stair*, published in 1933. It cannot, however, be claimed that, after he had abandoned French Symbolism, he was much affected by French poetry. He was not interested in Surrealism, and he did not care for the poetry of Valéry—in fact he does not seem to have appreciated any twentieth-century French poet. It may be that the realism of language and imagery of Corbière, Laforgue, and Apollinaire had some influence on his changed vocabulary after *The Green Helmet*, but it is more likely that this came from the general shift in poetic inspiration in England, just before and after the First World War. A poem from *The Winding Stair*, entitled *Vacillations*, and composed in 1931, owes something to the fashion for trivial everyday realism:

> 'My fiftieth year had come and gone,
> I sat, a solitary man,
> In a crowded London shop,
> An open book and empty cup
> On the marble table-top.'

He was writing increasingly in the modern conversational idiom. In 1926, in a letter to Herbert Grierson, he said: 'My own verse has more and more adopted—seemingly without any will of mine—the syntax and vocabulary of common speech.'

It was nevertheless very different from the common speech adopted by the French poets at the time—or by the English, on their model—for he was always more metaphysical, even when colloquial, than his contemporaries. Edmund Wilson wrote, in a passage quoted by Day Lewis, in his *Notable Images of Virtue*:

> 'His words, no matter how prosaic they are, are always somehow luminous and subtle. . . . He succeeds in dignifying such subjects, as perhaps no other contemporary poet has done, at the same time that he never ceases to deal with them without sentimentality and in the plainest language.'

Yeats, however, remained a solitary figure, aloof from the general tendencies of his age in poetry, and it was as if he were, unconsciously, fulfilling what he had, in his youth, prophesied about Irish poetry: that when it came, it would be 'distinguished and lonely'. That description could be applied to him. Yet, in his solitude, at the top of his winding stair, and in his lonely tower, he was the greatest, richest, noblest, and most varied poet writing in the English language during the first half of the twentieth century, the most spiritually satisfying.

Next to Eliot, Edith Sitwell is the English poet, in the years between the two wars, who was most saturated with French poetry. It is clear, from her *Note Book*, that she was intimately acquainted with the writings of Baudelaire, Mallarmé, Corbière, Rimbaud, and Laforgue, and that they affected her theories of art—her imagery and symbolism. There was no one single poet who exercised on her as much influence as Laforgue or Corbière had exercised on Eliot, but there are echoes in her work of the French poets, whom she read with sympathy. The ghost of both Baudelaire's *Un Voyage* and Rimbaud's *Les Poètes de Sept Ans* hovers in her *Sleeping Beauty*:

> 'When we were young, how beautiful life seemed!—
> The boundless bright horizons that we dreamed,
>
> And the immortal music of the Day and Night,
> Leaving the echo of their wonder and their might
>
> Deep in our hearts and minds. How could the dust
> Of superstitions taught in schoolrooms, lust
>
> In love's shape, dim our beauty? What dark lie,
> Of cruelty's voice, could drown this God-made harmony?'

But, as was also the case with Baudelaire, age dimmed her 'innocent paradises'. She shared the longing of Baudelaire and Rimbaud, to recapture the pure and unalloyed sensations of childhood. She says that her aim in writing *Façade* was the same as Cocteau's when he composed his *Parade*, and that it was the 'poetry of childhood taken over by the technician'.

Echoes of Corbière and Laforgue are also heard in her use of the folk-song, or nursery rhyme—as for instance in *The Sleeping Beauty*:

> 'Do, do,
> Princess, do,
> The Fairy Chatte blanche rocks you slow.'

Or in *Aubade*:

> 'Jane, Jane,
> Tall as a crane,
> The morning light creaks down again.'

Or in *Popular Song*:

> 'Lily O'Grady,
> Silly and shady,
> Longing to be
> A lazy lady.'

Her use of *correspondances* is similar to that of Baudelaire and, in her Preface to her *Collected Poems*, she talks of the manifestations of the world being 'correspondences whereby we may speak with angels'. Her further use of *correspondances* between the different senses is similar to that of Mallarmé. The end of *Romance* is in the Mallarmean manner:

> 'So fading from the branches the snow sang
> With a strange perfume, a melodious twang
> As if a rose could change into a ghost—
> A ghost turn to a perfume on the leaves.'

Of a dog she says that 'his smell was as dark and damp as grottoes'.

When Edith Sitwell began to write during the First World War, it was the time when it was obvious that a change in poetry had become necessary, in imagery and rhythm, owing—as she said in the Preface to her *Collected Poems*—'to the rhythmical flaccidity, the dead and expected patterns of some of the poetry immediately preceding us'. It was then that she and her brothers founded *Wheels* in 1916, in opposition to *Georgian Poetry*, in order to point the way to more interesting and adventurous experiments. Most of her poetry during the nineteen-twenties was technically experimental, and it followed on the lines of such poets as Corbière, Laforgue, and Apollinaire. She declared that her *Façade* was composed of 'abstract poems—that were patterns of sound'. Her experiments in technique are reminiscent of those of the French poets; as, for instance, in *Fantasia for a Mouth-Organ*:

> 'I had a mother-in-
> Law; no other kin
> Could be so kind, said
> He.

> She wrung me on the mangle
> When the hot sun's jangle
> Bent the North Pole to South, and
> The
> Wind hyperborean
> Dried the Marmorean
> Wash for a nominal
> Fee.'

All through the nineteen-twenties Edith Sitwell had felt a growing discontent with the ugliness of contemporary reality. This culminated in her *Gold Coast Customs*, published in 1929, which is in a deeper vein than any of her previous poetry, and foreshadows her future works during the sufferings of the Second World War. Its inspiration is similar to that of *The Waste Land*. The poem was written in anguish, and she said that she would not willingly 'relive that birth'. It is the denunciation of the hideous emptiness and bestiality of modern life, and she has shown the contrast between the 'haves' and the 'have nots', between the primitive people and their exploiting overlords.

Her greatest and deepest poetry was composed during and after the Second World War, in a period outside the scope of this study. During the war, with suffering and compassion, her disgust and disillusionment eventually blossomed into idealism and Christian hope. In *The Shadow of Cain*, published in 1947, she expressed the confidence that, in spite of pessimism, there are still grounds for hope, and that Christ did not die in vain. The collections composed after the outbreak of the war contain some of the finest and most deeply moving poetry of our age.

A new spirit in literature manifested itself in the poets who reached adult life in the nineteen-thirties—especially in the Oxford Quartet, Auden, Day Lewis, Spender, and MacNeice. They had been disturbed, as everyone else had been, by Eliot's *The Waste Land*, but they did not want to remain imprisoned in it for ever, neither did they wish to follow its author to his new heights, whence came his traditional Christian Tables of the Law. They believed that they could escape from the impasse of *The Waste Land* into social service. They were all very much concerned with the affairs of the age, and determined to remedy them. As Louis MacNeice said in *Modern Poetry*, published in 1938:

> 'It is probably true that, for the production of major literature, or literature on a large scale, a sympathy is required in the writer with those forces which, at the moment, make for progress.'

And Stephen Spender, discussing the spirit of the nineteen-thirties in *The Creative Element*, published in 1953, wrote:

'Regarded as a literary phenomenon, the movement of the 1930's reflected a shift from individualist vision towards an ideological orthodoxy based on a political creed. The shift was inevitable, because the events of the 1930's, which showed the interrelatedness of class interests at the base of society, shattered the myth of a completely isolated individual—anti-bourgeois and outside everything—who was the individualist writer. For with the unemployed in the industrial cities of Europe, and with intellectuals in concentration camps in Germany and Italy, he was no longer an outsider, unrelated to anything but his work, responsible to nothing but his artistic conscience. . . . The *poète maudit* of the earlier part of the century was transformed into the "intellectual" opposing fascism and supporting the Spanish Republicans of the 1930's.'

These intellectuals were called upon to take sides and their sympathies were enlisted. At the same time they saw, opening out before them, the possibilities of a different kind of literature, based upon social hope. Then they came under the influence of the French novelist, André Malraux, who had travelled along the same path as they were following, and whose novel, *L'Espoir*, was a banner of new hope for them.

Like their contemporaries in France, all the poets of the nineteen-thirties were interested in Freud, Sade and Marx, and most of them became—for a time at all events—members of the Communist Party, and many of them were implicated, on the Republican side, in the Spanish Civil War in 1936. Like Gide, at this time, they believed that salvation could only come from the Soviet Union.

John Lehmann's *New Writing*, founded in 1936, represented the new ideal of the time. Later he was to say that his aim had been:

'To review what had been one of the most interesting developments in our literature for many years: the growth during the early nineteen-thirties of a group of poets and prose writers who were conscious of great social, political, and moral changes going on around them, and who became increasingly convinced that it was their business to communicate their vision of this process, not merely to the so-called high-brow intellectual public, to which their predecessors had addressed themselves, but to the widest circle of ordinary people engaged in the daily struggle for existence.'

The new writers felt that they must abandon their habit of addressing themselves to a small élite, and write lucidly, without any paraphernalia of erudite allusions or private jokes. They were now approaching the working-classes and the broader masses of the people, in the belief that among them the real drama of our times was being played out.

The realism practised by the new poets was a direct development of the attitude to reality of Corbière, Laforgue, and Apollinaire—which they may only have known second-hand through Eliot—to which they have given a Communist slant. Of all French poets the one with whom they had most affinity in spirit, if not in literary style, was Arthur Rimbaud. Most of them, like Auden and Spender, wrote of him with interest, and they were particularly attracted by his personality and his destiny. His disgust with the world around him was the same as theirs, his violent iconoclasm, and his desire to sweep away all vestige of the past, so as to build a better world. He too wanted to leave decaying Europe behind him, and to go out towards a new people unspoilt by so-called civilization. He cries:

'Et toute vengeance? Rien! . . .—Mais si, toute encor,
Nous la voulons! Industriels, princes, sénats:
Périssez! Puissances, justice, histoire à bas!
Ça nous est dû. Le Sang! le sang! la flamme d'or!

Tout à la guerre, à la vengeance, à la terreur,
Mon esprit! Tournons dans la morsure: Ah! passez,
Républiques de ce monde! Des empereurs,
Des régiments, des colons, des peuples, assez!

Europe, Asie, Amérique, disparaissez,
Notre marche vengeresse a tout occupé,
Cités et campagnes!—Nous serons écrasés!
Les volcans sauteront! Et l'Océan frappé . . .

Oh! mes amis!—Mon cœur, c'est sûr, ils sont mes frères:
Noirs inconnus, si nous allions! Allons! allons!
O malheur! je me sens frémir, la vieille terre,
Sur moi de plus en plus à vous! la terre fond!'

Cecil Day Lewis said in 1934, in *A Hope for Poetry*, that the verse of his own generation had, as immediate ancestors, Owen, Hopkins, and Eliot. The influence of Hopkins was largely in the realms of technique, and he owed nothing to French literature, but, through

Owen and Eliot, the poets of the nineteen-thirties imbibed many of the theories of French poetry. Like their counterparts in France, they believed that the new poetry should speak with a new language and new rhythms; that the imagery should be drawn from modern life, its vocabulary from modern speech, and that the rhythms should be those of colloquial idiom.

10

FICTION

THERE was less direct influence of France on English fiction between the two wars than on poetry—at least the influence was less acknowledged.

The novel, at the end of the nineteenth century in England, had been much influenced by French Naturalism, but that had been somewhat diminishing since the beginning of the twentieth century, or rather, it had become modified, and a form of indigenous realism, more in keeping with the traditions of the country, had sprung up, the kind of realism found in H. G. Wells, Bennett, and Galsworthy. These novelists had developed their own way of using the realistic material which they found in their own country. As the century opened, the novel seemed to settle down to realism in some form or other. Fiction was the picture of the life of the time, and Wells, Bennett, and Galsworthy continued in an English way what had previously been done in a French way. They would probably have disclaimed any influence from France, or any interest in what happened in that country.

In France, after the decline of Naturalism, and the failure of the Symbolist Movement, the novel, although efficient, proficient, and well written, was developing on orthodox and conventional lines, and was not experimenting in an interesting manner. There was no reason why England—or indeed any other country—should look to France at this time for inspiration. Naturalism was out of date, as it attempted to depict only the outside of characters, while, with the new developments of psychology, those who were interested in progress wished to take advantage of this new science, in order to render the hidden depths of character.

The English continued to read French novels, to translate them, but not to imitate them. Some depth-charge was needed to blow fiction out of its rut. This happened in 1913 when Proust published the first volume of his work, *Du Côté de chez Swann*, which was a world-shattering event. He had submitted it to *La Nouvelle Revue Française* publishing house in 1911, but it was refused, and he eventually brought it out at his own expense with Grasset. It did not arouse any exceptional interest or excitement at the time, and he did not become well known until after the publication of the second volume, *À l'Ombre des Jeunes Filles en Fleur*, which appeared in 1918, and was awarded the *Prix Goncourt* in 1919. Then suddenly his name was made, and the various volumes of his work came out, at short intervals, until his death in 1922—but three of the seven volumes were published posthumously.

The admirable English translation by Scott-Moncrieff began to appear in 1922, but he died before its completion, and the last volume was finished, after his death, by Stephen Hudson. It is through this translation that Proust made his real impact on English letters. But English readers did not need to wait until its publication to appreciate Proust, for he was well known in literary circles in England—especially in Bloomsbury—by the end of the First World War.

Proust was the most important novelist in Europe at the close of the war, and his influence was more far-reaching than that of any other writer—even on English fiction, in spite of the denials of Pamela Hansford Johnson in *The New Statesman*, on 9 August 1958, and of C. P. Snow, in *The Times Literary Supplement*, on 15 August 1958. His influence was often unconsciously experienced, for it had floated, like pollen, on the air, settling in different places, and fertilizing indigenous plants, without the recipient being aware of it.

As far as France is concerned no more revealing or richer document exists for the first fifty years of the Third Republic than *À la Recherche du Temps Perdu*, and it is for that period what Balzac's *Comédie Humaine* is for the Restoration and the July Monarchy.

Proust was as much opposed to the ideals of the Naturalists as any Symbolist, for he considered that they had penetrated no further than the shell of the individual, leaving the core, his most interesting part, untouched. Realism, he thought, was as devoid of beauty as it was of truth, since beauty is revealed not by external images, but only by the penetration which can break through the world of appearances. As he himself said:

'la littérature qui se contente de "décrire les choses" d'en donner seulement un misérable relevé de lignes et de surfaces, est celle qui, tout en s'appelant réaliste, est la plus éloignée de la réalité et nous attriste le plus'.

The function of the true novelist is to interpret the outward signs, and to make clear what they indicate. This was also the doctrine of the Symbolists.

Our real life, Proust thought, is consistently concealed from us, and art is the only channel by which it can be revealed to us. So-called realism is useless as a medium of expression, since it confines itself to the description of external forms, and is concerned only with the photography of a superficial inner life, which we have grown accustomed to accept. But art is omnipotent for it *recompose la vie* and makes it into something different, with the same materials. Proust agreed with Baudelaire in seeing that beauty exists, not in the thing itself, but in what the artist brought to the subject. He thought that art was a 'reconstruction', a 'recreation' of the subject at its most intense and most meaningful moment.

In his great work he depicts a nervous and highly intelligent and sensitive being who wanders through life, seeking happiness everywhere, which he fails to attain, in family or sexual love, or in pleasure, or in the rivalries of society, but only reached it at the end in the sincere and whole-hearted practice of creative art.

Proust's attitude to his art has affinities with that of Baudelaire and the Symbolists—he is indeed a product of the same 'état d'âme', as they would say. It could even be claimed that, in his work, Symbolism reached the novel and took shape in it—as if it had been awaiting this incarnation. He makes use of Baudelairean *correspondances*—that is to say, that he expresses the response of one sense through appeal to another, rather than by direct description. It was important, as Mallarmé used to say, to 'décrire non la chose, mais l'effet qu'elle produit. La suggérer, voilà le rêve.' Proust, like the Symbolists, believed in the non-existence of what has not yet been re-created by the artist. In *Sodome et Gomorrhe* he says: 'La réalité n'existe pas pour nous tant qu'elle n'a pas été recréée par notre pensée.'

His Symbolism is an effort to recapture the lost past—or rather only mislaid, for nothing is ever really lost, and sensations of the past are like radio-active material which nothing can annihilate. His Symbolism was an effort to recapture the paradise lost, the paradise of the unalloyed and pure sensations of childhood, which Rimbaud considered the true source of poetry. The aim was to discover the path that led back to childhood, through the thick undergrowth of education, tradition, and convention, which have obstructed and hidden it. Proust says: 'Les vrais paradis sont les paradis qu'on a perdus.' It resembles what Baudelaire used to call 'l'enfance retrouvée à volonté'—only Proust did not believe that it could be recaptured at will, but only through unconscious effort, or, more correctly, by an unforeseen 'illumination', when a vivid memory of the past is suddenly flashed across the inner screen of vision.

The real subject of Proust's *À la Recherche du Temps Perdu* is the record of the destruction by time, and the secret process of preservation by memory—what he calls 'le temps destructeur et le souvenir sauveur'. It is not however every moment which memory embalms in its cocoon, but only the most significant, those which have been lived most intensely emotionally, those which have been burnt into the inner consciousness as if with a branding iron. This unconscious memory is very different from the recollection of facts which we have committed to memory. In *Le Temps Retrouvé* he talks of:

> 'l'extrême différence qu'il y a entre l'impression vraie que nous avons eue d'une chose, et l'expression factice que nous nous en donnons quand volontairement, nous essayons de nous la représenter'.

The unconscious memory is entirely involuntary, and the treasure chest is unlocked by the key of some chance, unexpected experience— the taste of a *madeleine* dipped in tea; the feel of a clean, crisp linen towel; an uneven paving-stone; or a long-forgotten book discovered, by chance, in a library. Baudelaire realized the importance and significance of this process and, deliberately, forged keys to unlock the chest of memory—as in his poem *La Chevelure*—but he was also aware of its involuntary aspect, and in *Le Flacon* he describes how, in a ruined and deserted house,

> 'Parfois on trouve un vieux flacon qui se souvient,
> D'où jaillit toute vive une âme à qui revient.
>
> Mille pensers dormaient, chrysalides funèbres,
> Frémissant doucement dans les lourdes ténèbres,
> Qui dégagent leur aile et prennent leur essor,
> Teintés d'azur, glacés de rose, lamés d'or.'

Voluntary memory dries up what it touches, since it is utilitarian, but unconscious memory comes with a sudden shock, as if in opening a drawer full of memories, the existence of which had long been forgotten—or rather they were no longer in the usually accessible drawer of conscious memory.

Proust said that man had long been trying to batter down doors which opened on to nothing at all, when the doors which really opened on to something could slide back, at the touch of a finger, without any effort. It was useless, he thought, to return physically to the places we had known in the past, for we were no longer the same person, and so our reactions would be different—we are the sum of very many different individuals all with different personalities. These different selves were, however, never lost, but lay embalmed in unconscious memory, and they could suddenly revive, through involuntary memory, or in a dream, or in a trance. But the things we had seen in the past remained for ever linked, not only with the objects that surrounded them at the time, but also with that self of ours which was then present, and which did not die. This 'resurrection' of our lost self could happen in the case of each of our different selves.

Proust does not seem to have known the writings of Freud, but he reached many of the same conclusions concerning dreams and the unconscious. In an interview with J. E. Bois he said:

'Mon livre serait peut-être comme un essai d'une suite de romans de l'inconscient—mon œuvre est dominée par la distinction entre la mémoire volontaire et la mémoire involontaire.'

He thought that these rich flashes of memory should not merely be accepted as a pleasing gift, but that they should be utilized to draw conclusions. The reflections which he makes when he experiences these flashes of illumination are interesting and revealing psychologically. He believed that only by penetrating deeply into his own mind, by subjecting the whole of his past to the most intense and ruthless scrutiny, could his intelligence fully illuminate the laws and the motives which must have governed his existence, but which, hitherto, had remained unconscious and unexplored. Like most Frenchmen Proust was, at heart, a moralist.

Proust's investigation into this form of memory reached depths of consciousness not yet plumbed in the novel, and very greatly enlarged its psychological possibilities.

Proust, like Gide, was interested in the 'cas déconcertants' of modern life, and what the latter used to call 'les régions non nettoyées' of man's nature, the jungle undergrowth. He too studied homosexuality, but with none of Gide's complacency, and, in *Sodome et Gomorrhe*, he was a merciless moralist, who flagellated the vice with the relentless fervour of an Old Testament prophet—Gide considered this unscientific and prejudiced.

Proust was an acute observer of the foibles, vices, and vanities of the society in which he moved, and it is easy to understand why Saint-Simon was amongst his favourite authors, for he has done for the Faubourg Saint-Germain what Saint-Simon did for Versailles.

The individual as seen by Proust is a highly complex being, made up of all his different selves which have not fully coalesced—he thought it was only defective memory in most people which prevented them from realizing that this dissociation existed. His people are never of one piece, are never governed by that 'faculté maîtresse' with which Balzac made unity in the characters he created.

Proust has frequently been accused by French critics of writing a complicated and unclear style. Nevertheless, in evocation and symbolical powers, he was a great master of French prose. Like many of the French painters—like Le Nain, Chardin, Cézanne, or Van Gogh—he was able to take a simple, everyday object and imbue it with significance and symbolism, revealing the powers it contained of embalming significant memory. In a letter to Princess Bibesco he declared that a sensation did not interest him in itself, but only in its possibilities of recalling something else, and becoming its symbol. In Combray, in *Du Côté de chez Swann*, he mentions the tears which, as a child, he had been able to restrain as long as he was in the presence of his father, but had allowed to flow freely when he was alone with his mother; then, when composing his book as an adult man, he writes of the memory of these tears:

> 'En réalité ils n'ont jamais cessé, et c'est seulement parce que la vie se tait maintenant davantage autour de moi, que je les entends de nouveau, comme ces cloches de couvent, que couvrent si bien les bruits de la vie pendant le jour, qu'on les croirait arrêtées, mais qui se remettent à sonner dans le silence du soir.'

In his method of psychological depiction Proust used a kind of 'monologue intérieur', as it came to be called. It has usually been claimed that this form of writing was invented by Édouard Dujardin in his *Les Lauriers sont coupés*, published in 1888. Proust's use of it is however nearer to the method of indirect speech used by Flaubert to depict the inner consciousness of the characters he was portraying. He used this method to reveal what the characters themselves would have been incapable of expressing coherently in words. This was immediately clear to those who saw the dramatized version of *Madame Bovary* which was put on by Baty at the Théâtre de Montparnasse, just before the late war. It was apparent that Charles and Emma had become totally different characters from what they had been, as Flaubert created them, between the covers of a book, who would have been incapable of exteriorizing the dreams and fantasies which come and go, without rational form, through their minds but which, in a play, can be rendered only in direct speech, and this completely transforms the nature of the characters. There is a masterly passage in the novel, where Flaubert indicates the differences between husband and wife by placing, side by side, their parallel and contrasting day-dreams. This loses almost everything when transferred to the stage.

In the nineteenth century Flaubert's realism was noticed—abused or praised—but his original use of indirect speech passed unobserved, yet it was one of the most important developments in the depiction of character, which permitted a more profound study of psychology than had been possible with Balzac's external method of reproducing only what expressed itself outwardly, in physiognomy, facial expression, gesture and speech. Balzac's method had the disadvantage of permitting the satisfactory depiction only of strong, elderly, or voluble characters, those who had been visibly marked and scarred by life; it was not suitable for rendering sensitive characters, for showing that side of human nature which does not reach visible expression on the surface, or those who have not yet developed a strongly marked exterior.

In English literature, the chief exponent of the *monologue intérieur* is generally accepted as James Joyce. He certainly considered that he owed it to Dujardin, and he acknowledged his debt. Yet it had been used before him in English fiction by two women novelists. In a modified form by May Sinclair in *Audrey Craven*, published in 1897, and, more fully, by Dorothy Richardson in her *roman fleuve* entitled *Pilgrimage*, the first volume of which, *Pointed Roofs*, was composed in 1913 but published only in 1915. It was followed by eleven further volumes, and ended, in 1938, with *Dimple Hill*. All these volumes deal with the inner flow of consciousness through the mind of one single personality. It is not clear whether its author obtained the idea from Proust, but, in 1938 when publishing a collected edition of the work, she denied, by implication, having had knowledge of him when she embarked on her first volume, for in the Preface she says: 'News came from France'—that was when she was composing her first volume—'of one Marcel Proust, said to be producing an unprecedentedly profound and opulent reconstruction of experience, focussed from within the mind of a single individual.' Her first volume appeared in 1915, after Proust had published *Du Côté de chez Swann* in 1913, but before he was well known.

James Joyce and Virginia Woolf are the two main pillars which support the edifice of the modern novel in England. They were of the same age, born in 1882; she was a week older, but lived two months longer, and they both died in 1941.

They both wrote in the Proustian mood—though, from their own testimony, they would seem to have reached their conclusions independently from the French master. In *The Common Reader* Virginia Woolf said that she had known Proust first in 1922, and by then she had already published *The Voyage Out*, *Night and Day*, and *Jacob's Room*. She did, however, know Joyce's writings—even *Ulysses*, when extracts from it were printed in the United States in *The Little Review* in 1919. She could have imbibed much of the French atmosphere unconsciously from him.

Joyce, although he had already written in the same mood before the publication of *Du Côté de chez Swann*, had, from childhood, been saturated with French literature, and had lived in Paris. Also he was an Irishman, and this made him more ready to accept inspiration from France than from England—indeed there is very little of the English tradition in his writings.

At seventeen, just as he was entering the University, he read *À Rebours*, and was much stirred by the decadent picture of life that it gave, and also by its conception of an existence dedicated to art. In the same period he read *Les Poètes Maudits* by Verlaine, and, through it, got to know the poetry of Mallarmé and Rimbaud, who were to have an influence in the formation of his literary doctrine. While at college he translated Verlaine and Maeterlinck, and Gorman, in his biography of Joyce, published in 1941, prints his translation of *Chanson d'Automne* by Verlaine, which is superior to most of those which have been published. At the same time he was reading Gérard de Nerval, as he mentions in *Stephen Hero*. Two years later, when he was nineteen, he read *Là-Bas* by Huysmans, and planned to write an autobiographical work, describing an intimate state of mind. By this time he also knew *The Symbolist Movement in Literature* by Arthur Symons, and it had on him an impact similar to that which it was to have on Eliot, opening new vistas for him.

It was after reading *En Route*, the continuation of *Là-Bas*, that, according to Symons, Joyce made the sudden discovery that the novel could compete with poetry, as well as with great *Confessions* and philosophy, that it could reach its consummation in the revelation of the subconscious. That had also been the belief of Proust.

In May 1902, when he was twenty, Joyce published his first piece of writing, an essay on Mangan, which was printed in *Saint Stephens, A Record of University Life*. In this article he showed a wide acquaintance with French literary movements—especially with Symbolism—and he discusses the poetry of Baudelaire and Verlaine. Indeed his views on the function of the poet are taken from Baudelaire, when he defines him as 'the mediator between the world of reality and the world of dreams'.

After taking his degree, in November 1902, Joyce went to London, and was introduced by Yeats to Symons, who encouraged him in his study of French literature. In December that year he crossed over to Paris, and enlarged his knowledge of the writings of Mallarmé beyond the poems which he had read in *Les Poètes Maudits*, for he now read *Divagations*, which helped him to crystallize his own theories. By this time his admiration for the work of Huysmans had waned, and he had learnt in Paris that he was not amongst the more advanced and interesting writers technically. In a review in the *Daily Express*, in Dublin, on 1 October 1903, he wrote that 'Huysmans is daily becoming more formless and more obviously comedian in his books, that Paris has begun to be wearied by the literary oblate'.

During that year in Paris he spent his time in the creation of a dozen or more plotless sketches, flashes of mood and place, flashes of life, which he called *Epiphanies*, which seemed to have some resemblance to the *Illuminations* by Rimbaud—some of them went to the making, later, of *Dubliners* and *The Portrait of the Artist as a Young Man*. He was ostensibly studying medicine in Paris, but he does not seem to have pursued his studies very far. He was living in great poverty, at starvation level, and this did not induce the state of mind necessary for academic work.

He returned to Dublin on account of his mother's last illness and death. There, in 1904, he began to compose the stories which were to become the collection entitled *Dubliners*, and also *Stephen Hero*, his personal confession.

This was an important year for him, and he realized its significance, for it was on a day in 1904 that he focussed the whole of the action of his *Ulysses*.

In October 1904 he left again for the continent, and spent the next ten years, until the First World War, at Trieste. It was there that he finished *Dubliners*, begun earlier in the year. He found, in Dublin, a publisher called Maunsell, who was prepared to bring it out, but who, eventually, was afraid of the censorship on account of the outspokenness of the language, and did not go through with the contract. It was only to be published ten years later, in 1914.

The influence of Maupassant is felt throughout most of the collection, and it is from him that Joyce learned the importance of direct observation, and careful attention to significant detail, but he is less ironic and more compassionate than his French model, and *The Dead* —especially its ending—is more poetic and imaginative than anything that Maupassant ever wrote. This story must surely be one of the loveliest ever written in any language.

'Generous tears filled Gabriel's eyes. He had never felt like that himself towards any woman, but he knew that such a feeling must be love. The tears gathered more quickly in his eyes and in the partial darkness he imagined he saw the form of a young man standing under a dripping tree. Other forms were near. His soul had approached that region where dwell the vast hosts of the dead. He was conscious of, but could not apprehend, their wayward flickering existence. His own identity was fading into a grey impalpable world: the solid world itself, which these dead had one time reared and lived in, was dissolving and dwindling.

A few light taps upon the pane made him turn to the window. It had begun to snow again. He watched sleepily the flakes, silver and dark, falling obliquely against the lamplight. The time had come for him to set out on his journey westward. Yes, the newspapers were right: snow was general all over Ireland. It was falling on every part of the dark central plain, on the treeless hills, falling softly upon the Bog of Allen and, farther westward, softly falling into the dark mutinous Shannon waves. It was falling too, upon every part of the lonely churchyard in the hill where Michael Fury lay buried. It lay thickly drifted on the crooked crosses and headstones, on the spears of the little gate, on the barren thorn. His soul swooned slowly as he heard the snow falling faintly through the universe and faintly falling, like the descent of their last end, upon all the living and the dead.'

Reviewing the collection in *The Egoist*, in July 1914, Ezra Pound wrote: 'Freedom from sloppiness is so rare in contemporary English prose that one might well say simply, "Mr. Joyce's book of short stories is prose free from sloppiness" and leave the intelligent reader ready to run from his study immediately to spend three and sixpence on the volume.' And then he goes on to say that Joyce writes a clear hard prose, in which he deals with subjective things, but presents them with such clarity of outline that 'he might be dealing with locomotives or with builders' specifications'. Ezra Pound thought that his most valuable qualities came from French influences. 'I can lay down a good piece of French writing,' he said, 'and pick up a piece of writing by Mr. Joyce without feeling as if my head were being stuffed through a cushion.' He compared him to Flaubert, in his universality and classicism, and showed how, in dealing with normal things and with normal people, 'he writes as a contemporary of Continental writers'

Shortly after reaching Trieste Joyce abandoned *Stephen Hero*, and began work on another personal confession, which was to become *The Portrait of the Artist as a Young Man*. By this time he had also planned *Ulysses*, but as a further story for *Dubliners*. However, in 1907 Symons managed to persuade Elkin Mathews to bring out a collection of verse by Joyce, entitled *Chamber Music*, and this was, in fact, his first published work. His poetry does not possess the originality of his prose—it is even less poetic—but the collection achieved the good result of bringing him into contact with the most advanced poets of the time in England, and he got to know Ezra Pound, Eliot, Aldington, and many others. This permitted him later, when the Imagists became a school, to be published by them, and it thus happened that his *Portrait of the Artist as a Young Man* was serialized in *The Egoist* between February 1914 and September 1915. It appeared in book form in 1916, published by *The Egoist* press.

The *Portrait* is in the form of a realist-impressionist novel, which has no English counterpart, and it brought something new to fiction in this country. It is the kind of self-analytical portrait—or 'roman personnel'—which the French have frequently favoured. But Joyce's chief affinity here is with Flaubert, whose writings he knew well—especially his correspondence, from which he has drawn much of his aesthetic doctrine. Joyce declares that the artist 'like the God of creation, remains within or behind, or beyond, or above, his handiwork, invisible'; while Flaubert had said that the artist, like God, must be in the centre of his creations, invisible and that, like Him, he must 'faire et se taire'.

Joyce looked at the petty-bourgeois, with whom he must spend his days, with Flaubert's eye of disgust, and realized, like his French master, the dreary monotony of the lives of minor civil servants, the squalid sameness of this life, where people all dressed alike, thought alike, acted alike, and he recognized, with the same horrified fascination as Flaubert, the immensity of their gross stupidity and insensitivity.

Pound praised here, what he had already praised in *Dubliners*, the accuracy of his style, which was 'the nearest in English to Flaubert, with no padding, or pages of slush'. He declared that this novel had become the 'prose bible' of a few people, in spite of Wells' allegation that its author suffered from a 'cloacal obsession'. *The Portrait of the Artist as a Young Man* may possess the accurate attention to realistic detail found in Naturalist fiction, and its recoil from existing conditions, but it is inspired as well by deep compassion, by a moving sense of poetry, and the contrast found in Baudelaire's antithesis between good and evil—between *Spleen et Idéal*—where disgust and aspiration are linked together in a spiritual perception of beauty.

When the First World War came Joyce moved from Trieste to Switzerland, where he remained, from 1915 to 1919, in Zürich. There he finished *Ulysses*, and extracts from it were published in the United States, in *The Little Review*, in 1919—publication was, however stopped, on account of protests against the obscenity of its language.

After the war, with the help and encouragement of Ezra Pound, Joyce migrated to Paris, and lived there for the following twenty years, until the German occupation in 1940.

When he arrived in Paris he made the acquaintance of Remy de Gourmont and Léon-Paul Fargue, who was the poet of Paris in somewhat the same way as he himself was the poet of Dublin. He also met Jules Romains, who had been the creator of the '*Unanimiste*' school before the war, as well as Proust and the Surrealists.

For the past two years he had been trying in vain to negotiate the publication, in book form, of *Ulysses*, but, both in England and the United States, he had been unable to find a publisher who was prepared to take the risk of publishing it. It was eventually brought out, in 1922, in Paris by Sylvia Beach, the American owner of the publishing house Shakespeare and Company, but its import was banned both in England and the United States.

Reviewing Eliot's poems in 1917 in *The Egoist*, Ezra Pound quoted some remarks made by Remy de Gourmont to demonstrate the incontestable superiority of Flaubert's novels over all others, but they could equally be applied to James Joyce's *Ulysses* :

'Il n'y a de livres que ceux où un écrivain s'est raconté lui-même en racontant les mœurs de ses contemporains—leurs rêves, leurs vanités, leurs amours, et leurs folies.'

There is very little in *Ulysses* which derives from the English tradition in fiction, but it has many affinities with France. In form it is classical in its integrated structure and its strict unity of time—twenty-four hours. But, in the same way as Racine, Joyce has succeeded in making use of the whole life of the characters depicted. In its plan it has the almost architectural inevitability of *Madame Bovary*, and it is as strictly composed. Like all great psychologists—whether in drama or fiction—like Flaubert when writing *Madame Bovary*, or Racine when composing *Bérénice*, Joyce wished to liberate himself from the tyranny of plot, from the artificial convention of a story—he succeeds in this aim.

The *monologue intérieur* which he uses in this work is an extension of the method employed by Flaubert, Édouard Dujardin, and Proust, but it has been taken to its most extreme limits, and it is difficult to imagine any other writer attaining the heights reached by Joyce, especially in Molly Bloom's final monologue. This *tour de force* by itself would ensure artistic immortality to its author. After reading *Ulysses*, Eliot said, as reported by Virginia Woolf in *A Writer's Diary*: 'How could anyone write again after achieving the immense prodigy of the last chapter?'

The language of *Ulysses* has an effectiveness not yet reached in fiction. Flaubert had considered that each subject, or theme, needed its own individual language and idiom; but Joyce went further, in believing that every person, every mind, and even every subconscious state, required its own particular accent, and, in his use of language here, he achieves almost miraculous virtuosity, in a style which has not yet reached that excess, that degeneration of language, when it is impelled beyond the bounds of reason and verisimilitude, as in *Finnegans Wake*.

Ulysses, like *The Portrait of the Artist as a Young Man*, represents an unsentimental and clear-sighted indictment of the age; but, as all Joyce's works, it is inspired by deep compassion for the human predicament—even though his gorge may rise as he contemplates the antics of mankind. In its picture of the corporate and complete life of a city *Ulysses* may owe something to the Unanimist Movement. In the same way as Jules Romains he makes the whole town assume a collective unity, a unity fiercely lit, at times, as if by a Rimbaud-like 'illumination'.

After Joyce's death an important document was discovered amongst his papers, dated 1919, at the time when he had just completed *Ulysses*, and was planning his next work; it is a notebook, in which he noted the authors who interested him and transcribed passages from their works —Mallarmé, Rimbaud, Léon Bloy, and others—and it is interesting to note that the only English author who figures in the list is Walter Pater. The most important of the passages transcribed come from Rimbaud and Mallarmé. Mallarmé's *Crise de Vers* and his *Coup de Dés* are amongst the chief sources of Joyce's next work, *Finnegans Wake*. He is known to have possessed a copy of the *Coup de Dés*, the first edition of which was published posthumously only in 1914, although it had appeared in the periodical *Cosmopolis* in 1898.

Joyce spent the last nineteen years of his life working on *Finnegans Wake*, which appeared little more than a year before he died, in 1939— though two extracts from it had been published earlier. It possesses the same kind of classical unity in form as *Ulysses*, for its action takes place in one single night. Everything happens, outside time and space, in the mind of Earwicker, who falls into a drunken sleep, after finishing what was left in the glasses of his customers, in the low pub over which he presides as landlord. In his sleep he endures all the tortures of the *Angst* and feeling of guilt of the nineteen-twenties. Thus *Finnegans Wake*, like *Les Chants de Maldoror* of Lautréamont—Joyce must have known this work though he does not mention it, for the first complete edition was published by his Surrealist friend, Soupault, in 1920—becomes the epic of modern man, with his distress and failure.

In this work Joyce has attempted to explore the subconscious world of dreams, to invent symbols which should evoke the incoherent state of sleep—it is the kind of world inhabited by Gérard de Nerval during his periods of mental instability, and which he evoked in his *Aurélia*. The scenes in *Finnegans Wake* have the absence of logic and lack of correlation of events which occur in dreams.

The author tried here, as Mallarmé had done, to rise beyond the ordinary logical use of language, beyond its limitations, to purify it, and to give it back its pristine significance which the vulgar tribe of men had debased; or, as Mallarmé expresses it in *Le Tombeau de Poe*, he attempts to 'donner un sens plus pur aux mots de la tribu'. He wants—again like Mallarmé—to strip words of their usual meaning, and to use them contrapuntally, as notes in music. He would have liked to invent a new language which would incorporate everything at once, speak to all the senses in one. This was also Rimbaud's ambition when he said, in *Alchimie du Verbe*, in *Une Saison en Enfer*: 'Je me flattai d'inventer un verbe poétique accessible un jour ou l'autre à tous les sens.'

Finnegans Wake is an obscure work, rendered through symbols which are not easy to interpret without a key, and Joyce could have echoed Rimbaud when he declared of his own work: 'Je réservais la traduction.' It is the veritable 'forêt de symboles' which Baudelaire evokes in *correspondances*, but a jungle forest which has not yet been cleared or charted.

Virginia Woolf followed along the path which Joyce had taken. In *A Writer's Diary*, on 26 January 1919, she records having read the extracts from *Ulysses* which had appeared in *The Little Review* and, in *The Common Reader*, she mentions having read as well *Dubliners* and *The Portrait of an Artist as a Young Man*, when they were published in London in 1914 and 1916 respectively. In 1920, when she had just read only extracts from *Ulysses*, she refers to it with some appreciation, though she thought that its author's form was self-narrowing and restrictive. She was, at that time, composing her own novel, *Jacob's Room*, and, in *A Writer's Diary*, she reflects that what she is trying to do 'is probably being better done by Mr. Joyce'. However, after she had read the complete work, when it appeared in 1922, she was no longer appreciative, but wrote:

G

'I should be reading *Ulysses*, and fabricating my case for and against. I have read 200 pages so far—not a third; and have been amused, stimulated, charmed, interested by the first two or three chapters; and then puzzled, bored, irritated and disillusioned by a queasy undergraduate scratching his pimples.'

Then she mentions, with amazement, Eliot's favourable opinion:

'Tom, great Tom, thinks this is on a par with *War and Peace*! an illiterate, underbred book it seems to me; the book of a self-taught working man, and we all know how distressing they are, how egoistic, insistent, and ultimately nauseating. When one can have cooked flesh, why have the raw?'

She repeats again later that the book is 'underbred, pretentious, brackish!' Twenty years afterwards she had not changed her opinion and, writing reminiscently in *A Writer's Diary*, after she had heard the news of Joyce's death in 1941, she said:

'I bought the blue paper book, and read it here one summer I think with spasms of wonder, and then again with long lapses of intense boredom. And now all the gents are furbishing up their opinions, and the books, I suppose, take their place in the long procession.'

Yet it must have been through Joyce—perhaps indirectly—that she came into contact with the new form of novel in France, for she claimed to have known Proust's work only in 1922. It was, in any case, only in 1925, with *Mrs. Dalloway*, that she reached her full maturity and originality as a novelist, and by that time the Proustian idiom was well known in England, even through Scott-Moncrieff's translation. Moreover, from her earliest days she had been soaked in the French atmosphere. Most of those with whom she associated were ardent Francophiles—Roger Fry, who had sponsored the first Impressionist exhibition in England; T. S. Eliot, who had introduced the poetry of France into England; Lytton Strachey, one of the most fervent admirers of France; and her brother-in-law, Clive Bell, who published the first study of Proust in England in 1928.

As soon as Virginia Woolf began to write she became disgusted with the way the novel was progressing in England, in the hands of Wells, Bennett, and Galsworthy. In 1919 she wrote an essay on contemporary fiction which was, later, published in *The Common Reader*, in which she expressed her dissatisfaction with the novel in England, which, she declared, was designed to represent life as the author saw it, but which succeeded only in obscuring, or even falsifying, it. 'Mr. Wells, Mr. Bennett and Mr. Galsworthy,' she said, 'have excited so many hopes and disappointed them so persistently that our gratitude largely takes the form of thanking them for having shown what they might have done but have not done.' She added that 'the sooner English fiction turns its back on them, the better for its soul'.

The reason why these novelists had disappointed her was that they were materialists and concerned not with the spirit, but with the body, and they spent such immense skill and industry making the trivial and the transitory appear the true and enduring, that true life escapes them. Then she asked herself the question: 'Is life like this? Must novels be like this?'

She too, like Flaubert, Proust, and Joyce, would have liked to be able to dispense with a plot, and, if she could have her way, she said, 'there would be no plot, no comedy, and no love interest or catastrophe in the accepted style, and perhaps not a button sewn on as the Bond Street tailors would have it'.

She realized that, in Proust and Joyce, she would find examples to help her to accomplish her ideal. Although, personally, she did not care for Joyce's work, she realized that he was important. She writes in *The Common Reader*:

'Whatever the intention of the whole, there can be no question, but that it is of the utmost sincerity, and the result, difficult or unpleasant, as we may judge it, is undeniably important.'

The reason for the importance of Joyce, she thought, was that, in contrast with the well-established novelist, he was spiritual, whereas they were materialists, and he was concerned at all costs

'to reveal the flickerings of that innermost flame which flashes its messages through the brain, in order to preserve it, he disregards, with complete courage, whatever seems to him adventitious, whether it be probability or coherence, or any other of the signposts which for generations have served to support the imagination.'

Her chief aim was to communicate the impression made by one individual on another, and to reveal the personality partly through his own consciousness and partly through the impact that he made on others, his projection on others. That is why she found narrative and

G*

comment on the part of the novelist disturbing. That was also the aim of Flaubert when he said that the author had no right to give his opinion about anything. She followed the method of Proust, and expressed the inner flow of consciousness, and to do so used symbolism in the Proustian manner. She avoided realism as far as possible, for she thought that it expressed only the inessentials.

Mrs. Dalloway, published in 1925, was her first successful novel in the new style, and her use of the *monologue intérieur* permits her to escape from the limitations of ordinary chronology, or ordinary narration, as she moves backwards and forwards in the minds of her characters. But it was in *To the Lighthouse*, published in 1927, that she reached her highest peak as a novelist, the perfection of her symbolism, in order to give a true picture of the inner minds of the characters she is depicting. With its restricted space of time and limited canvas, she has given complete knowledge of the group of people.

This is her supreme achievement in the novel as such, but she wanted more. She wished fiction to possess 'something of the exaltation of poetry, but much of the ordinariness of prose'. *The Waves*, published in 1931, which is not as satisfactory a novel as *To the Lighthouse*, is a prose poem in which we are concerned with shades of feeling and consciousness. Here she achieved her end of eliminating the conventional plot, and it is, more even than Joyce's *Ulysses*, concerned with the inner ebb and flow of day-dreams, inner musings—not the dreams of complete unconsciousness.

Like Proust, Virginia Woolf saw the individual as made up of several selves, all existing separately, and having little relation one with the other. Bernard, the main character in *The Waves*—the spokesman for the author—says:

'It is not one life that I look back upon; I am not one person; I am many people; I do not altogether know who I am . . . I am more selves than Neville thinks. We are not simple as our friends would have us to meet their needs.'

Her main conviction was that what is visible in a character is only the smallest part—for it is the submerged part of the iceberg which is most significant. She did not use Proust's way of unlocking, and releasing, the hidden past, or the different imprisoned selves, but she was conscious of them, and that they might, suddenly, rise to the surface and be unpredictable.

James Joyce and Virginia Woolf were the most significant novelists writing in English during the period between the two world wars, who brought to England the new form of psychological novel which was practised in France, and which had reached its noblest expression in the writings of Proust.

Joyce was more saturated with French influences than Virginia Woolf. He spent thirty-five of his fifty-nine years on the continent—more than twenty years in Paris—and most of the literary works from which he drew sustenance were French. Virginia Woolf, on the contrary, remained more in contact with the English literary tradition; she lived in London, and does not seem to have read much French literature outside Proust, from whom she undoubtedly absorbed inspiration—she certainly followed in the furrow dug by him. In *A Writer's Diary*, on 8 April 1925, just after she had published *Mrs. Dalloway*, she wrote:

'I wonder this time whether I have achieved something? Well, nothing anyhow compared with Proust in whom I am now embedded. . . . And he will, I suppose, both influence me and make me out of temper with every sentence of my own.'

There were other writers in England, as well as James Joyce and Virginia Woolf, who looked to France for literary guidance. One of those who thought that, outside France, no literary salvation was possible was Charles Morgan, who had an uncritical admiration—even veneration—for everything French. Not that he ever said anything very original or illuminating about France and her literature, or that he brought thence much of great value to England, but he assumed the task, the vocation, of tending the fires before the altars of French culture. His own well-ordered, and somewhat self-conscious, prose owed much to France, to the France of the past, to the great classical writers. But he remained a foreign body in English literature who was not assimilated.

Much new material for fiction was imported from France. The most popular theme was that of the pathological case, which had been first used by the Goncourt brothers, and later by Proust and Gide—as well as by many other novelists. Psychoanalysis afforded a rich source of new material in this field. Flaubert was almost the last writer to depict characters of classical universality. The favourite subjects for the twentieth-century novelist were homosexuals, lesbians, nymphomaniacs, dipsomaniacs, homicidal maniacs, and those with all sorts of complexes and obsessions. They all came from the psychological regions which Gide had called 'les régions non nettoyées de l'homme'.

Interest in the pathological case led to interest in the criminal type, who is another form of the pathological case—or so the psychiatrists claim. Attraction to the criminal is first seen in Gide, in *L'Immoraliste*, later in *Les Caves du Vatican*, in *Si le Grain ne Meurt*, in *Les Faux-Monnayeurs*, and in his *Journal*.

The hero as a 'voyou' was a very popular figure—particularly in the nineteen-thirties. It was this facet of Rimbaud's personality that interested so many readers in England, who admired his lawlessness, his refusal to submit to any authority. The aesthete was no longer fashionable, and young men no longer wandered about with a bunch of violets in their hand—they were far more likely now to have a set of house-breaking tools! The novelist who most frequently studies the criminal type is Jean Genêt, who began writing in the nineteen-thirties —though his works were to be published first during the Second World War.

The *crapule* hero—as the French called him—was coarse and obscene in his language, and used expressions not previously heard in polite society. One of the most characteristic of such novels was *Voyage au Bout de la Nuit* by Céline, published in 1932. The disgust of Céline against life and society developed later in the nausea of Sartre—his first novel, published in 1938, is, in fact, entitled *La Nausée*. Characters of the same family are found in Graham Greene's novels—especially in *Brighton Rock*, which appeared in 1938.

Criminality led to a sensation of guilt—we have seen that this was the main emotion in the inter-war period—as disillusionment turned to disgust, accompanied by a consciousness of sin. This is exemplified in the novels of Mauriac, Bernanos, and Julian Green, who rely on sin and guilt for the mainspring of their action. They are called Catholic writers—not merely because they happen to be Catholics by religion, but because their religious beliefs influence their attitude to psychology. Their English counterpart is Graham Greene, in such novels as *Brighton Rock* and *The Power and the Glory*—though his most characteristic examples appeared only after the war, *The Heart of the Matter* and *The End of the Affair*. However, *Brighton Rock* is a Catholic novel in the same way as Mauriac's novels are Catholic. The theme is salvation, and the possession of the soul by evil. The theme is also based on the assumption that what happens to a child in his early life will condition what he will become as a man. Pessimism, despair, and violent death follow inevitably on early corruption. The novel demonstrates the belief that a society which is not touched by true Catholic grace has abandoned charity and is incapable of real morality. Like Mauriac, Graham Greene requires the impetus of sin and guilt in order to be able to write.

Graham Greene, who owes so much to the French Catholic writers, has become, since the war, the English novelist most read in France, and the one whose influence—especially on youth—is most widespread.

As a consequence of the immense slaughter of young men during the First World War, youth, in the inter-war period, was worshipped, and never before were adolescent characters so popular in fiction, both in England and in France. Psychoanalysis encouraged the depiction of children from a different point of view than hitherto. They were no longer seen as trailing clouds of glory, but as living a secret life of their own, with its own standards, which weere often in contradiction to those of their adults. Examples are seen in Gide's *Faux-Monnayeurs*, in Cocteau's *Enfants Terribles*, in *Les Thibault* by Roger Martin du Gard, in *Le Blé en Herbe* by Colette—and in many others. In England they are found in *A High Wind in Jamaica* by Richard Hughes, in the *Jeremy* trilogy by Hugh Walpole, in the Irish novels by L. A. G. Strong —and later in the works of L. P. Hartley and Jocelyn Brooke; also in those of Elizabeth Bowen and Rosamond Lehmann.

The nineteenth century had been the age of the individual, and it was then that great characters—good and evil—are the heroes of the novels—as in Balzac and Dickens. In their works what is emphasized is what distinguishes one particular individual from another, and each could echo what Rousseau had said, at the beginning of his *Confessions*, that he resembled no one who had ever been created. But, with the advent of psychoanalysis, and other so-called scientific methods of investigating the human personality, the individual decreased in importance. The hero was no longer significant as himself alone, for was he not merely the product of his physical condition—his glands, his heredity, his unconscious, and his surroundings? He was now studied as part of a family, or the inhabitants of a block of flats, or the members of a community—as in the works of the *Unanimistes*, who saw a building, or a town, as developing its own collective personality, in which the individual members were of little account, except as a fragment of the whole. This is seen particularly in the novels of Jules Romains, in a single work such as *La Mort de quelqu'un*, or in a series of novels like *Les Hommes de Bonne Volonté*. This last is an example of the *roman fleuve*, which was a very popular form of novel at the time, and was well suited for evoking this collective psychology. Other examples are *Les Thibault* by Roger Martin du Gard, *Chronique des Pasquier* by Georges Duhamel, *Les Hauts Ponts* by Jacques de Lacretelle—and others. In England the form was also practised by Hugh Walpole, by John Galsworthy and Compton Mackenzie.

With the disappearance of the great individuals there arose the little man, the ordinary man, who takes his protective colouring from the mass, from his surroundings, and disappears into it. The hero is an undistinguished little man—usually with an inferiority complex—who settles down into the second-rate and has no ambition for anything better. A characteristic example, in French, is the hero of the Salavin cycle by Georges Duhamel, the unheroic hero, the apotheosis of the little insignificant man. He is found also in *La Mort de quelqu'un* by Jules Romains, where he is so insignificant that he is met only after his death as a corpse, who, for the short time that his funeral takes to pass through the town, impinges on the consciousness of a set of people, is the focus of their temporary thoughts, uniting them into a strange entity, a group of people who share the wonder, as the hearse passes, as to whom the coffin holds. It is the account of the burial of a nobody, whose name is not given; he is just anyone—'quelqu'un', he has merely died, and is being disposed of.

The short story developed late in England, and there were few examples worthy of note until the twentieth century—George Eliot and Trollope were exceptions in the nineteenth century. On the other hand, France, since her earliest days, had a well-established tradition of the short story, and had produced many examples of high artistic and psychological quality. It was natural that England, when developing this literary form, should look to France for examples, and especially to Maupassant, the most distinguished master of the short story in the second half of the nineteenth century. However, at the same time there was, affecting this form of English literature, as well as the influence of Maupassant, that of Chekov, and it would be difficult to say which was the stronger impact. Their respective influences were closely linked and blended together to form something new in England. Very often the influence of the Russian grafted itself onto the previous influence of the French writer. Most English writers were affected in the same way as H. E. Bates when he wrote: 'For me Chekov has had many lessons; but it is significant to note that I learned none of them until I had learnt others from Maupassant.'

The most skilled and talented short-story writers in England during the period between the two wars were Somerset Maugham and Katherine Mansfield.

Somerset Maugham was born in Paris, the son of an Englishman attached to the British Embassy. He was brought up in France, attended a French school, and was bi-lingual from childhood in French and English. He read French from his earliest years, and, in *East and West*, said that he had read Maupassant with avidity as a boy. It was only natural that, when he began to write, he should look to France. His sardonic and ironic cast of mind had more in common with the realistic and materialistic Maupassant than with the more spiritual and poetic Chekov, and, in fact, he is the English writer who most resembles Maupassant.

Somerset Maugham is intellectual and logical, clear-sighted and disillusioned, and, like Maupassant, he notices individual quirks of behaviour; like him also he is aware of the gross selfishness of most human beings, but he possesses less humanity. There is not much grandeur or nobility, imagination or passion, in his view of life, but his craftsmanship is always perfect. He himself was contemptuous of the praise of his technique, and, in *East and West*, he complains:

'There is evidently something that a number of people do not like in my stories and it is this they try to express when they damn them with the faint praise of competence. I have the notion it is the definiteness of their form. . . . This particular criticism has never been made in France where my stories have had with the critics and the public much greater success than they have had in England. The French, with the classical sense, and their orderly minds, demand precise form and are exasperated by a work in which the ends are left lying about. . . . This precision has always been slightly antipathetic to the English.'

Katherine Mansfield had less knowledge of France and French literature than Somerset Maugham, and probably knew little of either before she arrived in Europe, but thereafter she stayed for long periods in France—she even died there—and felt affinity with the French people. She was obviously influenced by Maupassant, but there is no doubt that she was also greatly affected by Chekov, and that his spiritual qualities, his qualities of soul, were more sympathetic to her than the materialism of Maupassant. Characteristics from the two masters of the short story—Maupassant and Chekov—fused in her, and became inextricably blended, so that it is hard to separate one from the other. There is something of Gallic irony in *At the Bay*, and its visual descriptions are more French than Russian—she has managed here to transpose Maupassant's method to the New Zealand scene. Also the ending of *The Doll's House* possesses the kind of pathos which he understood, and she can frequently be as merciless and as cruel as he. Her writing, however, shows a delicate tenderness at times—a kind of virginity even—a feeling for poetry, which is found nowhere in Maupassant's work, which brings her nearer to Chekov, and which also places her achievement, in spite of its limitations, on a nobler and more moving plane than Somerset Maugham could ever reach.

11

DRAMA

FROM the beginning of the Third Republic until the First World War France did not shine in the theatre as she did in poetry and fiction. Frederick Lumley, in *Trends in Twentieth Century Drama*, even declares that, before 1914, the French was the most backward and the most closed theatre in Europe. This is not a fair judgment—certainly as far as production was concerned. But the dramatists were undoubtedly continuing along the same well-worn paths and persisting with the well-made play—plays like those of Sardou and Scribe. They were well written, well acted, and well produced, and they ensured a good evening's entertainment, but there was nothing in them to feed the mind or the artistic sense, nothing new or experimental.

Fiction, on the whole, had replaced the theatre in the interest of intelligent and cultivated people, and was used as the particular form of literature in which the age expressed itself, and the conclusions it had reached concerning life. Fiction was the more serious *genre* and the one with the widest appeal. In fact drama had been in decline since the beginning of the century, and the only dramatist of permanent artistic and psychological value was Alfred de Musset.

The Romantic Movement had introduced certain new experiments in the theatre, but the gain had been in production and acting, rather than in actual play-writing. It is in the nineteenth century, with the expansion of mechanical and histrionic techniques, that a great generation of actors arose, for the first time, who had learnt their trade on the Romantic stage, and then found that the plays available did not, in fact, take any advantage of their acquired skill. This was an era of great individual actors, who, later, returned to classical plays in order to find an outlet for their new art. Rachel, the greatest classical actress known to fame, was, paradoxically, a product of the Romantic School who, when she was fully trained, discovered that the parts she was given by the new playwrights were neither interesting nor subtle enough to exploit fully the powers she had gained, for their psychological portrayal was non-existent. But she found, in the drama of the classical giants of the seventeenth century, in the plays of Racine and Corneille, characters worthy of her powers of exteriorization. Her triumph was a personal one, which did not affect the theatre as a whole.

The plays which followed on Romantic Melodrama were either the bastard classical drama of Ponsard, the frivolous trivialities of Meilhac and Halévy, the sanctimonious moralizing of Dumas Fils, or the didactic realism of Brieux.

The Symbolist Movement, making a complete break with the past, also brought new theories to the theatre. The plays of Maeterlinck and Claudel were original in plan and conception, but, for their satisfactory production, they require different stage management, and a different view of the function of both actors and stage. The theatre itself required to be revolutionized.

This happened when Antoine founded Le Théâtre Libre in 1887, which lasted until 1894. He was much interested in the Russian and Scandinavian theatre, and he brought new life to the stage in France by performing translations of Ibsen, Hauptmann, Tolstoi and Turgeniev.

Antoine was followed by his pupil and disciple, Lugné Poë, who radically altered the form of drama in France, and whose influence was to continue for nearly half a century. He started, with the poet Paul Fort, in Le Théâtre de l'Art, with a group of writers and actors who wished to create something more idealistic on the stage than had hitherto been seen. He supported Maeterlinck, and performed two of his plays at Le Théâtre de l'Art—*L'Intruse* in 1891 and *Pelléas et Mélisande* in 1893. He also encouraged Claudel at the beginning of his career.

In 1893 Le Théâtre de l'Art was renamed Le Théâtre de l'Œuvre, and Lugné Poë became its director, and it continued, under his direction, until the nineteen-thirties. He opened with what was described as a magnificent production of Ibsen's *Rosmersholm*, and it was he who launched the world première of *Salomé* by Oscar Wilde, in March 1896, and also *Ubu Roi* by Jarry, in December the same year.

Lugné Poë was much interested in international drama, in what was being written in Scandinavia, produced in Russia, and he was particularly favourable to the new Irish theatre which was developing at that time, under the auspices of the Abbey Theatre in Dublin, and he thought that, out of Ireland, salvation for the theatre of Europe might come. He put on many foreign plays, by Ibsen, Strindberg, d'Annunzio, Chekov, Synge—and many others.

Lugné Poë was the real pioneer of the new drama in France, and he was followed by others with similar ideals. Just before the First World War there was much interesting experimentation in the theatre—as in literature—amongst the founders of the advanced magazine, *La Nouvelle Revue Française*. An important off-shoot of the review was Le Théâtre du Vieux Colombier, founded by Jacques Copeau in the significant year 1913, which saw the birth of so many of the post-war movements. Copeau declared, when he founded his theatre, that he wished to free the stage from the exploitation of big business.

His theatrical innovations were based on two main principles, improvement in the technique of acting and stage production; and a repertory of well-written plays.

The First World War broke out before Copeau had been able to carry out his plans for a new theatre, with new conceptions of stage production and new authors, but his ideas were to bear fruit once peace came again.

If at the end of the nineteenth century the theatre in France did not enjoy much prestige, in England, at the beginning of the twentieth century, its glory was no greater, and its decline persisted longer than in France.

At the end of the nineteenth century in England, as in France, efforts were made to bring new life to the theatre. In 1901 the Independent Theatre in London was founded on the model of Antoine's Théâtre Libre. This was a beginning, though it did not have any immediate effects.

There were some critics—as William Archer—who looked towards the French stage. He greatly admired Maeterlinck and, in September 1891, he published an article on him in *The Fortnightly Review*, entitled 'A Pessimist Playwright'.

In 1895 Lugné Poë was invited to come to London with his company of *Le Théâtre de l'Œuvre*, and they performed *L'Intruse* by Maeterlinck and *Rosmersholm* by Ibsen. These plays did not excite much interest or curiosity in the general public—except in Archer and Bernard Shaw, who realized the importance of their experiments in the theatre, and that they were revolutionary in their stage production.

In 1898 Granville-Barker started the experiment of producing plays of literary interest, and of non-commercial value, on Sunday evenings at the Stage Society. In 1906 an important event for the English stage was the visit of the Abbey Theatre players to Manchester; and another the creation of a repertory season at the Duke of York's Theatre in London in 1910.

The leading playwright in England, in the years immediately preceding the First World War, was undoubtedly Bernard Shaw, who was probably the finest dramatist in the English language for over a century. He did not however look to France for inspiration, for he was an Ibsenite, the foremost in England.

Before any of these ideas had had time to take root the First World War broke out, and this naturally checked the development of drama in England. The only kind of plays that had a chance of production were such theatrical successes as *The Bing Boys*, *Chu Chin Chow*, or *The Garden of Allah*. There was no other kind of drama to satisfy more literary tastes.

The end of hostilities did not bring an immediate revival in the theatre in England, and it had to wait until new ideas from France had had time to percolate into the country. Gordon Craig, who was a reformer very much like Copeau, published his theories for the reformation of the English stage in his *Theatre Advancing* in 1921, but they went unheeded, and he left England a disappointed man, never to return again. After the war middle-class realism continued on the English stage, relieved by the fantasy of Barrie which made playgoers believe that they had been exercising their minds. No one asked any interesting questions concerning the future of the theatre. Frederick Lumley wrote, in *Trends in Twentieth Century Drama* : 'The English theatre has sunk to an incredible impotence and has almost ceased to play any creative rôle in world drama.' It was to revive only when it had drawn inspiration from the new experiments which were being carried out in France.

In 1919 Jacques Copeau returned with his company from the United States, where he had spent the latter part of the war, and he opened his theatre again in the Rue du Vieux Colombier. He collected the same company, in the main, as he had had before the war. He hoped that he would now have ample time before him to carry out his projects for the renovation of the theatre. He borrowed some of his theories from the Moscow Art Theatre, and also from the Diaghileff ballet, which had come to Paris in 1909, and had now settled in Monte Carlo. In his attempt to *rethéâtraliser* the stage he wanted to draw from all the arts in order to obtain the best effects—from the ballet and the cinema, that is to say the silent cinema, with its reliance on significant gesture—and he liked all his actors to be trained in ballet as well as dramatic technique.

Copeau had been much interested in the theories of Gordon Craig, and had considered inviting him to come and direct his company at the Vieux Colombier, but, as he says in *Cahiers du Vieux Colombier*, published in 1921, one of Craig's conditions was that the opening of the

H

theatre should be postponed for ten years, so that he could train up the company from the very beginning. Copeau admitted that Craig's position was logical, but he considered that the first duty of his company was to exist, and so he refused Craig's condition.

He collected together an excellent company—amongst the best actors in Paris at that time—Louis Jouvet, Charles Dullin, Valentine Tessier, Suzanne Bing, amongst others. His first season ended with his pre-war success, the translation of *Midsummer Night's Dream*.

Copeau's tastes were broad, his knowledge of literature was extensive, and he performed a great variety of plays—from the Russian, English, Italian, Spanish, and French. He was particularly good at encouraging French talent, and he produced many plays by new French authors—one of his triumphal successes was the performance of *Le Paquebot Tenacity*, by Charles Vildrac, in 1920, a play all in delicate half-shades of feeling—the kind of mood which was later to be reflected in French films. He also put on works by his former associates from *La Nouvelle Revue Française*—plays by Gide, Schlumberger, and Roger Martin du Gard.

The plays at the Vieux Colombier were very simply—and even austerely—produced, with no unnecessary complications. The actors were trained with the utmost severity, each of their movements was calculated to produce the effect which the producer had contemplated, all fitted into the cast to make a whole, and the aim was to prevent the development of stars.

It was a severe school requiring of its members an iron discipline, which some eventually found irksome, and many broke away.

Louis Jouvet, whose chief aim was to collect a good company of actors, and who was more interested in French than foreign plays, moved to the Comédie des Champs Elysées, taking with him Valentine Tessier. They made a very successful combination, and acted together for the next fifteen years or so.

Charles Dullin also left Copeau, but his main interest was in the training of actors, in production, and in the performance of plays from a variety of countries, from all ages. He migrated to Montmartre, to open the Théâtre de l'Atelier—the name means workshop, and that is what he intended it to be, a workshop of theatrical experimentation. One of his great successes was the performance of Ben Jonson's *Volpone* in 1928, with himself in the name part.

Jouvet and Dullin were missionaries from the Théâtre du Vieux Colombier who spread its ideas over a wider radius.

There were other producers in Paris at this time, besides the disciples of Copeau, interested in new ideas, and in discovering plays worthy of performance. There was Gaston Baty, who directed a company first at the Studio des Champs Elysées, and finally at the Théâtre de Montparnasse. He liked plays taking place in a dreamland, in contrast with the realism of the commercial theatre, in a poetical setting. His outstanding successes were Simon de Gantillon's plays—*Cyclone* in 1923 and *Maya* in 1924. There was also the Russian-born Georges Pitoëff, and his wife, who was one of the most delightful actresses in Paris at the time. Their taste was for foreign plays—which he translated himself—memorable amongst which were *Henri IV* and *Six Characters in Search of an Author* by Pirandello, *Saint Joan* by Shaw, and *Uncle Vanya* by Chekov.

All these actor-producers, Copeau, Dullin, Jouvet, Baty, and Pitoëff, raised the French theatre from one of its most humble positions to one with the highest achievement since the great classical period of the seventeenth century. No other country in the world, in the period between the two world wars, produced such a galaxy of fine dramatists, producers, and actors as France, and no other country was so imaginatively fruitful in the theatre.

Nevertheless, in 1925, Copeau left the Théâtre de Vieux Colombier, discouraged by the defection of Jouvet and Dullin, also worried by lack of money for his schemes, and retired to his native Burgundy, but he did not abandon his interest in the stage. He founded a school for the training of actors in Burgundy, called 'Les Copiaus', who studied dramatic art and technique with him, under his guidance. He was joined in this project by his nephew, Michel Saint-Denis, who had worked with him in Paris as stage manager and assistant producer, and who now helped him to train the 'Copiaus'.

In 1929, after four years of work, Michel Saint-Denis formed the 'Copiaus' into a company which he called La Compagnie des Quinze, and brought them to Paris to produce on the stage. He was joined by André Obey, who wrote plays especially for them, four in number: *Le Viol de Lucrèce*—which, later, served as the basis of Benjamin Britten's opera—and *Noé*, both produced in 1931; *La Loire* and *La Bataille de la Marne* in 1932. They are symbolical plays in which setting, grouping, and movement play an important part, which make use of a chorus poetically, but which are not very dramatic, nor very profound psychologically, though they afford great scope to the producer.

In 1935 Michel Saint-Denis took the Compagnie des Quinze over to London where they performed the plays of Obey. This was an important date, with repercussions for the English stage. Michel Saint-Denis considered that he could there be a missionary for French theatrical conceptions. He left his own company and opened in London, at Islington, the London Theatre Studio, on the model of the experimental theatres in Paris, which had flourished there since the end of the war.

He brought to England the same kind of organization which had prevailed at the Vieux Colombier, and he opened what might be called a dramatic factory at Islington, where he installed workshops, rehearsing-rooms, ballet-rooms, and a little theatre of the same size as that at the Théâtre de l'Atelier in Paris. The training was varied and as severe and strenuous as in France. The apprentices spent a long time at rehearsing, and each actor was obliged to be proficient in all the parts of the play. They were catholic in their tastes, and studied the drama from all periods of world civilization, and from all countries—Sophocles, Euripides, the Russians, Shakespeare, the Irish School, and all periods of the French theatre. Later, when his school was trained, he produced plays with his company, and amongst their successes were *Noé*, *The Three Sisters*, *Midsummer Night's Dream*, *Electra*, and *The Witch of Edmonton*.

It was sad that his work was cut short by the Second World War, when the London Theatre Studio closed. Michel Saint-Denis remained in England, and was Jacques Duchêne in *Les Trois Amis* on the B.B.C. radio programme *Ici Londres* during the war. When the war was over he became producer and director of The Old Vic Theatre Centre, for the training of actors.

English drama, between the two wars, was going through a sterile phase, when nothing interesting was being produced—except Shaw and O'Casey but, by the nineteen-thirties, Shaw was old and not progressing any further; while O'Casey had cut himself off from his source of natural inspiration by severing his ties with Ireland. James Bridie, from Scotland, was writing work that was original and interesting—though more in promise than achievement—but he did not owe anything to France, and this was perhaps his loss, for, in the severely professional standards of the experimental theatre in Paris, he might have acquired a more proficient technique—lack of which was his chief weakness as a dramatist.

What the English stage sadly needed at this time was well-established and well-trained groups of actors, with the highest standards, who would give an opportunity to new dramatists to obtain a hearing for their plays, when these rose to a higher plane than popular farce or musical comedy. It is the large number of such groups in France—Le Vieux Colombier, L'Atelier, La Comédie des Champs Elysées, Le Théâtre de

Montparnasse, and Le Théâtre des Arts—which gave so much scope and encouragement to the galaxy of dramatists who sprang up and flourished in the nineteen-twenties and -thirties in Paris. In this way Cocteau, Giraudoux, Romains, Bernard, and, just before the outbreak of the Second World War, Anouilh, were all given their chance.

The English theatre, in the same period, lacked the fillips of such encouragement. There were, nevertheless, signs in the nineteen-twenties and -thirties that the country was beginning to take an interest in the quality of the plays produced, and in the method of their production. In 1926 the Festival Theatre at Cambridge was founded, on French lines. In 1928 J. B. Fagan, from the Abbey Theatre in Dublin, founded a repertory theatre at Oxford, called The Playhouse, which was directed on French lines—as indeed were the Abbey and Gate theatres in Dublin. Fagan produced plays of the highest literary and dramatic quality from most European countries—this was the glorious period of the Oxford Playhouse. The same year the Canterbury Festival for poetic drama was founded, for religious and poetic plays to be performed in the cathedral itself. Eliot's play, *Murder in the Cathedral*, was performed there in 1935, and, with its background of the great church, and its poetic style, it may owe something to *L'Annonce faite à Marie* by Claudel. 1929 saw the beginning of the Malvern Festival. In 1933 was founded the Group Theatre to try out new forms of dramatic art—especially amongst the younger English writers. They performed, in 1933, *The Dance of Death* by Auden and Isherwood, in 1935 *Dog Beneath the Skin*, by the same authors, and, in 1936, their best play, *The Ascent of F.6*. These plays are very typical of the spirit of the nineteen-thirties, with their mixture of politics and psychology, and their bitter criticism of all the values of the day. The Group Theatre also performed *Out of the Picture* by Louis MacNeice in 1937, and *The Trial of a Judge* by Stephen Spender, in 1938.

None of these plays, nor their production, can stand comparison with the quality of the plays produced in France during the same period. Although they are interesting experiments—especially *The Ascent of F.6*—they are amateurish, and dramatically unadventurous. It was nevertheless sad that the war cut short this interesting beginning.

In the meantime, those who wished to enjoy the true and noble pleasures of the theatre made the journey to Paris, where the most advanced and stimulating theatre in Europe was flourishing and playing to full houses.

The impact of the French theatre on the English, in the period between the two wars, was in acting and production, rather than in the actual plays of the new dramatists. The effect of the writers themselves had to wait until after the war, when Christopher Fry was to be influenced by the drama of Giraudoux and Anouilh, and Graham Greene by Mauriac.

12

CONCLUSION

FRANCE had emerged from the First World War with enhanced prestige, which she sustained during the period which separates the two wars, for this was one of her most glorious eras, intellectually and artistically. Herbert Read, writing in *The New Statesman* on 28 November 1958, says that 'there is no doubt that for the years in question, the years between the two wars, the critical intelligence of Europe was the French intelligence'. More visitors than ever landed on her shores, and all who came found, not only the graces of culture and civilization, but that *douceur de vivre* for which she is famed, and which is not escapism from life, for the French have a genius for living.

The result of these closer ties was that there was more sympathy for France in England, when the Second World War broke out, than at any other time in their joint history, and more sadness at the separation which occurred after the Fall of France in 1940. During the century which had passed the English had learnt to appreciate the true qualities of the French people, and Cyril Connolly said in *Horizon*, in June 1943:

'I do not think that any writer can live in France without acquiring something of that serious and lucid power, which we have been discussing, and lacking which so much English work is a salad without dressing, a nostalgia left over from the Victorian age.'

He added that what sustained him during the sad time of separation was looking forward to his first visit to France after the war.

Did this *douceur de vivre*—as some have claimed—weaken the human fibre, and make the French incapable of resistance? It should, however, be remembered that she had suffered so terrible a drain during the First World War that she came out of it weakened physically, not only by the loss of the flower of her youth on the battlefields, but also by those who were never born. After the war she not only did not reproduce herself, but actually diminished in numbers, and when the census was taken in 1921 it was discovered that her population had fallen since 1911, notwithstanding the recovery of Alsace and Lorraine in 1918. Hitler fully realized this, and planned the next war to take place at the moment of France's greatest physical weakness, when her supply of men of military age would be the lowest in her history—that is to say in the late nineteen-thirties. It was no wonder that her leaders, in 1939, were, as Daladier said, 'avares du sang français'—there was so little of it to spare.

There was nothing but grief in England at the tragic circumstances which cut her off from France. Cyril Connolly, to keep the link from being entirely severed, founded *Horizon*, which was precisely the kind of literary and artistic magazine which he had always admired in France. All through the war this review kept interest in France alive in Britain. It published texts smuggled over from France—as for instance *Le Silence de la Mer* by Vercors, and *Le Crève Cœur* by Aragon—it published articles by refugee writers, and by admirers of France.

The defeat of France in 1940, the ensuing armistice, and the German Occupation of the country were a bitter blow to her friends on this side of the Channel. It also permitted anti-French sentiment to develop in some quarters; it created doubt of France, and brought back the feeling towards her which had existed during the previous century. There were some who said that she was finished, not only as a power, but as a force as well; that she no longer counted in Europe; there were others who even questioned her previous prestige, and tried to denigrate it. Many started to criticize, to discover weaknesses, and described the moral degeneration of the country; it was claimed that her defeat was due to the fact that she had grown demoralized and soft through too luxurious living, and too great insistence on the arts and graces of life. This was, of course, false. There were the idle rich in France, as elsewhere at the time, but the vast masses of the French people were serious, frugal, and extremely hardworking. France was defeated because, in company with other free democratic nations, she was utterly unprepared for war—no country in Europe, at that time, could have withstood the might of the German armies.

Even now, after twenty years, France has not yet recovered, psychologically and spiritually, from the humiliation of her defeat in 1940, and has not yet grown scar-tissue over her wounds. Nor has Paris yet regained entirely the position it had enjoyed between the two wars, as the cultural centre of the world. But what is clear is that no other centre in Europe has taken its place.

France has often gone through bad times before, and has recovered from them. George Sand, at the moment of France's defeat in 1870, prophesied the 'réveil général qui suivra, à la grande surprise des autres nations, à l'espèce d'agonie où elles nous voient tombés'. The general re-arising—as Arnold called it, when quoting the passage in *Mixed Essays*—which did indeed, to the astonishment of other nations, follow her humiliation after the Franco-Prussian War, was responsible for one of her most prosperous and glorious periods, under the Third Republic, when she shone in all intellectual and artistic fields.

It is perfectly true that France has often been conquered and trampled underfoot in the past, but has always risen again, and this has been true after the late war, as well as after others. In spite of her drained resources in 1945, when not a single bridge in the whole country was left standing, she has made enormous strides forward. She is now a growing country, with an increasing population, whereas, at the beginning of the century, she was not even reproducing herself. As long as her population remained so small she could not expect to wield an influence commensurate with the importance of her civilization, and moreover, her small population, considering the material wealth of the country, made her a tempting prey to her rapidly increasing neighbours. Since the end of the late war the policy of the Government has been to encourage a larger population, and the economists repeat that her lands could easily support one of ninety millions. The plan has been to aim at a population of fifty millions by 1960, and seventy-five by 1990. If this project were to succeed then France would be in the most favourable position to influence the development of Western Europe. This is not merely the idle dream of population planners, for it has already some basis in reality. In 1948 there were a million births—double the number of deaths for that year—the highest birth-rate for more than a century.

In 1950 France celebrated the two-thousandth anniversary of the founding of Paris and this can be taken as the symbol of the everlasting qualities of the French people.

It is, however, on spiritual and moral qualities that the survival of a people depends. Since time immemorial France has been the repository of the great general ideas by which man lives. Her greatest writers have been moralists—in the widest meaning of the word. She will once more be able to secrete the general ideas which give hope of the future, and the will to growth. She has the power of seeing things whole, and she still possesses this hard-headed realism—idealistic realism—for she knows that life must be lived, and that it cannot be lived without the spirit.

France stamps all her citizens with one special characteristic, a laughing acceptance of life as it is. The French are realists, but not of a

H*

grim, dour kind, realists in that they make the best of circumstances, and do not seek to hide the truth from themselves. They are intellectually honest and temperamentally adult. They refuse to be crushed by the cares of life which they think—as Laforgue used to say—'trop quotidienne'. They have a clear-sighted power of seeing things as they are without sentimentality. Eliot wrote in *Essays Ancient and Modern*, in 1936, 'in the honesty with which it faces the "données" of the actual world, this French tradition has a unique quality in European literature'.

These qualities can be seen in their painters as well as in their literature—in Chardin, Cézanne, and Van Gogh, as well as in Racine, Flaubert, and Baudelaire. They are a tough and adult people who have come to grips with life, and have made their peace with it. They do not imagine that it can be evaded—and, even if they could, they would refuse to do so—as Baudelaire, when he wrote 'Quiconque n'accepte pas les conditions de la vie, vend son âme'. They understand the human heart as no other people, for they have plumbed the depths, and can look at things without illusion—but also without disillusionment. That power of seeing things as they are, without flinching and without expressed judgment, but with understanding and compassion, is one of the most fundamental characteristics of French literature, and it is seen today in such writers as Camus. It is natural that the greatest French writers are those who have studied the human heart in all its ramifications, for they are psychologists second to none in world literature. The English are inclined to consider that such analysis is hair-splitting about motive and guilt, but it has produced such dramatists as Racine, such moralists as Pascal, such novelists as Stendhal, and such poets as Baudelaire.

Some pessimistic thinkers claim that there are signs that our Christian European civilization is coming to its end. If this is true then the historians of the future, when they look back on it from the distance of the *siècles révolus*, will undoubtedly say that the most universal manifestation of these two thousand years has been French culture, French classicism, and that this could, in world history, be placed beside the great civilizations of Greece and Rome. It could be claimed that the only unity produced by the Christian civilization has been a French one, and that the unity of Europe, such as it is, has been one in which France played the predominant part, which reached its zenith in influence and international prestige, as a result of the Golden Age in French culture, in the seventeenth century, so that, in the eighteenth century, every French work of note swept across Europe, from the shores of the Atlantic to the mountains of Ural, and could be printed in France, Germany, Italy, Switzerland, or Russia—it mattered little which. French civilization is the most homogeneous that the world has known and, in many ways, it is the greatest of all civilizations which have come and gone, if everything is taken into account—variety, artistic values, and human ideals.

Later, when this unity was weakened under individualistic Romantic pressure, France no longer played the predominant part in Europe, and there ensued a long period of nationalism in the various countries, as well as in literature and art. It is true that she still played one of the most important parts artistically and intellectually, but she had ceased to be a unifying element. Today, when thoughtful people are weary of nationalism and are looking for a new unity, France can still play her historic part, for she has never lost her belief in universality and unity.

Antiquity has long since ceased being a living force in European culture, but France, with her Graeco-Roman roots, can be the basis of the modern humanities, and become the needed bulwark against international communism. It is important, now that European civilization is seriously threatened and attacked from all sides, that this should be understood. Britain, torn between her rôle in her Commonwealth and her position in Europe, cannot adequately perform this task—she is a world power, but not really European. The only country which can achieve this in Europe today is France—Germany is too divided, Russia even less European than Britain, and the rest too weak. Without France, there will remain no Europe.

Julius Caesar compared France to a human body in which no organ is missing and none superfluous. This is true of her literature as well, which is, intellectually speaking, an *aliment complet*, as scientists say, which possesses all the vitamins and other elements necessary for growth and survival. There is no century when she has not produced some of the greatest international figures in literature. Spain, Italy, Germany, Russia, the Scandinavian countries, have passed through long stretches of time when no great figure at all has emerged, but this has not been true of France. Her mediaeval literature is the richest in the world; since the Renaissance, there is not a century without its literary giants. In the sixteenth century there were Rabelais and Montaigne among the thinkers, and Ronsard and Du Bellay among the poets; in the seventeenth century there were Descartes and Pascal, Racine and Molière, Madame de Lafayette, and Saint-Simon—to mention only a few who were unsurpassed elsewhere; in the eighteenth century there were Voltaire, Diderot, and Rousseau; in the nineteenth century there were the great novelists like Balzac, Stendhal, Flaubert, and Zola; the Art for Art's Sake and Symbolist Movements from which world poetry is still drawing sustenance. The twentieth century produced Bergson, Proust, Claudel, Gide, and Valéry. In every age there is something for every taste, and there has been no single period, in her long history, when it has been unnecessary to look to France intellectually.

Nowadays, with so much vanishing everywhere in the world, it is more than ever important that Britain and France should draw near to one another. Britain is the link between Europe and the West, and France is the gateway for the West to enter Europe. It is essential for the survival of Europe as Europe that they should be in sympathy with one another. Without a strong France there cannot be a future for Europe; she is necessary, with her generalizing qualities, and no one else but Britain can ensure her connection with the rest of the Western world. It is therefore of paramount importance to forge stronger links between Britain and France, to keep alive what is left of Europe. Cyril Connolly, writing in *Horizon* during the late war, said in June 1943:

'It is after the war that the opportunity to benefit from French culture will arrive. Whatever may be the political relations between England and France, and I am certain it will be very close (for it is only through alliance with France that England can be united with Europe again, and Europe remain a great power), I hope that their cultural relationship will be one of absolute union.'

However we consider the matter, the future of Britain in Europe is inextricably bound up with that of France, and they cannot do without one another. It should be possible, in the future, for the two countries to reach agreement for, when all is said and done, they share the same civilization, with only local differences. Saint-Simon, writing in 1815, declared that 'la réorganisation de la société européenne demandait l'union continue de la France et de l'Angleterre, nations qui ont la même civilisation'. And G. K. Chesterton remarked, paradoxically, that the reason why the wars between France and England had been so bitter and prolonged was because they had been, in fact, civil wars.

All through the centuries the stream of a common culture did not cease to flow backwards and forwards between Britain and France, fertilizing intellectual and spiritual life, to form a single civilization. Sometimes the stream flowed more strongly in one direction, and sometimes in the other, but never running dry. Chaucer was indebted to *Le Roman de la Rose* and Shakespeare owed much to French literature; while Rousseau and Voltaire, on the other hand, borrowed much from England; and, during the first half of the nineteenth century, the most vital currents in French literature came from Britain; but, during the second half, the stream flowed the other way, and French culture impregnated English literature—this influence continued, uninterrupted, until the advent of the Second World War.

The pattern of the second half of the twentieth century has not yet emerged, but, since the end of the late war, Graham Greene, who was previously influenced by Mauriac, has been the writer most read by young people in France; while, on the other hand, in both Britain and France, Sartre has been for post-war youth what Gide had been for a similar generation in the period which followed the First World War.

SUGGESTIONS FOR FURTHER READING

PART 1

INTRODUCTION

MATTHEW ARNOLD: *Collected Poems* (Oxford University Press, 1909).
MATTHEW ARNOLD: *Mixed Essays* (Macmillan, 1908).
IRIS SELLS: *Matthew Arnold and France* (Cambridge University Press, 1935)

ART FOR ART'S SAKE

CHARLES BAUDELAIRE: *Œuvres Complètes* (Paris, Pléiade Edition, 1952).
THÉOPHILE GAUTIER: *Mademoiselle de Maupin* (Paris, Charpentier, 1927).
THÉOPHILE GAUTIER: *Poésies Complètes* (Paris, Charpentier, 1924).
HENRY JAMES: *French Poets and Novelists* (Macmillan, 1878).
WILLIAM GAUNT: *The Aesthetic Adventure* (Cape, 1945).
G. TURQUET-MILNES: *The Influence of Baudelaire in France and England* (Constable, 1913).

SWINBURNE AND PATER

A. C. SWINBURNE: *Collected Poetical Works* (Heinemann, 1924).
WALTER PATER: *The Renaissance* (Macmillan, 1924).
WALTER PATER: *Appreciations* (Macmillan, 1888).
G. LAFOURCADE: *La Jeunesse de Swinburne* (Paris, Association G. Budé: Editions Belles Lettres).
T. WRIGHT: *Walter Pater* (Everett, 1907).

REALISM

GUSTAVE FLAUBERT: *Œuvres* (Paris, Pléiade Edition, 1951).
EDOUARD MAYNIAL: *Flaubert* (Paris, Éditions de la Nouvelle Revue Critique, 1943).
JACQUES SUFFEL: *Flaubert* (Paris, Éditions Universitaires, 1958).
E. & J. DE GONCOURT: *Germinie Lacerteux* (Paris, Charpentier, 1885).
GEORGE MOORE (Ebury Edition of the Collected Works, Heinemann).
ÉMILE ZOLA: *L'Assommoir* (Paris, Charpentier).
ÉMILE ZOLA: *Nana* (Paris, Charpentier).

GEORGES-PAUL COLLETT: *George Moore et la France* (Paris, Droz, 1957).
J. M. HONE: *The Life of George Moore* (Gollancz, 1936).
ANGUS WILSON: *Émile Zola, an Introductory Study of his Novels* (Secker & Warburg, 1952).

SYMBOLISM

J. K. HUYSMANS: *À Rebours* (Paris, Charpentier, 1929).
STÉPHANE MALLARMÉ: *Œuvres* (Paris, Pléiade Edition, 1945).
PAUL VERLAINE: *Œuvres Poétiques* (Paris, Pléiade Edition, 1948).
VILLIERS DE L'ISLE ADAM: *Axël* (Mercure de France, 1923).
GUY MICHAUD: *Message Poétique du Symbolisme* (Paris, Nizet, 1947).
ARTHUR SYMONS: *The Symbolist Movement in Literature* (Heinemann, 1899).
EDMUND WILSON: *Axël's Castle* (New York, Scribner's Sons, 1943).

THE YELLOW NINETIES

JOHN GRAY: *Silverpoints* (Bodley Head, 1893).
ROBERT HICHENS: *The Green Carnation* (Heinemann, 1894).
OSCAR WILDE: *Intentions* (Methuen, 1912).
OSCAR WILDE: *The Picture of Dorian Gray* (Simpkin Marshall).
W. B. YEATS: *Collected Poems* (Macmillan, 1958).
W. B. YEATS: *Autobiographies* (Macmillan, 1955).
W. B. YEATS: *Ideas of Good and Evil* (Macmillan, 1903).
OSBERT BURDETT: *The Beardsley Period* (Bodley Head, 1925).
ALBERT FARMER: *Le Mouvement Esthétique et Décadent en Angleterre* (Paris, Champion, 1931).
HOLBROOK JACKSON: *The Eighteen-Nineties* (Cape, 1927).
A. N. JEFFARES: *W. B. Yeats, Man and Poet* (Routledge, Kegan & Paul, 1949).

PART II

INTRODUCTION

ANDRÉ GIDE: *Œuvres Complètes* (Paris, Gallimard, 1932–9).
ANDRÉ GIDE: *Journal* (Paris, Pléiade Edition, 1940).

POETRY

GUILLAUME APOLLINAIRE: *Œuvres Poétiques* (Paris, Pléiade Edition, 1958).
TRISTAN CORBIÈRE: *Les Amours Jaunes* (Paris, Club Français du Livre, 1950).
T. S. ELIOT: *Selected Poems* (Faber & Faber, 1954).

T. S. ELIOT: *After Strange Gods* (Faber & Faber, 1934).

T. S. ELIOT: *The Sacred Wood* (Faber & Faber, 1928).

JULES LAFORGUE: *Œuvres Complètes* (Paris, Mercure de France, 1922–30).

WARREN RAMSEY: *Jules Laforgue and the Ironic Inheritance* (Oxford University Press, 1953).

EDITH SITWELL: *Collected Poems* (Macmillan, 1958).

EDITH SITWELL: *Aspects of Modern Poetry* (Macmillan, 1934).

C. M. BOWRA: *The Heritage of Symbolism* (Macmillan, 1943).

E. J. H. GREENE: *T. S. Eliot et la France* (Paris, Boivin, 1951).

GLENN HUGHES: *Imagism and the Imagists* (Oxford University Press, 1931).

FICTION

JAMES JOYCE: *The Portrait of the Artist as a Young Man* (Jonathan Cape, 1956).

JAMES JOYCE: *Ulysses* (Bodley Head, 1937).

KATHERINE MANSFIELD: *Selected Stories* (Oxford University Press, 1953).

SOMERSET MAUGHAM: *First Person Singular* (Heinemann, 1931).

MARCEL PROUST: *À la Recherche du Temps Perdu* (Paris, Pléiade Edition, 1955).

G. D. PAINTER: *Marcel Proust*, Volume I (Chatto & Windus, 1959).

VIRGINIA WOOLF: *To the Lighthouse* (The Hogarth Press, 1927).

VIRGINIA WOOLF: *The Waves* (The Hogarth Press, 1931).

VIRGINIA WOOLF: *The Common Reader* (The Hogarth Press, 1925).

RICHARD ELLMANN: *James Joyce* (Oxford University Press, 1959).

DAVID HAYMAN: *Joyce et Mallarmé* (Paris, Cahiers des Lettres Modernes, 1956).

DERRICK LEON: *Introduction to Proust* (Routledge, Kegan & Paul, 1940).

DRAMA

PAUL CLAUDEL: *L'Annonce Faite à Marie* (Paris, Nouvelle Revue Française, 1912).

JEAN COCTEAU: *La Machine Infernale* (Paris, Grasset, 1934).

JEAN COCTEAU: *Les Parents Terribles* (Paris, Gallimard, 1938).

T. S. ELIOT: *Murder in the Cathedral* (Faber & Faber, 1935).

JEAN GIRAUDOUX: *La Guerre de Troie n'aura pas lieu* (Paris, Grasset, 1935).

JEAN OBEY: *Noé* and *Le Viol de Lucrèce* (Paris, 1931).

PIERRE BRISSON: *Le Théâtre des Années Folles* (Paris, Editions du Milieu du Monde, 1943).

GORDON CRAIG: *Theatre Advancing* (Constable, 1921).

FREDERICK LUMLEY: *Trends in Twentieth Century Drama* (Rockliff, 1956).

JOHN PALMER: *Studies in the Contemporary Theatre* (Martin Secker, 1927).

INDEX

E

F